# ORAL HISTORY

# AND

# MY APPALACHIA

## J. LEONARD GREER

# DEDICATION

In recent times it has become popular to blame all our social ills on poverty, living conditions or even prejudices. This can be misleading at best and can become little more than an excuse. The eight Greer children experienced all these and more but went on to become honorable and productive citizens, without exception. If they could do it, so can anyone else who has the will.

# In Honor and Memory of:

The
Greer Children as
Adults

2006

*Clockwise from upper left corner:*
*Leonard, Johnny, Elton, Jack,*
*Gail, Emma Mae, Lena, and Grant*

# CONTENTS

# ACKNOWLEDGEMENTS

As is usual, these efforts are not mine alone. The topics are mine for my remembrances reach back more that eighty years. Many of my best sources have long been gone. The heritage libraries of Ashe, Watauga, Wilkes, Johnston, and Wake Counties are wonderful resources, and I have used them often. Books have been an invaluable resource because many authors have unusual information and perspective. I highly recommend the books listed in my bibliography for further study. They have often supported my family's oral history.

Few works, such as this one, are possible without the help and support of special individuals. This one is no exception. My wife Marny has researched and typed for me on many occasions. She is a wizard with old photos, and we hope to use a lot of her work. She has computer experience while I do not. This has helped on occasion, though I do not consider the internet a good or dependable resource for what I want to do.

Nona Lawrence has been indispensable in the process. We were co-workers in Watauga County's Maintenance Department, and she is as familiar with my handwriting as anyone can be. When I called upon her to turn my handwritten copy into something readable, she graciously accepted the challenge. I thank her and all the others who have been of help. I cannot list them all but must credit one more; Grandson Harley Cole proofread the manuscript and made valuable suggestions, "Thank you Harley".

# Introduction by the Author

This work covers over eighty years of life in Appalachia. With beginnings in the Great Depression and World War II, things had to get better and they did. The economy of the area improved, but this was only a small part of the total picture.

Most of Appalachia is divided among several states which are predominately "off-the-mountain." Their mountain areas were ignored to say the least. Even worse, mountain people often endured a second-class citizenship and unnecessary isolation. They became different, and it was not all economic by any means.

These differences were most noticeable to the outsider. Wife Marny came to Boone, NC in 1971 at the age of twenty-six and she relates:

> "It took a long time for me to be able to understand the accents, phrases, and vocabulary of this area. This area was very foreign to me, being that I grew up in the Central Valley of California. I think it is important to remember that the language and lifestyle of the area were so different, and we need to remember the time before the outside world moved in and changed it all. But the lost culture of the area should be remembered, especially by the families who originated there."

These writings were first intended for the Greer and Miller families. The changes witnessed in my life have been largely of "overcoming." To many it has been as simple as "Appalachian State University 34 and Michigan 32." To me it has also been the coming of "oneness" with the rest of the country. As we continue in an age of reflection on our past, I hope these writings have something to contribute.

# 1

## A New Land

Environmentalists of today often seem bent on returning the land to a natural state or at least limiting the effects of human habitation. Both are probably worthy goals, but I wonder if they realize just how much the lands the pioneers found had already been altered? Huge areas of forest land east of the Mississippi had already given way to the Indian practice of burning during hunts and to increase forage for large game. The buffalo and elk had responded favorably by grazing out forest land vegetation that survived the Indian burning.[1] These native pastures reached even to the mountain peaks along the Blue Ridge and into the river valleys to the east. One could become lost for days on the treeless barrens of Western Kentucky and Tennessee. The huge pine forests of the South were also a product of Indian burning. The hardwood undergrowth was largely controlled by fire and a monoculture of pine prevailed in much of the South.

A popular misconception of the early wilderness is that there was little or no open land. This was far from the truth. Hunting and gathering was not a dependable living, even for Indians. They developed an agriculture of corn, beans, melons, and squash to supplement their hunting and gathering activities. These cultivated areas were often up to 200 acres and occupied the activities of women, children, and some of the men.[2]

Early settlers learned farming from the Indians. They planted their corn on burned off land in the hills. The areas between the hills would be dug or beaten down with a grubbing hoe. Warm season beans and squash would later be planted in the corn. (The squash were more like today's pumpkins and would keep all winter or longer if dried.) Corn, squash, and beans were basic to the Indian diet as well as nuts and berries from the woods and fields. Opossum and raccoon were common in the diet. In fact, early written accounts give the raccoon as being a universal favorite. Fish and other small animals caught by the women, as well as the men were part of their diet. But crops were the dependable food source.

Far more land on the upper New River was once occupied and tilled by Indians than we now know about or could even imagine. During my boyhood much of the land was tilled by the local farmers. Fields were far more frequently plowed in those days and Indian artifacts came to the surface surprisingly often. In some hot spots, arrowheads could be picked up by the score after a rain. However, there were few serious collectors. Boys often carried arrowheads in their pockets for trading purposes. I still have in my possession a few blue glass beads picked up when I was a boy while hoeing corn planted on one of these sites. I do not think I ever found more than five and why I kept them I do not know. I read now of blue glass beads made in Italy for export to the early Virginia settlers. Early traders with the Indians found them to be much in demand. Are these some of those beads? They could just have easily been lost by an early white girl working in the fields. Someday I hope to know for sure.

Even the historians do not seem to be aware of such a great Indian presence in the area. They seem to believe that Indians were only a small factor in our local history. It is true that they were crowded westward ahead of the push of the white settlers, but they were here at least until white diseases killed most of them. Entire Indian communities must have died at once, otherwise so many valuable tools and weapons would not have been left in some locations. Some Indians were still present when the early white settlers arrived, as Indian fields, peach orchards and burial sites were still very much in evidence.

Very evident were Indian burial grounds. Early Indian occupation of the area was not so far removed that the early whites did not find such burial sites. Such sites were often reference points or place names. Indian Grave Gap is a local landmark in Caldwell County. A gravesite on Meat Camp is given as a reference point on the early road from Deep Gap to the gap of Rich Mountain. In Ashe, several Indian cemeteries were kept in use by white settlers. The Calloway Cemetery on Highway 163, for example, is believed to have first been an Indian cemetery. For the most part, Indian cemeteries were viewed with some respect and not a little superstition. At the time of my childhood ghost stories were still told by some older persons about areas where Indian cemeteries once existed.

Many would explain the abundance of Indian artifacts by saying they were buried with Indians for use in an afterlife. I believe this was mostly myth. Sites where artifacts are to be found are simply too common. They occupy nearly all of the land areas that lay reasonably well for cultivation in our area. This includes mountaintops and lower elevations anywhere the land was not overly steep and rocky. It would have taken a lot of dead Indians to create such a presence even if the Indians could have afforded to bury such huge numbers of axes, arrows, etc. with their dead. Artifacts in our area are more in keeping with the sudden death of a village population as might have come about with the introduction of white men's diseases such as smallpox.

Indian men did most of the hunting, traveling, and making war. They developed paths which often ran for hundreds of miles. When hunting they often used fire to drive game. They may have even burned areas to eliminate brush and improve hunting in the future. Such burns may have influenced the development of mountaintops, which were often open timber and meadow or grassland. These open areas were likely connected by Indian and game trails to the more commonly cultivated fields at lower elevations. Only good hunting seems to have drawn the Indians to the more exposed higher elevations. Old Fields Bald on the Ashe-Watauga line is a notable exception. There the Indians mined soapstone to make lamp-pots and bowls. The open land also likely attracted elk. Artifacts indicate a significant Indian presence at any rate. White settlers in their turn would be drawn to this remote open land. They would clear much more adjoining land, along Long Hope Creek for example.

The effect of grazing animals on opening the land is hard to gauge. It is quite likely that mountain balds were most influenced because they were preferred by the elk. Very early white observation was that buffalo were not common east of the Mississippi until after much of the Indian population died off due to white men's diseases. Then the buffalo moved into what had been Indian fields. The remaining Indians and early whites armed with firearms would later wipe them out in short order for their meat, hides and tallow. Once they obtained guns, the Indians appear to be as wasteful of big game as the whites. At any rate, the presence of buffalo did not last for long east of or along the Blue Ridge. Daniel Boone would never see a buffalo until he reached Kentucky.

The Blue Ridge Mountain area had many open areas, and these were the first to be used by the white settlers. There were meadow and old field areas and also glades. The place names "Old Fields," "Balds" and "Glades" still survive in large number on our topographical maps. Bishop Spandenberg, who traveled the area in 1750 recorded "much meadow land suitable to the grazing of cattle". After hunting and trapping, this was the first use of the land. Cattle were much needed to furnish meat, hides and tallow. Besides food, hides became leather and tallow became candles. Drovers moved cattle to summer grazing along and across the Blue Ridge prior to the permanent settler. All settlers would follow the lead of the Indians. Just look at the county seats of the five northwest North Carolina counties: Sparta is at the north end of Glade Valley; Wilkesboro borders on the Mulberry Fields; Jefferson is at the Old Fields of the New; Boone is at the Big Glades of the Three Forks; while Newland is at the Old Fields of the Toe River. Former Indian fields had been great elk pastures but were pasturing Yadkin Valley cattle in summer by the 1750's and 1760's.

These open or grassy areas were usually interconnected by a wandering system of game trails. These trails themselves were likely to develop into open woodland or glades. The old Indian fields had a character of their own, however. They were usually an open area of grassland and brush land near a stream or creek but usually not along a river of size. They would lay along Indian trails or game trails if the Indians no longer occupied them. The effects of Indian farming would show on the land. Long farmed areas or areas of thin soils would often be given over to a crab orchard. In the days before vigorous European grasses or the use of lime and fertilizer, this land was often bare and eroded prior to being occupied by briars and crab apples. Early land entry locations record their existence at the "Ashe Old Fields" and at the "Great Glade of the Three Forks." (The original Brushy Fork area there seems to have referred to a crab orchard near the Boone glades.)

River bottom meadows were more likely to have resulted from flooding caused by beavers. They also could have resulted from being severely grazed as winter yarding areas for big game which may have used them for many years consecutively. These meadows, too, are often mentioned in deed descriptions where land entries were made. Often also are entries given in relation to someone's grazing operation. The name "Salt Rock" or "Salt Log" remains on our maps long after we have forgotten the reason they are there.

The cattle herders grazed their cattle upon open land in a pattern that would prevail during the settlement of the entire continent. Land was not titled for years. Much of western North Carolina had been granted to Granville but that land office seems to have shut down about 1767. The county of Rowan became the most populous county in the state, but few had deeds for their land. Only with independence would the government begin to recognize claims and even then, many of the original claimants would end up losing their homesteads.

Benjamin Cleveland ranged cattle west of the Blue Ridge very early. He would follow up these activities by entering many hundreds of acres of choice land when it finally became available. His claims included 300 acres at the West Jefferson town site to be and the glade on the New River. He would never receive title to most of his entries. In another county yet to be, the town site was also cattle pasture. The Boone Valley and surrounding mountain tops were being grazed by Benjamin Howard who then lived on the upper Yadkin.

As mentioned, off-the-mountain areas did not escape modification by the Indians either. Lawson in his book, *New Voyage to Carolina*, is our best account of early coastal and piedmont land and its Indians. He describes good hunting in woods kept open by burning and rich farmlands. In some places though, the burning had created monocultures of pine not natural to the land. In my life span I have witnessed east of the mountains a return from piney woods to hardwoods. The piedmont now has a fall leaf color that lasts even longer than in the mountain's forests.

What Lawson describes is an Indian who hunts, farms, and lives a life not very different from the pioneer. All he needs to catch up is a rifle and a steel axe. By the time of the Cherokee removal the Indian would live little differently from the white man.

A good local example of an Indian village was the Old Fields of Gap Creek on the south fork of New River. It has several hundred acres of fertile river bottom land. A village at the mouth of Gap Creek even had a mounded area for a council house built up above any expected flooding. This seems to have been a very common way of locating the Indian village site. Johnson J. Hayes in his book, *Land of Wilkes*, indicates this site would have been occupied even after 1750.

It seems now that the white man found open forests interspersed with fields and glade that were tied together with long used trails. Contrary to a popular misconception, getting around was usually a horseback proposition. Hunters, trappers, traders, herders, and sugar makers would come early on. The axe settler was far down the line.

Johnson J. Hayes' *Land of Wilkes* indicates that Christopher Gist was living with the Indians at the Mulberry Fields on the upper Yadkin in the 1760's. *Neighbor to Neighbor* by Ballard and Weinstein says that Bishop Spangenberg would have found some Indians at Gap Creek.[3] Spangenberg himself noted that the area would be good for missionary work among the Indians. Indians, or at least mixed blood Indians, were said to still be in the Gap Creek area when Benjamin Cleveland first claimed it. Having grown up on a hardscrabble farm, it is hard to believe that Indian fields could have survived nature's healing process for long. Today most students of local history seem to think that Indian presence in our area pre-dated settlement by whites by centuries. This might be true for any large Indian population, but there is too much evidence of an Indian presence for this to be totally true. There is a lot of evidence of a significant Indian presence until about 1760 when smallpox ravaged the northern tribes. An Indian presence survived even after white settlement. Orphan children of mixed blood were sent to the Cherokee school in Western North Carolina for example. (Wilburn Waters' siblings went there.) When the government attempted to reimburse Cherokees for their confiscated lands several, as many as eight, local residents filed claims for payment. Though it is not certain that any ever received anything.

Although altered by the Indians, the character of the land was still largely determined by nature itself. But was it what we imagined it to be? Not likely. The trees of the forests were tall and shaded out most of the understory. They lived maybe hundreds of years, much longer than it took for the fallen to decay thus contributing to a more open forest.

No description of the land would be complete without including its rivers. John Lawson's book gives us the first good written account of a portion of the Yadkin and its valley. He was most likely not the first white explorer, but he did leave good written detail. He describes fertile river lowlands with farmed fields sometimes reaching hundreds of acres where the corn grew thick-stalked and productive. These fields were created by girding trees and the use of fire. Some were even fenced. The Indians apparently had already acquired steel axes, iron pots and other metal tools from white traders before Lawson's visit and they were usually quick to adapt to the new lifestyle. Guns were much more efficient than bows and arrows. Lawson notes that they even had horses but that they were treated more as pets than as work stock.

Lawson notes that tributary streams often flowed through grassy meadows while the uplands were forests of chestnut oak. The natives told of mountains covered with chestnuts themselves. Lawson correctly foresaw a time when both would feed huge herds of hogs. The Yadkin Valley as described was a paradise in waiting for settlers who would follow the Indians. If one has ever stood on the overlook on Highway 25 between Sparta and Elkin, NC, it is easy to understand why. The area would become the most populated area of the state, but it would not have much in common with its eastern neighbors. Most of its settlers would come down the great wagon road from Pennsylvania, Maryland, and Virginia.

West of the Blue Ridge flowed another river. This river defied conventional expectations by flowing north. It drained a more rugged area more of interest to hunters and grazers than farmers. Higher elevations and colder temperatures meant that crops were often subject to frosts. It also meant that fewer settlers would enter the area by following the New River upstream. The main flow of settlers would cross the Blue Ridge from the Yadkin settlements. They were led by the hunters and trappers and often wanted more distance from the predominantly English settlements in the coastal areas. They were of many national origins but were most often Scottish in nature at least. It seems that a little Scot's blood goes a long way, for even in the Scottish Lowlands other nationalities had long been present. Although two, three or even four generations in America, they largely kept Scottish ways.

While Lawson gives us perhaps our best hands-on descriptions of 1700 Carolina, not all would hold true until the mid-century settlements of the Blue Ridge territories. This area would still hold an abundance of wild game but with two notable exceptions. The wild cattle (buffalo) Lawson describes were gone. Belue in *The Long Hunt – Death of the Buffalo East of the Mississippi* gives an approximate date of their demise as 1730.[4] This was before the influx of settlers into the Yadkin Valley.

The loss of the migratory passenger pigeon was more sorely felt. In the fall they appeared in the Carolinas in numbers that blocked out the sun. Their flights roughly corresponded to the limits of the beech trees which provided a favorite food for them. The beech groves rarely grew farther east than the piedmont. Lawson describes the Indian use of this game in the Yadkin River area. They would go among the roosts at night and kill them by the thousands with long poles. From the carcasses they would render a tasty oil called "pigeon butter." Even a small village could harvest 100 gallons or more.

Another often forgotten feature of the virgin land was the prevalence of lots of rattlesnakes. Indian reverence for the rattlesnake is likely a myth, but it also seems unlikely that they were any threat to the rattlesnake population. Settlers, on the other hand, held them to be a menace that needed to be eliminated and they were eliminated except in remote and less frequented areas. Many were the snake stories that are largely lost in our history.

The New River headwaters seems to have been particularly well supplied with rattlesnakes in pre-settlement days. Benjamin Cleveland loved to go into the mountains to hunt elk. Legend has it that while on a hunt on the north fork, he found himself surrounded by rattlesnakes. Being on a rock ledge on the riverbank, he threw himself backwards into the river to escape. It appears that Cleveland had wandered into a denning area where the snakes congregated in great numbers. Another such area once existed near Boone on Rich Mountain. Aunt Frances

Miller told how rattlesnakes were eliminated from the entire area by attacking this den. Boone area residents of the time did them in. An article form Arthur's *History of Watauga County* confirms her account. Arthur's history relates that Jordan McGhee and a Holland Hodges killed 432 rattlesnakes in 1856. My Aunt Frances Miller may have had the same total, but she described it differently. She gave Jordan McGhee credit for the idea, but he had two helpers whose names I cannot remember except that one was a Hodges. They built tree stands at the dens and entered them before the snakes got warm enough to stir. They used the stands every spring for about four years. The first year the kill had been less than three hundred, but the total climbed rapidly until the final count was over four hundred. This location is near the Rich Mountain fire tower.

The tendency to den in huge numbers make the rattlesnake vulnerable and they did not reproduce rapidly. There were late to mature and gave live birth to a limited number of offspring. Their use of their rattle helped expose them. In recent years there have been efforts to reintroduce them to their former territories. I think this is misguided. A copperhead bite is usually survivable even without treatment, but a rattlesnake bite is much more serious.

# 2

---

# Our Ancestors

## The English

The English must be considered the dominant American settler but only because of their ties to their mother country. They were the power structure and controlled access to land. Others would be subject to them. This was especially true of other British subjects such as the Scots and the Welch. The colonists were often anglicized even though they would develop a new and different national character. Some, such as the Pennsylvania Dutch, would play a very significant role but must defer to the English who controlled language, government and land ownership. In some areas the English even sought to control the religion as they had in Great Britain. This point of contention was carried over into the Colonies and would become a unifying argument in opposition to the English crown. Even many English longed to make separation of church and state a hallmark of our country.

The English likely could be considered the predominant or standard settler. But they dominate only if you factor in the influence of other British such as the Scots and the Welch. The English were about as likely to have left England for religious freedom as any other nationality. Nevertheless, the English controlled the government, the language, largely the early economy and even religion in some states. Englishmen were most likely to be planters, merchants and dealers in real estate being opened for settlement in most of the colonies. Pennsylvania was the most notable exception where the population contained Germans and others.

The English were most likely to remain loyal to the crown. At least until many became alienated by the crown's economic policies and lack of input into the government. Still, alienation to the crown among the English was nowhere universal. It was truly a civil war. The move for independence was strong in New England, yet when the war was won many of them resettled in Ontario, Canada to be under their king. The middle Atlantic states were more of a mix of peoples. It is interesting that this area is the anchoring point from which most of the military activities radiated. The states south of Virginia had ties closer yet to the crown. Trade with the mother country remained more important to the plantation economy during the Revolution and for decades to come. The strongest opposition to the British came from settlers in Wilkes and over-the-mountain men. These were predominately third generation settlers with strong ties to the more independent Scots. They were outside the plantation economy and the established governments had rarely responded to their needs.

A surprising number of English families in our area have Quaker backgrounds. The Boones were the best-known example. Quakers are still widespread in Yadkin, Stokes and other northern tier of North Carolina counties with Guilford County becoming a center of influence though many were to later move to non-slave states. Quakers were common in the mountains even. Unlike the Anglican English these Quakers remembered religious persecution in England and Ireland. They too became an important element of American independence, though not all Quakers supported the movement by any means. Our perception in this area of the Quaker Church is of a pious people being farmers or other simple professions. This was not altogether so even in the early days. The Pennsylvania Quaker society was highly developed with a vigorous professional and merchant society. (The Boones were first weavers.) Many Quakers in the Philadelphia area were very wealthy. They pursued worldly gain with a miserly enthusiasm. These Quakers often felt their fortunes to be more secure with the English. During the Revolution many of them were forcibly removed to the Shenandoah Valley to prevent any possible collusion with the enemy. These prominent Quakers protested their fate endlessly as food, drink and lodging in the interior were not up to Philadelphia standards. What hurt even more was that they were forced to pay for this keep out of their own pockets.

As for the upper New River, I will not attempt to give English names. Englishmen rarely had the same bent for exploring as others. They usually were involved in real estate schemes and other enterprises when they did appear on the frontier. On the New River they were more likely to be second wave settlers though they did control the government as a rule and displaced Scots and others not prepared to cope with the power structure.

Becoming a nation after the Revolution was a struggle in itself. It is not politically correct to say this today, but strong measures were taken to make citizens of the Loyalist. Many would end up losing their property and moving to Canada. A loyalty oath to the new government was required or property taxes would be doubled. George Washington was a great military leader and he became a great president. He travelled the new country and worked hard to bring the colonies to be a unified nation. "George Washington slept here" became a common expression. The signs of division are almost invisible now, but not quite so. My wife Marny and I visited friends in rural Ontario, Canada a few years ago. They lived at a crossroads complete with a school site and a church. I noted that the cemetery grave markers listed common American names. Too my surprise the church was Baptist. Many such communities were founded in Canada as a result of our American Revolution.

Locally, there were plenty of Tories in the area. Strong areas of Tory activity existed along New River into Virginia. This is also said to be true of the upper Watauga. Some see a connection of English support in areas where the Episcopal Church was established early on. I am not sure if this is valid, but the Episcopal Church was an English institution. The extent of the division within the population of that day is often under-appreciated today. The war for independence became a most brutal affair that lingered for decades. The War of 1812 has been called the second war of independence. Even then Britain harbored thoughts of a British America by controlling the Mississippi Valley. The battle of New Orleans was fought with this in mind. It has been learned in recent times that the British military was to ignore any news of a treaty. The battle was fought after the war was over, but the Mississippi was the prize.

## The Scots

American Scots are usually lumped together as Scots-Irish though there were patterns to their immigration. Those who had the most impact on early mountain affairs might best be described as Scots. James Greer, for example, arrived in Baltimore, Maryland in 1674 on the ship, *Batchelor*. He had been born about 1627 in Dumfriesshire, Scotland. These early Scots cannot accurately be called Scots-Irish because Ulster Scot immigration did not begin for about fifty years later. By the time of the Revolution the descendants of these early Scots would have been third, fourth or even fifth generation Americans. They would be following the frontier west and were largely American patriots. James Webb, a recent author and Virginia senator, in his book, *Born Fighting*, lists among them explorers Daniel Boone, Lewis and Clark and Davy Crockett. Noted fighters he lists are Stonewall Jackson, Sam Houston, Nathan Bedford Forrest, Ulysses S. Grant, and even George S. Patton. [1] Webb says that Scots descendants comprised about forty percent of the Revolutionary War soldiers. In more modern times they produced Sgt. Alvin York and Audie Murphy.

My second group of Scots emigrants is the truly Scot-Irish, the Ulster Scots. They shared religious and economic oppression from the English as did the mainland Scots. They were just as Scottish as any. They usually shared only the Irish name with the Irish as the two did not mix well. They still do not today. They came in great numbers in the 1720's era.

There was still a third group of Scots who came to America. They were the Highland Scots. They formed a large community on the upper Cape Fear River in North Carolina. They had sworn allegiance to King George as a condition of passage. They took their oath seriously but seemed to have largely avoided taking an active part on either side during the Revolution. North Carolina is said to have had more Scottish surnames than any other state in the Union. The Highland settlements in the Fayetteville area was sometimes referred to as a "Mac-ocracy."

Without the early Scots there may have never been a War for independence. Theirs was not one so much as influence in high places as it was the independent nature of the common people. The roots of these frontier Scots went back to settlers in the first fifty years or so of colonization. These were largely immigrants to Maryland, Virginia and Pennsylvania who were brought over to populate tracts of land closer to the frontiers. The independent natured Scots made an excellent buffer between the English planters and the Indians. They were the lead elements of waves of Scots who would later leave Scotland and Ulster, Ireland. But the earliest immigrants were likely to come directly from Scotland to escape religious persecution and for opportunity. Later immigrants from Ulster had been persecuted both by the English Anglican and the Irish Catholic Churches. These immigrants are still referred to as Scot-Irish, but they were too stubborn to have ever done much real mixing with the Irish. When the Irish Parliament tried to restrict immigration in 1735, the Scots gathered on the docks by the thousands begging for passage to America.

The Scots in early America were highly visible wherever they happened to be. It was as settlers began to push west and south into the valleys of Virginia that they began to greatly influence the character of the "new America." Often, they were in the forefront mixing and trading with the Indians. Usually they dominated certain villages along the "Great Wagon Road." These Scots settlers were bold and adventurous but also often rowdy. In Pennsylvania they had excited Quaker and German indignation. In the valley of Virginia their villages were avoided when possible by pious German settlers travelling south to the Yadkin.

15

The early Scots were almost all Presbyterian, at least in Virginia. The Presbyterian Church is still often a rural church as opposed to North Carolina where they are more likely in towns. The Scots were not hampered with religious division as were the Germans who might be Lutherans, Moravians, Mennonites and Amish. With this solidarity of religion, they were said to pray without embarrassment "Teach me, O Lord, to think well of myself." It was not in their character to take a back seat to anyone. This was true even as the mountaineer was said to be "as poor as Job's turkey." All too often the Scots independence and his love of fighting and whiskey became his legacy. A lady at a small Settler's Museum off Highway 11 near Marion, Virginia told me just a few years ago that the German-Scott differences are still a matter of fact. A spouse of German ancestry may still be known to make disparaging remarks about a partner's Red Neck Scot-Irish ancestry.

On the Yadkin predominantly Scot-Irish communities do not appear to have existed although family ties among Scots themselves and their extended families were extremely strong. Early Presbyterianism ran deep but was not expressed in organized churches usually in the early days. With their great love for freedom and independence the Calloways and Greers, for example, made a conscious decision to join the Baptists. These Baptists had long opposed the colonial government and fled to the mountains of Wilkes to escape persecution. Benjamin Greer was a member of the Three Forks Baptist Church, but his Scots love for strong drink caused him to be expelled by the church. There is no record that he ever reconciled his differences with the Baptists.

Like the English, the Scots had a split personality. On the one hand, they pushed the frontiers and crowded the Indians. (Pity the poor Indians.) On the other hand, the late movers took their Presbyterian Church with its love of education with them. These Scots were to establish colleges all the way from Pennsylvania and Maryland to the Carolinas, though frontier Scots were generally lost out to other churches like the Baptists. They were to have an effect on churches wherever they went, however. Their fatalism and belief in pre-destination is now often more important to the Primitive Baptist Church than it is to a lot of Presbyterians.

It would be difficult to over-estimate the Scots presence on the early Blue Ridge frontier. By early I mean prior to the end of the American Revolution. Most area families do not go back that far and many of the originals have moved on. They turned their eyes to the West. Teddy Roosevelt said that our "Manifest Destiny" (to occupy the land from sea to sea) would not have been possible without the Scot-Irish. From long hunters and traders with the Indians they overran our borders to the west before we could get used to them being along the Appalachians or the Mississippi. From long hunters they became mountain men. Some of the earliest of Scot origin in our area were Brown(e), Blackburn, Calloway, Campbell, Carroll, Colvard, Cox, Cutbirth, Ferguson, Fletcher, Green, Greer and Lewis. Hard on their heels were other recognizable Scots names like Baird, Banner, Blair, Buchanan, Craig, Crichton (Critcher?), David, Douglas, Duncan, Elliot, Hall, Hamilton, Henderson, Hunter, Gordon, Graham, Grant and Morris, this only scratches the surface. Because of their association earlier with the English and the Irish it is impossible to draw the line. We can only assume that many others whom we think were English or Irish joined Scottish kin on the frontier.

Huge numbers of Ulster Scots (Scot-Irish) eventually made their way over the ocean to America. Their occupancy of those northern colonies had begun rather well. Those English Lords given possession of these lands taken by the English from Catholic Ireland were glad to have them. They were often veterans of service to the English in their armies. (This service has a long tradition in England and continues even today.) The Scots were good fighters and would be handy if it was necessary to defend the claims militarily. But most Scots likely relocated, as always, because they felt the opportunities to be better than in Scotland. The move was not far anyway. Only a dozen miles or so separated some of Ireland from Scottish territory. The early Ulster Scots fared reasonably well. They were not only herders but were weavers, doctors, educators and tradesmen as well. Their stay also experienced difficulties of religious persecution from both Catholic and Church of England. Coupled with drought and occasional famine even the early Ulster Scots began to find their way to America.

Often, we hear that these Scots were a low class of people who most likely came as indentured servants. This was probably true for a few, but it is largely a romantic notion. Even contemporary English historian Arnold Toynbee seems to believe that Scots have an affinity for being poor and living in squalor. He promotes the idea that Appalachian mountaineers are poor because of their Scottish heritage. His prejudice does not serve him well and history does not support this theory. It is true that poverty existed in both Scotland and Northern Ireland, but it was far more likely to have been induced by their English Lords than for lack of intelligence or industry. The truth is that most Scots were valuable citizens and were sorely missed by the English when they emigrated. The English feared for the local economy and its defense so much that they even tried to prevent the Scots from leaving by making it illegal.

The descendants of these Scottish immigrants have played a great role in building our nation. They were inclined to move onto the frontiers looking for opportunity and might outpace the development of churches and schools, but their children are just as capable as any when allowed the opportunity.

The Scottish settlers might be a weaver, blacksmith or other tradesman, but the Scot was most in his element, as long as he was a herder. I have often wondered if these Scots had over the generations became imprinted to this type work as were the Border Collies. I am continually amazed at my Border Collie's attempts at herding though she has not been exposed to cattle since a few-weeks old puppy. She helps me mow our lawn with a riding mower. I had long suspected that she felt responsible for the rounds it made. She confirmed this for me one day when I was mowing outside the fence on the road right-of-way. (She was not supposed to go there.) But when I stopped to pick up paper, she came through the fence in a flash to nip the mower's rear tires and get it going again.

Herding in Ulster and in nearby Scotland had not lasted, however. Their English Lords decided that the Scots should grow flax and become weavers. A trickle of Scots begins to show up in the new world by the mid sixteen-hundreds. They were joined by Scottish prisoners of war who were expected to be less problem politically in far-away American. The real flood tide however was to come after a siege of Catholic persecution. Derry had come under siege and the Scots almost starved. They had eaten the cats and dogs and started on the horses. When the siege was broken, they had only one pint of meal per person left and nine starving horses. While this event was far later than American independence one John Brown(e) of early Wilkes is said to have come directly from Derry County, North Ireland. (This was not the norm – most Blue Ridge Scots took two to three generations.) He was well established by 1779 at Brown's Ferry just up the Yadkin from Wilkesboro. Wilkes Countians met in his home to form a county government in 1779 and he was one of the first twelve judges chosen as part of the new independent government. His home and ferry are now marked as a historical site. He appears to have been the ancestor of the large number of Browns settling in the New River Valley.

## The Germans

A few Germans had immigrated to Pennsylvania prior to 1700. They made good citizens being good farmers and craftsmen. They would have a huge impact on gun, furniture and wagon making in the New World. Penn was impressed and sent an agent to actively pursue new immigrants in 1708 or 1709. Encouraged by the promise of religious freedom, German immigration increased to a floodtide. This did not please the earlier English and Welsh Quaker communities who often made the Germans and Scots unwelcome. The then Protestant government of England was generally anxious to have them in the colonies. The Germans soon learned of cheaper land in the great valley of Virginia and in Western North Carolina, and they began to move south. Normally they moved as groups rather than individuals. One of the attractions of the new territories was the opportunity to build their own communities with people of their own beliefs. They generally sought the best land but were said to bring even the poorer and stony lands into productivity. The Lutheran Germans would also enter from Charleston, South Carolina later on.

One of the German sects, the Moravians, was particularly interested in NC. Bishop Spangenburg was one of the earlier visitors to the vacant lands of what was to become northwestern NC. The German habit of recording the particulars of these ventures gives us a clearer picture of the land and the conditions of the time. After establishment of the Moravian settlement at what became Winston-Salem, NC, they wrote Pennsylvania migrants detailed instructions of how to avoid the wicked Scot-Irish communities as they were to travel along the Great Wagon Road in Virginia.

Locally, individual German families were also common in Rowan County before it evolved into more compact counties. The Germans were good farmers and solid citizens who were not usually any trouble in the community. Those outside their established communities were quickly anglicized. This did not mean that later German Lutherans would leave the close-knit Lutheran Church, however. The Germans were not usually participants in revolution or any other political upheavals of the time. The Pennsylvania Germans had sworn loyalty to the English King as a condition for entering the country. While they likely did not necessarily love the King, they took their oaths seriously.

German genes are far more common in our local mix than we often think. They had large families and were less likely to move on than the Scottish and English. A huge number of German names were changed to English spellings. Cabel became Cable, Deshmond became Dishman, Muller became Miller, for example. These are a few local family names, but the list goes on and on. Others are Aaron, Beam, Beard, Barringer, Brinegar, Eller, Fisher, Fraley, Grubb, Lemley, Roan, Shore and even many Smiths. The German emigrant has long been one of the most sought after of any in our national heritage. He would have many skills needed in the community such as blacksmithing and wagon making. Many were also millwrights, masons and carpenters. They seemed to prefer to practice all these trades as a sideline to their farming. The German saw the family farm as a small factory, and it all belonged to him. He was not inclined to work for wages for other people but expected to have a trade as well. All farm efforts were pointed toward having something to sell or feed his family. If it covered a lot of different enterprises, so much the better.

The family was the center of the German's world. He tended to leave politics to others and thought it stupid to go into the army if you did not have to. He would, however, answer the call of duty willingly when it was made by an authority that must be respected. His children would be in demand for military duty or any other enterprise of the times for they would be disciplined to the point of sternness. They would make good soldiers. They would have the necessary education, if it could be had, and would never remember a time when they did not have to work with both hands and head. The German children rarely grew up to be problems in the community for they were brought up in the church. Besides, papa would not stand for it.

Everything on the German farmstead was calculated to best use the resources at hand. This was especially true of the household labor. Women and children were expected to produce items for sale, even if they were in small amounts. This would begin with butter, eggs and from there on you can use your imagination. It was not unusual for the farm census to list goose feathers, lard, cured pork, sausages, molasses, honey, tree sugar and woven cloth goods in addition to cattle and any grains from the fields or fruit from the indispensable orchard. The women of the household would also use any spare time at the looms to make the cloth for family clothing or for trade as many of the country stores. If the family did good at home papa would work at one of his trades or run a gristmill, sawmill or threshing machine.

The strengths of the German family were often copied by others. There had been a great deal of mixing early on anyway, but those retaining their German names were very likely to retain the Lutheran Church also. If these church families could stay neighbors, it was that much better. The "drive" to prosper and to get ahead was the hallmark of some families, and not just those of German extraction either. Not infrequently, a mountain farmer became very frugal as he acquired more property. Some were so stingy in the old days that they would even ration what they ate in order to buy more land.

My connection with the German settlers is on my mother's side of the family. Her grandmother was "Grannie Marthie," Martha Winebarger, a daughter of Jacob and Salome "Sallie" Moretz Winebarger. Like most families of German extraction, Jacob arrived in the area after it was already settled. Their purpose was to practice trades that were much in demand. They were famous as millwrights and builders. Jacob's looms and spinning wheels were still a part of the Miller household when I was a child.

## The French

A significant proportion of our population has always been French although it has become less and less obvious over the decades. It comes from two primary sources. First would be the Canadian French or the remnants of the great French colonial presence in North America. These French once had a presence from the Great Lakes to New Orleans. Untold numbers would mix with the Indians, Spanish and the early settlers pushing west of the mountains. Those having the most effect locally, however, would come from another source. They would be seeking to escape the French Catholic oppression of their Protestant peoples. They were called Huguenots. The Parlier family is one that we would most easily recognize. The Lenoir family was probably the most prominent of our early history. The Waters, Buntings, Catheys, Hardins, Pendleys, Lamberts, Rambos, Sherrils and Vannoys are also supposed to have been French. There would be many others though the names have been anglicized and would not stand out in our now predominantly English society. Laurens, for example, would become Lawrence.

It is hard to overrate the part the French have played in our society. Like William Lenoir, they have proven themselves to be very intelligent and industrious. They are often found to be educators, scientists, or builders and mechanics.

The United States once had no national language. It is hard to believe now but there was once a drive to make French the national language. If our new country had succeeded in taking Canada in our early years, we might be speaking French today, at least as a second language.

# The Welshmen

It is hard to gauge just how big an impact the Welsh had on America. It is even hard to know if they were true Welshmen. Their families, like many others, may have been in England for generations. You will know however that the Welsh made an impact when you know that the Jones, Wilcoxes and many others were Welsh names. In some areas Welsh settlement was particularly noticeable. For example, they worked the lead mines near Austinville, VA early on. These important sources of lead were sometimes referred to as "the Welsh mines" in the early days. Later these mines would be worked largely by Negro slaves.

The Welsh also deserve mention for another reason. Many of them in this country early on were Quakers. They were very serious about their religion though they did not remain Quakers for long. It is said that the early Baptists and others often got their preachers from the ranks of the Welsh. The Welsh had long practiced a sort of chant to deliver the news from one of their communities to another. This also worked well for preaching even if the words could not be understood. The message seemed to arrive anyway.

## The Negroes

A portion of our population has always been black. Some early settlers were affluent to the point of owning slaves. These were not the earliest of settlers as a rule, however. Most slave owners acquired title to the better lands in a second wave of settlement that found the original settlers displaced. The earliest settlers either moved west or on to poorer farming lands. It is sad that these wealthy families now dominate our history to a large extent when; in reality, they were latecomers. It is even sadder that the presence early black residents are rarely mentioned today for they may have been the first permanent settlers. Negro Mountain, for example, is now said that it was a station on the Underground Railroad. Actually, it was named long before any such organization or system existed. It was home to early escaped Blacks who refused to be enslaved. The area has always had a few free Blacks though remaining free with the power of the state behind the institution of slavery was difficult.

Quite a few early Blacks refused their estate in life and ran away to the west. Many joined the Indians though they could end up living in slavery there also. Negro Mountain already had the name when early maps were first made. (These early maps were usually made by land speculators looking to make a buck when the land was settled. This was a pattern that marched across the continent. Their real estate dealings left a stain with still visible effects.)

I have no idea how early a Negro or Negroes lived on Negro Mountain. There had been little or no provision for the return of slaves from the frontier until the treaty ending the French and Indian War. Then a reward was offered the Indians for their return. It would not become the law of the land until 1793. My first factual information is from the pension application of a Revolutionary

War veteran. According to him the campaigns he was involved in on the New River used Negro Mountain as a landmark. Apparently, the name and landmark had already been in use for some years. Unfortunately, we have usually found the Negro presence on the frontier to not be of local interest. If we will but look, we will find several Mulattos among the small army of long hunters and mountain men who opened the west.

## The Indians

It would be hard to ignore an Indian presence in area history. It was never extensive, far more than admitted early on but probably much less than claimed today. On my father's side of the family my great-grandmother was Lula Waters Greer. She was a niece to Wilburn Waters, the famous part-Indian bear hunter. My grandfather, Ivory Greer, said his mother had a dark complexion and could have been black. It was not passed on, however, for Grandpa Ivory and his younger brother John Avery were blue-eyed and fair. Perhaps that is why grandpa was named Ivory?

Ashe County was very hard on any mixing of the races. An uncle of Lula's was tried in the court for having married a white woman. His defense was that his wife was also part Indian. Nevertheless, the judge released him only if he left the state. I believe this was the origin of a Waters family at Laurel Bloomery, TN.

Grandma Lula Waters left home soon after John Avery's birth. The family simply said that she ran away and nothing more. I am sure now that they knew more than this, but it was never talked about. For years I feared that it might have something to do with the climate of discrimination among the power structure of Ashe County at that time. In later years I tend to feel her disappearance was for ordinary reasons. I expect to get into this story in more detail later in this effort.

# 3

## Patterns of Settlement

The Cherokees were the first mountaineers and they defended their mountain homes with considerable force on many occasions. They also adopted white ways and attempted to defend their treaties even to the point of sending delegations to Washington. They lived in towns and villages among the mountains and in the river valleys of North Carolina, Tennessee, Georgia and South Carolina. They resisted early settlement and, later, their removal to the west by President Andrew Jackson. The removal began in 1828 and became an Act of Congress in 1830, but it never became a complete fact in the southern Appalachians. Cherokee persistence in now southwestern mountains delayed white settlement there. Settlement on the New River and other areas north of Asheville were earlier.

The early Cherokee was described as ingenious with keen wit and rare cunning. He could also be poker-faced while enduring hardship or even torture. He was said to have unflinching nerve. Said to be loyal and unselfish with those who could gain his confidence, The Cherokee was also said to be honorable in payment of just debts and obligations. (The same could not be said of a great many whites.) Early on, the Cherokee was unchallenged in his homeland by either Indian or white. He resented the fact that his traditional enemy, the Catawba, relented to white settlement so easily. The last battle between these two enemies occurred at the Warrior's Gap about four miles north of present-day Lenoir,

North Carolina, not far from US Hwy. 321. The problem between the two arose when the Catawbas began to allow settlement in the upper Catawba Valley near Cherokee lands.

Nevertheless, the Cherokees willingly opened their homeland and their villages to people that they liked. William Gist, the first permanent settler of Wilkes County, was living among them at the Mulberry Fields about 1750 (*Land of Wilkes* by Johnson J. Hayes). At that time, the Cherokees still occupied the Yadkin Valley west of the big bend. In their western towns the Cherokees usually offered a home and a chance to have a family to traders that they liked and trusted. These people were often given a monopoly on Indian trade and there was lots of trade. The Indians liked the white man's guns, axes, cooking pots and clothing as well as colored ribbons and beads. This situation was maintained for several generations even though the Indians paid a heavy price from sickness introduced by the white traders. They were not unaware of the cost. Guards were often posted on the travel paths to ensure any visitors were healthy so far as they could tell.

The Cherokees took up white-ways generations before their removal. If anything, they lived as well as the early whites. They lived in log cabins and farmed the land. They kept cattle, horses and planted peach orchards. Some even owned black slaves. Their ties with the whites were extensive. William Gist's son, Nathaniel, married a Cherokee Princess. Nathaniel would later be killed at King's mountain but his son, Sequoya, became one of America's greats. This genius invented the Cherokee alphabet. It was said they could learn to read and write in six weeks. They had their own newspaper and even read the Bible in their own language.

Unfortunately, The Cherokees became the pawns of competing governments. – the French and English. They were first courted by the French during the French and Indian War and later by the British during the American Revolution. The resulting friction between Indians and settlers gradually reduced Cherokee power until the regions west of the Blue Ridge would be settled. The Shawnees of the Ohio Valley continued to raid east of the mountains to stop the settlers, but their power was soon broken also as the frontiersman carried war to their towns north of Ohio.

The demise of the Indians was not an event which occurred overnight, but the fate of the Cherokees was largely decided from 1750 to 1800 in the northwest mountains. In 1750 the Cherokees still lived along the upper Yadkin and in the mountains to the west. Raids on settlers in 1750-51 led to many settlers, including the Boones, fleeing to Virginia. In the late 1750's and early 1760's Indian trouble required a vigilant defense by the frontier settlements. The results of that war secured all territory east of the mountains and the Great Wagon Road for the settlers. The treaty was also supposed to prevent settlement on the western watershed. This was not to be the case for long. By purchase of land from the Indians and other maneuvers, it soon became clear that colonial settlement would not be stopped short of the Mississippi. The Cherokees are still hanging on in small numbers in Western North Carolina even today, but the last known incident in the area was in 1800.

A young girl by the name of Lydia Walters was taken by Indians along the South Fork of the New River near present-day Brownwood as late as 1800. Lydia's beautiful golden hair is said to have saved her life, so she was made a slave instead of being killed. Lydia was traded from one Indian to another but earned her keep by working in the corn fields. At night she slept in a tree but woke occasionally to give the warning if wild animals had entered the field. In the summer she would steal an occasional ear of corn, but in the winter she often went hungry. One summer the Indians' spring went dry and they decided to dig a well. Lydia's owner would not help but he sent Lydia for water as soon as it was complete. The enraged well diggers attacked Lydia. They pulled out her hair and burned her on her neck with hot irons. She was disfigured and her golden hair grew back white. She was released after two years through an agreement worked out with the Indians, but she had changed so much that her family did not recognize her. In despair she spotted the family horse, called "Old Fox," grazing in the field. She said, "Look, there's Old Fox." Thus, her family knew for certain that she was their Lydia.

Another such event was the capture of Katy Sage. Her family settled in the Elk Creek drainage of the New River in Grayson County, Virginia. Katy disappeared while her mother washed clothing at the nearby spring. She was about five years old at the time, which was April 11, 1792. Katy was captured by Indians, or someone who traded her to the Cherokees, and was to be lost for fifty-two years. A "Granny Moses," across in North Carolina, had a vision to the effect that Katy was with the Indians, and also foresaw that the family would eventually re-establish contact. She was to be found living with Wyandotte Indians in Kansas over fifty years later.

Whites who became Indian captives appear to have been fairly common, especially women captives. Howard Greer tells me that his family remembered a lady in his line of Greers who had scarred feet. The Indians had burned her feet to keep her from running away. This was not usual, however. Many Indians adopted captives as a way to replenish declining numbers.

Of course, the most notable Indian capture was that of Mary Ingles at Draper Meadows on the New River in Virginia. She was carried all the way to the Shawnee towns in Ohio. She escaped and survived the long trip home. *Follow the River* by James Alexander Thorn is a remarkable account of this remarkable event. I have often given a copy to my nieces and others. I recently bought a copy to keep, at least until I find someone who needs to read it. For those who are into outdoor dramas, I recommend seeing the drama "The Long Way Home" at Radford, Virginia. Go early and visit the old ferry site on the New River where untold thousands used the ferry on the Wilderness Trail on their way to Cumberland Gap.

We should not automatically think the Indians to be totally uncivilized by these isolated incidents. Most Cherokees lived in towns west of the Blue Ridge in settlement days. Disease and militia raids decimated their ranks. The actions of the Shawnee, who raided all the way east of the Alleghanies, and the actions of renegade bands brought destruction upon the civilized Cherokee and the other civilized tribes. It is interesting to note that none of the above incidents were by Cherokees. The more serious were Shawnee who came all the way from the Ohio Valley. The others were wondering bands of renegades with only loose tribal ties.

A lot of people now tell me that they think they have Indian blood. (They once would have kept it secret.) Indian blood in an ancestry is very difficult to prove, but it is likely more prevalent than most area people think. Many mix-breed Indians melted into the local populations during the removal of about 1828. They often would not be welcomed by neighbors, but neighbors were scarce where most of them went. They already had English names in most cases. Waters, Ward, Sizemore and many other common settler's names have Indian blood. For those who wish to find their Indian kin, I recommend a search of the Guion Miller records of applications for payment for confiscated Indian lands. But be prepared to also find a history of discrimination. All dark-skinned people were listed as mulatto and joined their Negro brothers suffering from a discrimination that would be unthinkable today.

As the Indians were removed from the upper Yadkin, only small groups of the most destitute were left. Early Rowan records, before Wilkes was even formed, indicate a severe and growing problem. Court records detail an incident where Indians were removed at public expense. Instructions were to prevent the Indians from getting whiskey and to secure any property during the trip to prevent it from being stolen. More substantial Cherokees had already retreated west of the mountains at that time.

It is unlikely that any Cherokee born in the mountains ever really felt at home in Oklahoma. Up to a third died even before they got there. (The Trail of Tears) A lot of mountaineers can still relate to these feelings. My ancestor Samuel Greer, son of settler Benjamin Greer, lived in the Brownwood area from 1785 to 1872. He is said to have told this story. My grandfather Ivory Greer told it to me.

One winter day a commotion could be seen through the falling snow across the river. At intervals some movement in the bushes could be seen.

Samuel's curiosity finally got the better of him, and he poled his boat across to investigate. What he found was an old Indian who occasionally stood up to shake the snow from his blanket. When asked, the Indian said that he had "returned to the land of his heart to die." That was what happened a couple of days later and he was buried there.

My grandfather related this story. However true it may be, my grandfather did not read it for he was almost illiterate. He could very well have heard it from his grandfather Samuel.

## Indian Trails Become Roads

Our common perception of pre-settlement America is often not very accurate. We have long heard it was a "trackless wilderness" and we tend to believe it. We imagine an intrepid settler hacking his way through the forest to a site where he will fell trees and build a cabin. The truth is that by the time the axe settler appeared on the scene, the unknown wilderness had come and gone. The Indians had hunted over it, traded over it, fought over it and even farmed the land for centuries. By the time the axe settler appeared, the white men had already explored and even mapped most of it during the preceding one hundred years. It had not been as difficult as it sounds. They only had to use the system of paths and trails made by the Indians.

It would not be accurate to say that trackless forests did not exist, but the preponderance of the evidence supports a surprising lot of travel and interaction among the Indians. Theirs was a network of villages interconnected by trails, some of them hundreds of miles long. They used these trails and so did the early white men. (So would black men escaping from slave owners to fade into the wilderness.) Indian goods showed up hundreds of miles from their origin, but most of the really long distance travel related to the Indian sport of warfare. The "Great Warrior's Path" reached from central Pennsylvania deep into Georgia. (*The Great Wagon Road* by Parke Rouse, Jr.) Like an umbilical cord another trail reached from Southern Virginia through the Cumberland Gap. This would later often be called the "Shawnee Trail" for they would use it to raid into the Yadkin Valley.

Early knowledge of the new land and its system of trails came from the Indians. By 1646 Virginia traders had already grown rich as they pushed south into the Shenandoah Valley. The trail they used extended from central Pennsylvania all the way to the river valleys of the Carolinas and Georgia. In the north the western mountains barred easy settlement. Land was cheaper and the travel was easier to the south. Most of the upstate valleys, including the Yadkin, would be settled by people from further north rather than from the low country to the east. In short order they would turn the "Warrior's Path" into "The Great Wagon Road." This road would become the focus of defense against the French and Indians. When secured it would bind the colonies together and start patriots to dreaming of a new nation. The Shenandoah and Yadkin Valleys of the South would become a melting pot of Scots-Irish, German and English settlers. Together they would lose their national identities and develop a national character.

Early access into the interior was not important except for hunting and trade with the Indians. It was generally conceded to belong to the French anyway.

The French were on this land early. Early town sites had French names such as Louisville, Knoxville, Nashville, and Asheville, etc. These "ville" names linked to English surnames paid homage to the French who owned the lands. (Such names were less common east of the mountains, but some existed, probably due to a considerable number of Protestant French Huguenots in the population.) The French had expected little from the land except trade with the Indians. They did not often live on the land in either Western Canada or what became the United States unless they were intermarried with the Indians. French defense of the northern areas discouraged early western expansion. They depended on the Indians to do the same in the South.

After the French and Indian War western movement did not proceed at a very rapid pace immediately. It was generally expected that land west of the mountains would remain Indian. The Indians thought so. They had even agreed to return runaway slaves. They were to be rewarded with a rifle, shot and powder. Consideration for the Indians was not much deterrent to settlement, however. Travel access was still a major problem though. Wagon roads in the north were through wooded territory and often full of tree stumps. To be "stumped" became a common American term coming from a wagon becoming hung up on a stump. The far south at first did not receive population pressure to warrant much settlement. Besides, it was occupied by the "Civilized Tribes" and they received some respect. It was in the center of this long frontier that early settlement pressure was greatest and an entrance into western lands already existed. Sometimes called the "Shawnee Trail," the Virginians would develop it into "The Wilderness Trail" to Kentucky. Settlement in Kentucky seemed feasible because there were no permanent Indian villages here as there were to the south. The Cherokees sold part of Kentucky to Henderson and others but neither they nor the other tribes really claimed to own it.

Locally the Yadkin settlers had at least some early access to the west. An Indian trail ran up the Reddies River, across the Blue Ridge and into Southwest Virginia, all the while in view of the White Top Mountain. Daniel Boone used this route early on and had a campground where the trail crossed the South Fork of the New River. (This is where Highway 163 crosses the river today.) Boone likely crossed the Blue Ridge at Horse Gap near where US Highway 16 crosses the Blue Ridge today. (A gap still called Daniel's Gap is in the same area.) This trail accommodated Boone's horses and dogs. It is not often understood today that Boone's custom was to hunt with dogs and to transport his supplies and his skins and furs by pack horses. Boone's bearing would come from the "Meadow Mountain," or White Top, the first leg of his trip. This would take him to the settlements near present day Saltville, Virginia. There he would find the old trails across the Holston, Clinch and Powell Valleys to the Cumberland Gap. This was part of the "Warrior's Path" or "Shawnee Trail." The Cherokees usually got along well with the whites but both they and the Shawnees were concerned that the whites' settlements stay east of the mountains though no Indian tribe at the time claimed Kentucky and large areas of western Tennessee, except as a hunting grounds.

The early portion of this route was not something Boone had developed. He would later lead efforts to cut a trail through to the Cumberland Gap and to the Kentucky River. This would be only a "Trace". Wagon traffic would not be possible for another twenty years. The real "Wilderness Road" would be developed by the state of Virginia to facilitate travel to their westernmost county, Kentucky. It would reach from the "Great Wagon Road" running south at Fort Chiswell, Virginia, to the Cumberland Gap. (Fort Chiswell was established during the revolution to protect the lead mines near present day Austinville, Virginia.) The western access in this area through present day Wythe County was much better than in the North Carolina mountains. The latter would only become important after settlement of Eastern Tennessee and an increase in populations. It was likely spurred by the transport of salt from Saltville, Virginia to the Yadkin Valley. Trade, Tennessee was an important point on this route.

Boone was shown the trail through present day Ashe County by William Gist who lived with the Indians in 1750 at the Mulberry Fields on the Yadkin at present day Wilkesboro, NC. (Gist was America's earliest authority on Indians.

He was sought to negotiate with them during the French and Indian War.) Later, Boone was to cut a "trace" through a more southerly route to Kentucky, but this was after he moved his family to the Beaver Creek section of the upper Yadkin. There is no doubt that Boone knew of this shorter route from his hunting experiences. An Indian path likely existed but not a major one. It did not provide supplies nor grazing as did the old route. Why did he cut this "trace" then? I suspect that it was to please Richard Henderson who had hired Boone to lead settlers to Kentucky. Henderson was dreaming of a new state called Transylvania. He likely did not want to advertise his activities to Virginians more than necessary. But it had practical applications also. Boone's nephews had interests in land in the Three Forks area. Boone also traveled with his dogs. Most homesteads of that day were defended by dogs. Travel through settled areas involved inevitable dog fights.

I place Gist with the Indians for reasons I hope will be obvious. Gist was among Wilkes' very earliest settlers. He had been prosperous in Maryland prior to 1745 but had fallen on hard times. It took everything he had there to avoid debtor's prison. By 1750 he and his family were located with the Indians at the Mulberry Fields across the river from the mouth of what would be known as Moravian Creek. His time was prior to the Revolution but I place him as a patriot because of the tremendous influence he had on those events. His sons would later be heroes in that war.

Christopher Gist lived with and had the respect of the local Cherokees. He would also be respected by Indians west of the mountain even into the Ohio country for he was often in their lands. Land speculators employed him as surveyor and as their agent to secure land from the Indians. During the French and Indian Wars Gist would become the colony's first line of defense on the American frontier. He was employed to convince the Indians to support the British rather than the French.

Gist would work with many surveyors including the young George Washington. He is credited with saving the young George's life. During one of his trips Gist would eventually die from small-pox and be buried on the side of the road between Williamsburg and Winchester, Virginia. His influence would be long lasting, however. He had shown Daniel Boone the Indian trail through the upper New River Valley into Virginia after Daniel had exhausted the supply of bears on Hunting Creek. Gist's sons would remain in the area and fight for independence. Most importantly, his son Nathaniel would marry a Cherokee princess. Nathaniel would later die at Kings Mountain, but his son would be one of the greatest geniuses the country ever produced regardless of race. He would invent the Cherokee alphabet. His name was Sequoyah.

Today's historians seem to doubt any Cherokee occupation of the upper Yadkin and the New River. It is true that most of our recorded Cherokee history is about towns centered in present day western North Carolina and the Tennessee Valley. But we get occasional glimpses of early contact with Cherokee villagers along these watersheds. Cherokee tradition is that their lands reached to Virginia's White Top Mountain and even further north along the New River. It is clear that they felt defensive toward this area, before their population began its decline. Why else would they have fought the Catawba at Warrior's Gap or would they have attacked settlers moving into the upper Yadkin?

However, this resistance was not an organized action and was doomed to early failure. The truth is that the Cherokee was not a member of a unified tribe. He was member of a tribe, but he lived in independent, self-governing towns and villages. While the individual Cherokee could be a fierce warrior, he only had the support of his immediate village as a rule. Later, too late to be exact, he would attempt to band together. By this time the time was gone for anything but a rear-guard action. By that time also the civilized Cherokee tribe would limit their efforts to the courts and appeals to Congress.

The Cherokee also had other notable characteristics well worth noting here. Of particular interest is the status of both men and women. The men generally hunted and provided protection for family and village. They spent much of their time out on the hunting grounds. The villages, with their nearby cornfields and woods, were the territory of the women and the children. Here they would also provide much of the family's food by raising crops, catching fish and small animals and gathering nuts and berries. This would be the pattern of life until the Cherokee later took up white men's ways and began to live in the log farmhouses, till the soil, plant orchards and pasture livestock.

The Cherokee also differed significantly from other Indians in another way. The frequent absence of the men in effect made the women head of the household. Her responsibilities were the home and the children. Her husband had come to live with her when they were married, and her sons would also become members of their wives' families. When the woman's child rearing years were over, she often was raised to a unique position in the tribe. She sometime received the title of "Beloved Woman." These women were heard in the tribal councils with respect. There is no evidence that the council was under any obligation to grant their wishes though they sometimes did. At least often enough to give the most respected of them a lot of power. Cherokee princess Nancy Ward was a "Beloved Woman." She is credited with saving the lives of white captives.

The most amazing thing about the Cherokee is how well he adopted white ways. From almost the beginning, he sought to have firearms, cooking pots and woven clothing as well as ribbons and beads. They welcomed traders and sought to provide furs, etc. that were in demand. They paid a heavy price for their contact with the whites. Many other tribes fell into the same pattern. But the Cherokee probably made the best effort of any to deal with these problems. He developed a system for writing and published the news. He made significant efforts to participate in government. He also adopted white men's religion and even made it work for him in problem areas. Drunkenness, for example, fell into disrepute and largely ceased to be a problem for the Cherokee of that era.

Why then did the Cherokee fail to achieve a proper place in the new experiment with democracy? It is easy enough to lay it to white men's greed and prejudice for this is an accurate assessment of our history. However, we now seem to be entering into an era of re-examination and rewriting of our history. If the new works are not lost in the oceans of tradition which bind up our present history, we may at last realize a more honest account.

Perhaps we should start with a more honest account of how the white men came to be in America in the first place. Our first inclination is to say, "religious freedom." Most settlers from Quaker, Mennonite, various Scotch, French and other Protestant and Jewish faiths would indicate this to be so. It is to some extent. However, could religious discrimination have motivated and provided the means to relocate across a dangerous and stormy ocean? It is not likely that religious freedom nor the desire for adventure alone energized relocation on such a grand scale. It was true for the ordinary settler, but the common denominator of all reasons had to be the profit motive. Most emigrants had to have been part of some arrangement or scheme that was expected to leave the promoter better off economically. (The English shipped a few Scottish prisoners of war but not a very large number.) Reality is that business concerns in England were into the grandest real estate development in history and they needed customers. With home grown initiative it only grew greater after independence. It raged hell-for-leather across the continent and the Indian got steamrollered in the process. If the Indian got in the way he was removed, either forcefully or otherwise.

Settlement of the local area was much influenced by two rivers, the Yadkin and New. The Yadkin River valley was the attraction that drew the Boones and all the others down the Great Wagon Road from Pennsylvania. If you have ever stood on the Highway 21 overlook between Sparta and Elkin, North Carolina, you would never question why again. The Miller side of my family likely first lived in Pennsylvania or New Jersey. The Greer side of the family came by way of Maryland and Virginia. Both families ended up on the upper Yadkin of what became Wilkes County prior to the Revolution. Not much is known about this Miller family before, but the Greer family's journey is well documented. After Maryland they had lived on Tick Creek on the Roanoke River (now called the

Blackwater Prong) before settling on cub Creek near Moravian Falls in Wilkes. There is still a significant Greer presence in Virginia, but I suspect the original homestead may be on the bottom of Smith Mountain Lake. The John Greer of Cub Creek was already fourth generation American.

The Miller history is less clear, but it is known that they were part of the Jersey settlement that was involved in the Regulator Movement. A William Miller is mentioned in the book *Breaking Loose Together* by Marjoleine Kars; but there was more than one William Miller in that age. William Miller assaulted Justice William McBride of Roan, cursing "God damn you, your commission and them that gave it to you."[1] The Battle of Alamance greatly influenced the settlement of the mountain valley in the west. It also documents the dominance of the eastern establishment over the west that is so much of our history.

By the 1760's westerners outnumbered the eastern establishment; but, were at its mercy. Westerners had very different ideas on government in particular. They wanted to know what the tax laws said and who they applied to. They even wanted to know what the money was for, and who ended up with it. In fact, they were willing to send representatives to help figure things out. They were particularly offended by the governor's mansion, Tryon's Palace, being built for Governor Tryon at a cost of 115,000 pounds. They were willing to withhold their taxes to get a voice in the government. When one of their members had a horse seized and sold to pay his taxes, they boldly took the horse and saddle back and returned them to the owner. From there on things got bad.

These "Watchdog" activities earned the name of "Regulators." They gathered in large unruly groups to protest for they felt a God-given right to the freedom of assembly. Governor Tryon himself called over 1,400 well-armed militiamen to disperse an even larger, but poorly armed, group of Regulators. Tryon ordered the Regulators to disband or be fired upon. The reply was given, "Fire and be damned." Tryon gave the order, but the militia hesitated. He then said, "fire on them or fire on me." The militia complied and the Battle of Alamance was on.

The Regulators were poorly armed and were badly defeated. Twelve were arrested and six were later hanged. Tradition has it that they were all Baptists. At any rate the defeat had the effect of scattering the Baptists to the west far away from Tryon. Those who could tried to get to western Virginia. Some went up through Fancy Gap, VA and westward to settle only to find years later they were in the Tennessee portion of North Carolina. Others took their chances in the hills and foothills of the Blue Ridge. Wherever they went they only became more fanatical about their religion. Ironically, they would now bring a significant portion of English blood to the west albeit opposed to the Crown.

The Battle of Alamance contributed significantly to the growing needed for independence that many were beginning to feel. The New and Watauga River settlements and the upper Yadkin would become hotbeds of rebellion against England and its Monarchy. It became a bitter Civil War with neighbor seeking reprisal against neighbor with increasing cruelty. No one was safe from roaming bands of Tories. Benjamin Cleveland had a solution for this. He hung them on the "Tory Oak" at the old Wilkes County Courthouse.

During the time of the Regulators lands ceased to be sold by the Granville Grant offices. It would never be for sale again. The Greers and Lowes arrived on Cub Creek near the Mulberry fields about the same time about 1768. They could only squat on the good land that they had found and hope the situation would change for the better. Their situation was better than that of many others for John Greer, Jr. and his several sons were able to find land together. They had known and inter-married with their neighbors, the Lowes in Virginia. The Hampton and Demoss sons-in-law would also settle on adjoining property. Together they were a formidable group able to defend their interests.

No one would question the claims that the Cub Creek group had. This was fortunate for the land could not be entered until after the Declaration of Independence. The new state government appropriated the Granville Grant and started to accept filings on it in 1779. Even then it would be years, if ever before people received title to their land.

The few people west of the Blue Ridge largely moved to safer territory, at least temporarily, during the Revolution. About 215 families remained in the whole New River headwaters until the end of the war. After the war was over, however, there was a rush to file on land west of the ridge. Confusion prevailed. The land was known and mapped, and the big game mostly gone, but that was not the problem. There were many hunters' cabins and even improvements but who could be certain who they belonged to or whether the owner would ever come back? William Miller and Nathan Horton filed on lands in the Bamboo area of present-day Watauga County that had cabins on them. Both hunters eventually returned. They must have worked it out for early Wilkes court records show that they had business with one another in later years. Benjamin Greer must have had an amicable agreement with Reubin Stringer for he filed on Stringer's improvement and 100 acres. Stringer filed for an adjoining 150 acres the same day Benjamin filed his claim.

Others had far more difficulty in filing claims. None of them would get titles for years and how to hold a claim was a problem. To have a large family and agreeable neighbors helped, but friends in the county court helped even more. In the meantime, steps were taken to solidify the claim. Axe marks helped if they were fresh and had someone to defend them. So did a cabin, if it was occupied, but many were not and might be available for filing. One of the best signs that land was taken was a growing crop of corn. (This was worth more in Virginia where a settler was allowed to file on 100 acres of land for every acre of corn that he planted.) Real permanence, however, could best be had with another crop rarely thought of today. That was the planting of peach trees. The country is still full of place names like Peach Orchard and Peach Bottom Mountain. The peach of the time was the red and white Indian peaches. They matured quickly and were very tasty. They were not near so juicy as the modern peach and were easily dried for winter. If there was ever a surplus it would make good brandy. A serious settler would likely carry peach seeds or peach seedlings along with his bag of seed corn.

Other areas of the "country-to-be" would differ greatly from the population mix predominant locally. The Hudson River Valley had its Dutch and New Jersey had its Swedes. The true Irish and the Italians would contribute large numbers later on, but they were not numerous in early settlements. That is not to say they were never present, however. Lower Scotland and England had long been melting pots. A Tallifero family mentioned in early Wilkes records was Italian that had already been in England for three generations. Early records also mention a "Spanyard" living on the trail to New River.

Most of the Indian trails used by hunters and early settlers crossed the mountains with little regard to elevation. Game trails and the more open forests were the preferred routes. My Greer ancestors and others crossed the Blue Ridge at what is now Jeffries Park on the Blue Ridge Parkway. Benjamin Cutbirth found good land for settlement there and it was referred to as Cutbirth's Plantation. The trail descending to the Gap Creek area is now known as the Hege Greene Road. My Deep Gap, NC home was on the creek following this road. Above me was a water bottling plant. I believe the water source is the historic fire springs often given a reference point and campsite in early Wilkes County records. A lot of people would be surprised to know that a Wilkes court order to view a road from Lewis Fork through the deep gap of the mountain was not given until 1806, some thirty years after the early settlements.

One of the most prevalent misconceptions held by those of us brought up in the Boone, NC area concerns the travel routes used by Daniel Boone to reach Kentucky. It is almost certain that he came through the Boone Valley late in his travels, but it is also almost certain that he preferred other routes early on. What's more, there is little indication that he ever used today's route through Deep Gap. In fact, there is no mention of anyone using the Deep Gap route in early records in Wilkes County. It is not until after that county was formed in 1779 that

Benjamin Greer and others are asked by the county court to lay out trails down Gap creek to the Old Fields on New River. Even later they would be asked to lay out a route through the gap of Rich and Snake Mountains to the area of what is now Trade, Tennessee.

Boone's first trip to Kentucky did not cross the Blue Ridge in present day North Carolina at all. He had first heard of the Kentucky territory while serving as a teamster in Braddock's Army in 1755. A fellow teamster, John Findley, had been to Kentucky earlier. Boone became determined to see it for himself and made the journey in 1767. This was after the end of the French and Indian War and resistance to English settlement seemed to be breaking down. On his first trip, Boone went back up the Great Wagon Road through Fancy Gap, Virginia, to the area of Fort Chiswell. From there he headed west by way of Castle's Wood and into Kentucky's Big Sandy River country. Later his most used route would be up the Reddies River and across the Blue Ridge to the New River. Nathaniel Gist, a Boone hunting partner and also a French and Indian War veteran is believed to have shown Boone this route. It appears that the route through the present-day Boone Valley was not use by him until after Boone moved his family to Beaver Creek on the Yadkin. This was near where Elk Creek comes out of the mountains and that creek led to the Blue Ridge and Cook's Gap.

There are several reasons for believing the Ashe County route to have been an early route Boone most commonly used.

1. The existence of a well-traveled Indian trail connecting the Mulberry Fields on the Yadkin to the Indian Old Fields on the New River. (This route also was likely used by Shawnee raiders coming out of the Ohio Valley.)

2. Nathaniel Gist, Wilkes County's first permanent settler, lived with the Cherokees at the Mulberry Fields by 1750 and would almost certainly have known the route. He was a friend and hunting partner of Daniel

Boone and it said to have shown Daniel how to cross the Blue Ridge to the New River.

3. Open lands and game trails likely existed along the tributaries of the Reddies River all the way into the Blue Ridge and could have accessed Horse, Calloway, Benge or Daniel's Gaps. This may not have been the case with Deep Gap however. There is little territory along the upper Lewis Fork that appears to have been open land early on. Access to the Deep Gap up the north fork of Stoney Fork Creek seems to have been impassible. It is still difficult today. The marshy exit out to the Gap Creek watershed was not likely to have encouraged heavy animals to enter so no game trail likely existed except into Stoney Fork.

4. Early settlement patterns show that the Upper Reddies and Old Fields area on the South Fork of the New to have been settled first. Early settlers on the New were Boone kin and hunting partners. Benjamin Cutbirth and Benjamin Greer often hunted with Boone and both married daughters of Boone's older sister Sarah Boone Wilcoxen. Thomas Calloway, a Boone hunting partner, would form the Calloway settlement near where present-day Highway 163 crosses the New River in Ashe County. His son, Elijah Calloway, would also marry Boone kin. (This little band of patriots would survive the Revolutionary War by fortifying the Calloway home.)

5. Tradition and the Calloway cemetery are also evidence. Boone often used the area of present-day Calloway cemetery as a campground. It appears to have been an Indian field at the time and is believed to have already had a cemetery where Indians were buried. When Boone could reach this point across the New, his horses and dogs likely resigned themselves to the trail and gave up trying to return home. Boone liked this area very much. (It bears some resemblance to Boonesborough, KY.) Tradition has it that he hoped to live and to die there. A unique long and slender rock that he had found was to be the headstone of his grave. Thomas Calloway kept it

for twenty-five years against Boone's return. When that became unlikely, Calloway used the stone for his own grave marker. It can be seen today in the Calloway cemetery standing among Boone's friends and kin.

6.  Once on top of the Blue Ridge in the vicinity of Horse or Calloway Gaps, the "Meadow Mountain" (White Top) in Virginia was plainly visible. This was a known landmark which guided the way to the Glade Spring area leading to the Castle Wood fort and settlement. Some think that Bald Mountain on the present-day Ashe-Watauga County line might have been mistaken for White Top. If so, Boone and others might have gone through the gap of Rich Mountain. I doubt this. Bald Mountain turns a wooded shoulder to the east and cannot be identified as a bald by travelers coming from that side. (Bald Mountain was visible to Spangenburg as he came up from the south, however.)

7.  If, as some would have us believe, Boone used the Boone, NC route, some historical facts would have to be questioned. When Boone overstayed his leave in Kentucky is an example. His father, Squire, went to look for him. It is well documented that Squire retraced a route that went by the Virginia lead mines. This is much too far to the east for anyone traveling through the present-day Boone, NC area.

8.  Well-documented Boone campsites along what became the Virginia Creeper railway bed.

At one time I doubted that Boone developed a trail through the Boone Valley at all. There is no doubt that he hunted often in the area and was very familiar with it. No doubt that he used the meat camp on the creek of that name and used the herder's cabin on the site of the present-day Appalachian State University Campus. A trail to Kentucky through this area would not have helped him much until he moved to Beaver Creek on the Yadkin. By this time there would have been some settlement on the Watauga where supplies could be had. This route by then would have become a practical shortcut for horses but not for wagons. For that matter, it was twenty years after Boone cut a trace through the Cumberland Gap before that portion become a wagon road. Eventually 300,000 people would pass through that gap on their way west.

Boone had a great attraction to the "Great Glades of the Three Forks" (Boone Valley). It was here that he taught his eldest son, James, to hunt. It was here that he would have moved rather than Beaver Creek if Rebecca would have permitted. Boone was a hunter by profession, and he wanted to be near the game he hunted, but Rebecca knew that it was her garden that fed the family.

Boone interest in the area was not yet over, however. John Boone entered the good land adjoining Council's in the area of present-day Hardin Park School. Behind this school and the present day new Methodist church is a phenomenon that ties those early days and the Boone extended family to the days of my childhood. My Grandmother Miller on Howard's Creek referred to the gash in the eastern side of Howard's Knob as "Cutbirth's Chimney" or "Cutbirth's Smokehole" because of the frequent columns of fog which rose from it after a rain. Benjamin Cutbirth had married Daniel Boone's niece but the connection with the name Cutbirth meant nothing to grandma. But the fogs did. She observed that if the fogs went up the mountains to the west, wet weather would continue, but if they drifted east away from the mountain clearing weather was likely on the way. Today the chimney is sometimes called "Sampson's Chimney." The Cutbirth name is lost to recent generations though in early records Cutbirth was more prominent as a long hunter and as an area settler than Daniel Boone himself. Cutbirth for example, had left with a party from the New River area to west Tennessee the spring of 1767 before Daniel Boone left for Kentucky in the fall. Cutbirth's party consisted of himself and John and James Ward that we know of. They made their way all the way to New Orleans and sold their furs but were robbed on the Natchez Trail on the way home. It is interesting to note the relationship the Wards either had or developed with the Cherokee Indian tribe. A Cherokee Indian princess named "Beloved Woman" lived in an Indian town near where

Bean's Station, Tennessee is today. She married a Brian Ward and took the name of Nancy Ward. She is credited with saving the lives of whites captured by the Indians. She was much respected in their councils.

Daniel Boone would have lasting family ties to the present-day Boone Valley. Daniel and Rebecca adopted Daniel's brother Israel's children after Israel and his wife's death from consumption. Their names were Jesse and Jonathan. They lived in Daniel's household until the family moved to Kentucky in 1773. They would have been in their twenties by that time and had, or would, settle in the Boone Valley themselves. They were early members of the Three Forks Baptist Church but, like Benjamin Greer, were sometimes at odds with the rules of that church on drinking.

# 4

---

# Independence

It seems odd now that my family was still talking about Kings Mountain when I was a child. Apparently, they still saw it as a pivotal event of the most important war in our history. It seems odd also that the conversation did not claim ancestor Benjamin Greer killed Ferguson during that battle. It was not questioned but neither was it talked about. I am sure, however, that my elders would have felt that history, as recorded, made some mistakes and left some important things out. I will try to correct these. All wars involve great personal sacrifice and are therefore important. The American Civil War called for the greatest of sacrifices. So did the American Revolution. But I believe we are prone to overlook the most important war to the birth of our nation, the French and Indian War. We are inclined to think of the birth of our country as a matter of providence or fate and some of it was. But many elements of the French and Indian War on this continent had both intentional and unintentional long-lasting effects.

The major objective of the British and their American colonies was to establish firm control of the Atlantic seaboard west to the eastern continental divide. The second objective was to confine the Indians to the lands beyond the divide along with their French allies. To accomplish all this a major effort was mounted. English soldiers and hired German mercenaries were stationed in the colonies. The military capabilities of the colonials were expanded, and forts were built along the Great Wagon Road and in the northern lake country. From about 1754 to 1763 a long series of engagements were fought with the Indians and the French. These were bloody and often bumbling events, but in the end the British won probably more than they expected. The French conceded everything east of the high mountains and the Indians agreed as well. The war had really ended in Europe and the British were triumphant. But the colonies and the colonists would never be the same.

The French use of Indians against the British colonies was especially brutal in the north. Settlers following the Great Wagon Road south began to feel safer farther south into North Carolina. The Pennsylvania Dutch had never welcomed the rowdy Scotch-Irish anyway. They and many English and German settlers flooded south all the way into the Yadkin Valley of North Carolina. Among them would be family ancestors Greer, Miller and Boone.

The end of the French and Indian War left the birth of our nation well under way. The colonies moved quickly to consolidate their gains with new settlements. The war also played a pivotal part in dealing with the Indians, but important factors leading to the revolution were evident. They were:

1.  The colonials lost much of their respect for the British military. It was evident to the colonials that the British could be easily defeated by anyone fighting Indian style. Yet the British would not change their tactics. On the other hand, the British were also contemptuous of the colonial militia.

2.  The rudiments of a colonial army were being formed. The officers of the future revolution, including George Washington, were being trained. An English man wrote, "There is not a tavern keeper or stage owner in all Western Virginia, or a great woodchopper, who has not some military title. Anyone who so much as kills a rattlesnake is made a major on the spot." After bad experiences with untrained troops, George Washington would literally whip his into shape. Many were no more than runaway boys of 14,

15 and 16 years of age. Everything from drunkenness and lesser offenses was dealt with a required number of lashes. Serious offenses meant hanging or a firing squad. All this from an officer who was said to be seen later during the revolution on his knees in Valley Forge's snow praying for his men while tears rolled down his cheeks. Of such is the personal baggage of war whether experienced by the disciplined or the discipliner.

3. The colonists had become manufacturers and merchants of their own goods. Not only did they trade along the Great Wagon Road, but they also sailed the high seas. One particular development was the answer to the frontiersman prayer, the Pennsylvania rifle. The country that had the technology to make such an instrument would soon be able to perform other technological miracles. Not only is the American rifle a thing of beauty, it has long had a positive effect on our development as an industrial nation.

4. Last, I would list the most commonly listed reasons for the revolution, the raising of tariffs and taxes to be paid by the colonials. The British had grown weary of providing for the defense of the colonies. They took measures to recover their own costs and to place the burden of providing for their army on the colonists. Colonials saw the real conflict to be in Europe and resented every levy. Without representation in the government, independence seemed the only solution to many. They were never a huge majority, however. As many as half of the colonials remained loyal to the king, maybe even more in the south where trade with the mother country was greater. Whenever military events turned against the colonials, Tories were a threat in a large part of the colonies. The patriots would prevail only by sheer will and determination. A few well-directed political moves also helped. Tories were denied land ownership and were hounded by the militia if they were active in defense of the crown. By the same token, Patriots stood to lose everything and be hanged if they failed.

The Revolution was not really over everything we see in history books. It had been a long time coming. It had been brewing in Scotland for generations due to religion and the English mercantile system. The Scots long endured the persecution of their Presbyterian Church and the required payment of taxes to support the Church of England.

In the colonies passions still ran high on both sides. In Arthur Herman's, *How the Scots Invented the Modern World*, a mercenary Hessian officer said in 1778, "Call this war by whatever name you may, only call it not an American rebellion; it is nothing more than a Scots-Irish Presbyterian rebellion."[1] Feelings were deep almost beyond description. Herman also relates the experiences of an Anglican missionary who tried to preach in the Carolina mountains. He says the locals "disrupted his services, rioted while he preached, started a pack of dogs fighting outside the church, loosed his horse, stole his church key, refused him food and shelter, and gave two barrels of whisky to his congregation." The sooner a revolution the better.

The King's Mountain victory is properly credited to over mountain men, but the New River settlements also provided heroes. One account sometimes showing up in local papers is "The Ride of Martin Gambill". Gambill seems to have settled in what became Ashe County sometime after the Battle of Alamance. British Major Patrick Ferguson had sent a message to the western settlements promising their destruction unless they stayed out of the conflict with the crown. Colonel Isaac Shelby, Colonel John Sevier and other patriot leaders were offended by the challenge and made plans to oppose him. Gambill volunteered to carry a message to Colonel William Campbell who lived at Seven Mile Ford in Virginia. Gambill rode over 100 miles in a sparsely settled territory. It is said that he spent over 24 hours in the saddle with little food and no rest. He rode two horses to death but delivered the vital message.

Listing of New River participants in the King's Mountain action is not very complete. A staff person at the old courthouse museum in Jefferson once gave me a logical reason for this. He said the New River men had reported to the Sycamore Shoals assembly rather than to Cleveland who commanded their militia units. As a result, they had failed to be included in the rosters of either command.

King's Mountain is a long story but deserves to be told over and over again. My ancestors on both Greer and Miller side took part, Benjamin Greer as a captain in Cleveland's militia and William Miller as a supply officer for the same outfit. I do not say this boastfully. Such family connections were common in western North Carolina, eastern Tennessee and southwestern Virginia in my youth.

My account of the affair must be much abbreviated, but some things stand out. First, the participants assembled from a large, sparsely populated area. There was no means of communication except for people like Martin Gambill. Second, there was no overall command structure. One was agreed to while on the march apparently with some rancor and envy. Third, the units assembled on short notice. Horseback was the preferred transportation early on. Fourth, the band of patriots was huge when you consider the sparseness of the settlement of that time. Shelby's Virginians and Wataugans would number about 800 while Cleveland's sharpshooters were numbered at about 350. Other western North Carolina units and South Carolinians from the local area would push their numbers to about 1,600. Ferguson was expected to have less than 1,200. Fifth and last, has to be the depth of determination and spirit the patriots exhibited.

Ferguson would have the advantage despite patriot numbers. His was the choice of a defensive position. Once entrenched on the high ground of his choosing he was said to have boasted that, "God almighty Himself could not push him off." On the other hand, the patriots were hoping to have the advantage of surprise. In order to arrive before they were expected they had elected to push on at top speed with only those 910 men who were considered well mounted. They covered the last 45 miles during a rainy night and the following morning hours. By the time they began their assault they had not rested in the last 35 hours.

They had completely surrounded Ferguson though he may not have realized this. Shelby's forces would attack on the more gentle and open slopes on the north and the west. Area locals from North and South Carolina would attack from the east. Cleveland's men (perhaps the best trained and most experienced) would fight their way up the steep rear entrance to Ferguson's position. They fought Indian style from tree to tree conserving their ammunition and always keeping some rifles ready while others were reloading.

All units began a probing action about three in the afternoon. This was the plan, if it could be called that. But it was an action that these backwoods hound dog men understood. When their enemy turned to defend one flank he was assaulted on the other. Ferguson had been 'treed." He was being worked like a pack of hounds would work their prey. But time did not permit the patriots to continue toying with Ferguson until nightfall. Shelby's men charged the more gentle slopes to their front on horseback. These over-the-mountain men rolled Ferguson's defenses down the ridge where they would be crushed on the anvil that was Cleveland and others.

Cleveland's men had fought their way up to where the slope was more gentle and there was a better field of fire. When Ferguson realized that Cleveland's position was his only possible escape, he charged them. But the Wilkes men and others on their flanks held. Cleveland's men had been trained to shoot accurately and to kill the officers first. When Ferguson appeared on their front, he was reportedly struck by eight bullets. Several have been credited with shooting Ferguson. Among them has been my ancestor Benjamin Greer.

Probably the most amazing thing of all was the "foot cavalry" left behind 45 miles back. Urged on by the sounds of the battle they arrived on the scene before the mopping up was completed. Many accounts of the battle would leave one to think Ferguson's men were largely poorly trained colonists. This is misleading. All were American, but two companies were New Jersey – New York area regulars.

They were as well trained and equipped as the usual British soldier. They composed a majority of Ferguson's troops by some accounts.

King's Mountain was still a frequent subject of conversation in my family when I was a child. It seems odd now that the subject of Ferguson's death did not come up in these conversations that I can recall, although Arthur's *History of Watauga County* gave Benjamin Greer credit for shooting Ferguson. Arthur was the grandson of a King's Mountain veteran himself and interviewed many locals around 1912-15 who might have been knowledgeable of the facts. He deserves some credibility though it is highly unlikely that any one person can be said to have killed Ferguson. I believe that Pat Alderman's, *The Overmountain Men*, is the best researched and most scholarly account available today. He stops short of naming any one shooter. However, he does say that most historians credit Robert Young.

To me, there are several weaknesses to the Young story. First, Young was quoted as saying "We will see what Sweet Lips (the name he gave his rifle) can do." With the gunfire from 2,000 rifles and the yelling of 2,000 men, this does not seem plausible to me. The people who believe this story surely have never been exposed to much gunfire and especially not from black powder rifles. Rufus Myers, in his book *North Carolina's Northwest Frontier*, carries the Young story even further. He states that Young shoots Ferguson in the head.[2] Not only does the witness have excellent hearing, but he also has exceptional vision to follow a bullet from a particular rifle to an impact in Ferguson's head, and this above all the other gunfire and gun smoke.

I think it wise not to credit anyone. If factual, Young's shot to the head would have most likely been delivered at close range after Ferguson had already been wounded several times and was already near death. Only under such a circumstance could there have been a reliable witness it seems to me. Bobby Gilmer Moss in *The Patriots at King's Mountain* prints a disposition for a pension by one Joseph Starnes that he saw Ferguson's body and it had at least seven wounds. It is unlikely that a head shot was an early one.

For years I was haunted by a vague memory of another King's Mountain tale that did turn out to be a part of family oral history. Alderman's great book brought it all back with his account of Joseph Greer's ride to carry the victory message to Philadelphia. I had first heard it as a child from my Grandmother Greer's account of "Little Joe Greer's Ride." Grandma Greer knew more Greer history than Grandpa, for she was also a descendant of Benjamin Greer.

The best account of the King's Mountain Messenger" seems to be Pat Alderman's, *The Overmountain Men*.[3] It is well researched and well documented. Alderman records that Joseph Greer had one or more horses shot from under him by the Indians. Much of the trip had to be covered on foot. He had to swim several streams, some with floating ice. One night was spent in a big hollow log, hiding from a party of braves who had been following him all day. From his concealment in the log, he could hear them talking as they tried to pick up his trail. It is said that they actually sat on the log for a spell.

Greer was given a musket and a compass for the trip. Why would Sevier pick one so young for such an important mission? Actually, Little Joe was uniquely qualified. He had lived much of his young life on the frontier west of the mountains. His father, Andrew Greer, was an Indian trader and these were welcomed among the Indians for they desired the white man's goods. This might be of advantage though the British were currently promoting an Indian war against the Watauga settlements. Little Joe would be at risk but knowing the Indian towns and trails had to be an advantage. Little Joe would also have some knowledge of the Great Wagon Road up through the Virginia valleys to Philadelphia. It is possible that he and his father had traveled it to secure trade goods for their businesses.

On Greer's arrival in Philadelphia, he made his way to congressional headquarters. The doorkeeper tried to block him, but Greer pushed him aside and delivered his message to a very surprised body of delegates.

As a reward for his services, Greer was given a grant of 3,000 acres of land in what is now Lincoln County, Tennessee. He prospered there and accumulated much more land. Alderman says that one could ride in a straight line all day and not get off his land. (This property was due south of Nashville, Tennessee near the Alabama state line.) The original grant resulted from a request to congress by the first president, George Washington, to reward veterans. Washington himself was involved in western lands as a young man. He knew the new government was otherwise broke except for land. The grants ranged from 500 to 3,000 acres. Greer's contribution to the war effort must have been considered significant in that day for he received the maximum acreage.

Many mountain people would later feel that politically correct history had short-changed the importance of the King's Mountain victory in particular and the war in the South in general. Sevier must have been well aware that the war effort needed a huge morale boost. The treason of Benedict Arnold had devastated Continental leaders and Arnold, now a British general, was ravaging eastern Virginia almost at will. (Interestingly, then Virginia governor Thomas Jefferson was considered inept in the state's local affairs.) Sevier must have felt a need to encourage the congress and also draw attention to the needs and the possibilities in the South. Washington sent his favorite general, Nathaniel Greene, to fight a most unorthodox war for the times. By December he was in Charlotte, North Carolina beginning a war of attrition against British forces. Greene's strategy was to do as much damage as possible without risking the complete destruction of his own army. It would later be said that he never won a battle but that he won the war.

The Overmountain Men continued to be a part of Greene's battles but never to the extent of King's Mountain. That had been a spontaneous response of like-minded neighbors defending family and homes. Their major concern now was defense against the Indians that the British were using on the frontier. The western settlements were a world of their own anyway. Theirs was a community of largely local interests that went beyond the war and even North Carolina government. They were dreaming of a state of their own to be approved by the Continental Congress. If so, present day Ashe and Watauga Counties would today be in the state of Franklin. Through all this, North Carolina seems to either not know or not care.

Fortunately, the state of Tennessee did not totally forget Greer. A suit of his clothes is on display in the Tennessee State Museum along with a painting by Volosio. The painting shows Greer in complete Davy Crockett attire barging through the door with his message to Congress. Grandma Greer's account was accurate except that "Little Joe" was not little; he was said to have been near seven foot tall. Surely his ride deserves as much acclaim as Paul Revere and Martin Gambill's. At least, it garnered Washington's attention and support for one of his best generals, Nathanial Greene, for the war effort in the south.

Grandma Greer's account of Little Joe's ride covered only the essentials, and I was too young to appreciate the importance of the event. She possibly did not know much of the circumstances, but she did know that it deserved a more important place in our history than it received in North Carolina history. All too often the state's power structure could not see beyond the western foothills. The Watauga settlements had a Sullivan County land office under the new government but at the end of the war still had no court system or military to protect the frontier. (Max Dixon's *The Wataugans*.)[4]

No local history of the Revolution would be complete without accounting for Benjamin Cleveland. He was the driving force behind local war efforts arising out of the Wilkes County area. Unlike the Overmountain Men, he had official status. He was a militia colonel appointed by the newly formed state government. As such he administered a form of military justice that was often harsh and cruel. It was a civil war and each side preyed upon the other persons and possessions. Perhaps stern and cruel actions were called for.

Benjamin Cleveland was an early Wilkes settler. He established a plantation, "Round-About," on the Yadkin. (A shortened version is said to have rendered the present-day name of Ronda, NC.) Benjamin became prominent early on in efforts to resist British tyranny and to establish a county government in the area. He was a huge man whose training was in building, but rambling seems to have been more to his liking. He hunted extensively along the north and south forks of New River west of the Blue Ridge. He was said to have once found himself surrounded by rattlesnakes on a rock ledge on the north fork of New River. He forgot about elk hunting and jumped backwards into the river to escape. The location was called Rattlesnake Den when land entries were made in later years.

Cleveland had numerous land interests in what is now Ashe County. He once owned 400 acres at what is now West Jefferson. He also had interests on Pine Swamp and at the mouth of Gap Creek. The hewed log gap on Idlewild Road likely referred to a hewn log used to hold salt for his cattle. He placed these holdings and his Yadkin plantation at risk by prosecuting the Revolution. The *Wilkes County Heritage* gives accounts of his activities.

In the spring of 1777, Captain Cleveland and his men were sent to protect the Watauga settlements against the Cherokees and served until the treaty of Long Island was made in July of that year when they returned to the Yadkin valley. In the autumn Cleveland attended the North Carolina assembly to use his influence toward the dividing of Surry and forming a new county. In March 1778, Wilkes County was organized. Cleveland was made head of the commission of justices and colonel of the militia. He was also elected to represent Wilkes in the House of Commons, and in the state senate.

"Old Round-About," as Cleveland was often called, claimed that each of his men was equal to five ordinary soldiers. They did their full share toward freeing the colonies from the British rule.

When the call came to aid in the campaign against Ferguson, Cleveland gathered his men together on Rendezvous Mountain, in Wilkes County. About 350 men marched to Quaker Meadows, joined other patriots who took part in the campaign, and moved on to King's Mountain. The battle was fought 7 October 1780, and Col. Ferguson was killed.

Rendezvous Mountain is at the tip of a spur of the Blue Ridge chain which reached to a point nine miles from Wilkesboro. Cleveland's assembly area gives some insight into settlement patterns of the day. It was convenient to Cleveland's home and the Reddies River settlement. It was also not too far from the patriots, Calloways, Greers and others, just across the Blue Ridge on the New River. It also demonstrates that the early travel routes were not up Elk Creek of the Yadkin nor through what became known as Deep Gap.

Unfortunately, Cleveland has long held the reputation for cruelty for his hanging of Tories. Others go to great lengths to prove that his heart was not really in it. When a young son pleaded that one Tory be spared, Cleveland was said to have had tears in his eyes. He explained, "If I let him go, he will return to stealing and destroying our food and killing our people." He promptly hanged the Tory. Another Tory was later turned over to Cleveland's young sons while Cleveland was away. Not having any certain way to confine the prisoner, they asked their mother what do. She replied, "What would your father do?" They promptly hanged the Tory. The Tory Oak at the old Wilkes Courthouse lived until recent times. It could have related many stories of Tory and other public hangings. When it recently died a graft survived. Today you see Tory Oak Junior.

I am basically a farm boy turned carpenter. I never had much inclination to write until my age and health prevented me from following those passions. I never dreamed of doing poetry, but I found "Little Joe" easy. It is, however, probably two in one, the first and the last.

# Little Joe's Ride

Draw near all my readers
For you are about to hear
Of a ride much more daring
Than the one of Paul Revere

It was soon after the victory
On King's Mountain had been won
Colonel Sevier was very happy
But something must yet be done

Benedict Arnold was now a traitor
Congress was disheartened and sad
There had been so few victories
Now one was needed ever so bad

We must send the word to Congress
If we can find such a man
He must travel west of the mountains
For Tarleton still prowls this land.

There is one who knows the Indians
Though they be our enemies now
What you ask seems impossible
But this one just might know how

He is still only in his twenties
And he seems to know no fear
Though he is a big man
He is called "Little Joe Greer".

They gave Joe a gun and compass
So little did they know
For the mountains were uncharted
Finding a way would be up to Joe

Perhaps he used the French Board River
Looking for a mountain gap
He must get through them somehow
And do it without a map

Joe took no time for rest nor comfort
His mission must prevail
He found a way through the mountains
On some unknown Indian trail

Once the Indians almost got him
They did manage to shoot his horse
On foot they continued to chase him
Finally, they would lose the course

They sat on a fallen tree and rested
For Joe had disappeared in a fog
As they discussed his whereabouts
Joe lay hidden inside their hollow log

Joe swam the mountain rivers
Their waters were icy and cold
He must reach the frontier settlement
At the Watauga's Sycamore Shoals

With fresh horse and provisions
The mission must still prevail
He went up a Holston Valley
To reach the Wilderness Trail

From there he must reach Fort Chiswell
Astride the Great Wagon Road
Once an Indian trading path
Now it carried pioneer loads

The new horse was now worn and weary
But Joe rode on in hope
For he had Greer kin at Tick Creek
Near old Roanoke

The Shenandoah is always scenic
But Joe could not enjoy the sights
To miss the frequent Tory camps
He must often ride at night

Pennsylvania found Joe tired and weary
If only he could stop to rest awhile
But a few day's ride can do it now
For he has come five hundred miles

When Joe came to where Congress met
There a doorman blocked his way
But Joe was not to be deterred
He was determined to have his say

The doorman said "important men
Are the only ones I can allow"
But Joe knocked the man away
And went in anyhow

Congress sat in stunned surprise
But they did agree to hear
The letter Joe had carried
From Colonel John Sevier

It is still a matter of record
But its worthy of repeat
Everyone gave their attention
When Washington rose to his feet

Washington said "How can we lose
With men like this Joe Greer?"
Joe missed the compliment
Tired and sleepy he did not hear

Washington said "There's few troops to send
But I have the best general I have seen
I am ready to place my confidence
In one Nathaniel Greene"

By December Greene was in Charlotte
I know you have heard the rest
Cornwallis did not yet know it
But he faced an angry hornet's nest

The war was long and heroes plenty
There is so much to write about
For those who would retell the story
Please don't leave "Little Joe" out

--- J. Leonard Greer

# 5

---

# Crossing The Blue Ridge

It would not be accurate to say that the New River settlers all crossed the Blue Ridge. Some of the earliest came up-river from Virginia. Enoch Osborne had a fort early on a few miles downriver from the mouth of Wilson's Creek and a few settlers moved upriver, primarily on the north fork. The names of Helton Creek and Pond Mountain were well known while Boone was still a backwater community called Council's store. One Ashe family is said to believe that its ancestors came from far down the New River by boat. They surely do not fish. The New is just not that kind of river. The vast majority of the New River settlers would cross the Blue Ridge from the upper Yadkin in what was to become Wilkes County.

Early access did not follow the routes of today's modern highway to much extent. The Indian trails used paid little attention to elevation. The one used by Daniel Boone would climb Jake's Mountain and would cross the Blue Ridge at Cook's Gap. My maternal ancestor, William Miller, would use this gap also to reach the Bamboo area where he claimed a large tract of land. My paternal ancestor, Benjamin Greer, would cross in the Cascades area that is now the Jeffress Park on the Blue Ridge Parkway. Early on their route was known as "Stringer's Path" for an early long hunter and trapper whose cabin was near the mouth of Gap Creek on the south fork of the New River. This site had been the location of an Indian village and there were probably some persons of Indian blood still in the area. It seems strange now, but the Cascades area was the location of one of the areas earliest homesteads known as "Cutbirth's Plantation" owned by Benjamin Cutbirth. Greer and Cutbirth often traveled and hunted with Daniel Boone. Cutbirth and Greer had married sisters, the daughters of Daniel's older sister, Sarah Boone Wilcoxen. Cutbirth would eventually move to South Mill Creek upriver from present day Fleetwood. Other Wilcoxens would live in this area including mother, Sarah. After Cutbirth's move the trail would sometimes be called "Greer's Path." It passed down Hege Greene Creek to Gap Creek by where I once lived at Deep Gap.

These trails would meet the needs of the settlers for years. Some of these routes are still in use today. For example, the road up Meat Camp Creek through the gap of Rich Mountain to Trade in now Tennessee. (Trade was an early meeting place where traders and Indians exchanged goods.) Others, like Cutbirth's or Greer's path, would be lost to progress. These trails were often barely visible to the untrained eye but were plain to the Indian or the experienced frontiersman. Bridle paths would give way to roads that would be suitable for wagons. The Deep Gap route was apparently not one of these. It was not approved by the Wilkes Court for nearly forty years after Boone crossed the Blue Ridge for good.

The eastern North Carolina power structure barely acknowledged the existence of the western settlements. This would not change much until Wilkes would form its own county government. Forming of mountain county governments would never become easy to get by the eastern establishment. Case in point, of the seventeen mountain counties, only Watauga and Cherokee do not have names of important persons to ease the passage.

After independence, North Carolina began extensive efforts to organize state and local governments. A new county named Wilkes was authorized. The Tennessee settlements were supposedly a part of Wilkes County, North Carolina but it had little effect there.

A meeting to organize the government of the new county of Wilkes was on the first Monday in March of 1778. It was held at John Brown's house near Brown's Ferry at the "bent" of the Yadkin just west of present-day Wilkesboro. Brown's Ferry Road still crosses the Yadkin below Kerr Scott Dam. Brown, though having and English sounding name, was said to have come from County Derry, North Ireland. Little matter, for the others present were from Scots, English, Welsh and German origins. Likely the best educated was William Lenoir of French descent. A dozen judges were duly appointed, and their bonds posted. They were Benjamin Herndon, Elijah Isaacs, Charles Gordon, John Brown, John Parks, Jr., Joseph Herndon, James Fletcher, John Greer, Jr. (Benjamin's father), William Torval Lewis, Thomas Elledge, George Morris, and William Colvard. Posting bonds sufficient to bond the members of the court were Sammuel Becknoll, Thomas Tanner, Daniel Vannoy, Joseph Herndon, Benjamin Elledge and Benjamin Greer (for this father, John).

The court appointed Benjamin Greer as his father's constable in militia district 4 which was the Warrior Creek and Moravian Falls area. The other appointees have names of local interest, but the lists are too long to enter here. It should be mentioned, however, that William Lenoir became the first clerk to the board and Benjamin Cleveland was apparently left to his military duties. (He was also representative to the new state government.)

Benjamin Greer must have moved back down the Blue Ridge at least temporarily during the revolution if he had ever lived west of the Blue Ridge prior to the revolution. He still owned land on Cub Creek in the Moravian Falls area though he may have lived on the south fork of the New River as early as 1768. Just when he returned to the New River is not certain, but it could not have been long. He would replace Captain Vannoy as militia captain and later was appointed judge of the district. He held these positions for many years after the war. That is, until he caught "Kentucky Fever" and moved west.

The early Wilkes court and its people were an amazingly vigorous and progressive people. Not only did they pursue the War for Independence with vigor, but they met many other challenges as well. They entered into a crash program to re-enter the land as required by the new states Confiscation Act. The machinery was in place and ready to function as required in early 1779. They would also be ready to conduct the first federal census. They commissioned the construction of roads and provided for citizen road committees to provide for their maintenance. They even began a program to clear the Yadkin for river traffic all the way to present day Darby, which is near where Elk Creek empties. Considering the difficulties involved, their record was remarkable. Following the war's end, the Yadkin area became a political power to be recognized in the state though the power structure would always be in the east.

After declaring independence, the various colonies had to move quickly to replace colonial authority with their own versions of a democratic government. How they did this while the country was torn by civil strife and fighting a war against the mother country is one of the most interesting stories of our history. The new county government was formed in in Wilkes County in 1779. (Most of Watauga and all of Ashe and Alleghany were part of Wilkes at one time.) The county court with its system of pleas and quarter sessions was a miraculous institution for its time. The Wilkes County Library does a great job making this information available. I am proud of the part that my ancestors from both sides of the family played in forming the government.

Benjamin Greer was present at the formation of Wilkes County "By act of the General Assembly of North Carolina, Richard Caswell, Governor, at John Brown's (Brown's Ferry on the Yadkin just above Wilkesboro), the first Monday being the 2nd day of March in the year of our Lord and the second year of American Independence." The action taken was to form a government to administer the business of the county and for a court which would meet quarterly. (County Court of Pleas and Quarter Sessions) Each justice represented a militia district of the new county. They were:

| | |
|---|---|
| Benjamin Cleveland | John Parks, Jr. |
| Benjamin Herndon | Joseph Herndon |
| Elijah Isaacs | James Fletcher |
| William Terrell Lewis | William Lewis |
| Charles Gordon | John Greer |
| John Brown | Thomas Elledge |
| George Morris | William Calvart(now spelled Colvard?) |

Benjamin Greer posted in part the necessary bond to secure John's (his father) position as justice. Benjamin was appointed constable in John Greer's district (Moravian Falls-Cub Creek). William Ray became the first constable west of the Blue Ridge.

The county court elected Richard Allen as sheriff. Benjamin Cleveland was appointed "patroller" or "ranger" which was a position responsible for the defense and the militia.

John, Benjamin and others appointed to "view" a road from the courthouse to the Rich Cove of the Brushies. Aquilla Greer will later be overseer of this road.

John Greer brings suit against John Low of Bedford County, Virginia. This suit produces official depositions and is apparently handled eventually regardless of the distance and location across state lines. The previous Greer settlement was Bedford County Virginia and the suit appears to have been a land dispute.

---March 3, 1779 James Laws, Sr. appointed to replace Benjamin Greer as Constable.
---March 5, 1779 Benjamin Greer appointed to the "Committee on Insolvents" and
    made collector for Capt. Hargraves' district.

---December 8, 1780 Benjamin Greer appointed to collect taxes in his own district (Capt. Hargraves' district). This is still Cub Creek in Wilkes County.

---December 6, 1781 Benjamin Greer brings suit against James Jones (possibly a tax matter). No results given.

---June 4, 1782 Benjamin Greer has jury duty, as he often does. (Possibly the court drafts those present when jurors are short.)

---June 5, 1782 Benjamin Greer has two suits – Christopher Control (?) and Kedar Powell, possibly tax cases.

---January 28, 1784 Benjamin Greer on grand jury.

---January 29, 1784 Benjamin Greer is paid two pounds for services as tax collector.

---July 27, 1784 Benjamin Greer has jury duty.

---October 27, 1784 Benjamin Greer and others to view road from James Tompkins on Lewis Fork) to Greer's on New river. (This is the first definite indication that Greer is on New River. His moving date was likely between 1782 and 1784.)

---July 27, 1785 Benjamin Greer has jury duty.

---April 24, 1787 Benjamin Greer on jury duty.

---April 29, 1788 Nathan Horton, William Miller, Benjamin Greer and others ordered to view a road from Deep Gap at head of Stony Fork to Williams old place on New River. (This may have been aways down river from Three Forks Church and above the Horton place.)

---Benjamin Greer now Capt. Of this district. His 1790 census list gives a good indication as to who now lived on South Fork alone. It is estimated that less than fifty families still held on west of the Blue Ridge at the end of the War for Independence.

## Benjamin Greer's Eighth Co. 1790 Census.

| | |
|---|---|
| Jesse Council | Shad Estepp |
| Jordan Council | John Whittington |
| Aaron Ingland | Baker King |
| Andrew Wool? (Wall) | Jesse Green |
| Joe Stonecipher | John Humes |

| | |
|---|---|
| Daniel Eggers | Ezekial Beard |
| John Duncan | Sam Beard |
| Mary Banker (another widow?) | James Hoselan |
| Casper Cabel | Sam Hicks |
| James Tomkins | John Hoselan |
| Ben Bailey | Ben Ward |
| Joseph Sewell | Lewis Stephan (Stevens?) |
| Thomas Hampton | John Ward |
| Ben Cutbirth | Bashiba Smith |
| Daniel Cutbirth | Frederick Suers? |
| Sam Wilson | 77 white males over 16 |
| James Shepherd | 107 white males under 16 |
| Jake Calliway | 10 Negro slaves |
| Elijah Calliway | 3 white females heads of households. |
| Robert Judd | Other white females not counted. |
| Jeremiah Bloomer | |
| William Vannoy | |
| Richard Calliway | |
| Champion Given | |
| Thomas Linville | |
| William Whittington | |

---January 30, 1789 Samuel Castle appointed overseer of road from Tomkins Mill (south branch of Lewis Fork) to top of Blue Ridge. Benjamin Greer overseer of road down Gap Creek to New River. Note: This road into present day Ashe County appears to have been used as well as Cook's Gap to reach the south fork settlement.

---October 28, 1789 Benjamin Greer has jury duty.

---Benjamin again qualifies as Justice for 1790.

---April 27, 1790 Benjamin Greer sells Turner Hampton 200 acres.

---July 26, 1790 Benjamin and two others officiate at this session of court. Daniel Cutbirth becomes Constable of Capt. Greer's district.

---January 25, 1791 Benjamin Greer present as Court Justice.

---October 25, 1791 Benjamin Greer posts bond for Lewis Demoss to become Sheriff. (Demoss is a brother-in-law.)

---April 26, 1792 Benjamin Greer still Capt.

---April 29, 1792 Benjamin Greer present as Justice – returns his district tax list.

---July 29, 1793 Benjamin Greer still Justice of the county court. Court appoints committee to view road from Deep Gap to Gap of Rich Mountain possibly led by Greer's urging. (There may have been traffic through the gap by this time, but by way of the Stony Fork rather than Lewis Fork.)

---November 8, 1793 Capt. Greer's tax list is returned by Nathan Horton who is attending court as a Justice himself.

---May 10, 1794 Benjamin Greer assigned to fall court as judge.

---August 6, 1794 Benjamin Greer and committee to view road from Deep Gap to Gap of Rich Mountain now asked to view road on to Stone Mountain.

---May 6, 1795 Benjamin Greer in court as judge.

---May 2, 1796 Benjamin Greer not on list of judges but this is probably an omission.

---August 2, 1796 Benjamin Greer returns list of taxable property in Capt. Ray's district.

---June 30, 1797 Benjamin Greer still Justice of Wilkes County Court.

---Henry Hardin becomes a judge from Cranberry Creek area of New River.

I do not know just when Benjamin Greer's duties ended in the Wilkes Court, but the County of Ashe was formed in 1799. The Ashe County minutes for the early years have not been published in their entirety. I do not know if Benjamin was ever part of the Ashe Court. Possibly he was never happy with the division, but he had signed a petition to form the county.

## Other Interesting Court Actions

---December 6, 1779 Orders the perishable crops of Jacob Ketchum, deceased, harvested so the proceeds can be added to his estate.

---December 4, 1781 Ordered Joseph Tompkins relieved of tax on Negro slave "Dinah" because she is infirm.

---December 5, 1781 Orders James Jackson relieved from paying taxes, due to being an object of charity. (Jackson is a land speculator with hundreds of acres of land.)

---March 5, 1782 Ordered that all newcomers to the county after April 1, 1781 be exempted from paying taxes for the entire year of 1781.

---April 28, 1784 County to appoint a "Stray Master" to settle disputes over ranging livestock.

---July 29, 1784 Court orders that in the future three constables shall attend each court and each constable is to provide himself with a staff of tough wood, neatly shaven, six and one-half feet long and one and one-half inches thick. Eight inches of the top of the staff is to be painted black. Said staffs are to be carried by the constables at all times. The sheriff is to have a similar staff seven feet long but only one inch thick.

---July 27, 1786 Bounty's allowed

| | | |
|---|---|---|
| John Sale | 2 wolves | 40 shillings |
| John Duncan | 1 wolf | 20 shillings |
| Sammuel Park | 3 wolves | 60 shillings |
| James Calloway | 1 wolf | 20 shillings |
| John Hall, Jr. | 1 wolf | 20 shillings |
| Phillemon Crane | 1 wolf | 20 shillings |
| | 1 wild cat | 2 shillings six pence |

---October 26, 1786 The court begins qualifying surveyors.

---April 24, 1787 Court hears suit between families alleging to have had "words." (These suits are fairly common.)

---October 24, 1787 Jesse Council on the jury. (Jesse will be a frequent member of the court from this point on.

---July 29, 1790 Bounty law repealed.

The new County of Wilkes experienced a rush to file. No new deeds had been made since the Granville grant people had ceased operation years ago. As the colonies became sovereign states, they seized crown lands and even some property of Loyalists. Many already lived on property they did not have legal title to. Their claims were often validated but not always. Land speculators were not always quick to honor prior claims. Both ancestors William Miller and Benjamín Greer rushed to claim land. Both had county government connections which undoubtedly helped. As tax lister, Benjamin would list 1,000 acres each for himself and ancestor William Miller.

## Gap Creek – Old Fields

I do now know at this time when and how (Bowie) Fleetwood was named but the area figured prominently in early filings. Many referred to Gap Creek, Old Field's Creek or Stringer's Path down Gap Creek to the South Fork of New River as a means of identification. By sorting through the entry records carefully a crude picture of settlements can be worked out.

Examples:

---Francis Hargrave was an early settler who appears to have held land near the mouth of Old Fields Creek although I have yet to find the paperwork for this claim. (He was married to Benjamin's sister, Sarah.)

---April 17, 1778 – Timothy Perkins enters 400 acres both sides of the New River upper end of Old Fields crossing at Deep Gap Creek. (Perkins was possibly the first settler before the Revolution. At least he had the best land. A portion of these river bottoms was likely already cleared.) Perkin's entry seems never to have been recognized. He was a Tory. He would live on Helton Creek after the Revolution.

---May 4, 1778 – Benjamin Greer enters 200 acres adjoining Francis Hargrave including improvement. (Greer appears to be filing on land on which he already lives.)

---May 28, 1778 – William Sherry enters 50? Acres on New River about three miles above Old Fields Creek. (William Sherry later marked out and Samuel Wilcoxen written in.) This would have been on South Mill Creek. Samuel was a brother to Greer and Cutbirth's wives.

---May 28, 1778 – William Sherry enters 100 acres adjoining the line of the previous property.

---June 26, 1778 – Benjamin Greer enters 100 acres S fork New River where Stringer now lives. (This was likely an amicable arrangement.)

---June 26, 1778 – Reubin Stringer enters 150 acres on S fork New River. Stringer, then Jonathan Hankins and Thomas Farmer written in.

---July 20, 1778 – Joseph Couch enters 50 acres New River above Old Fields lower end called Adam's bottom. Samuel Wilcoxen written in. Could this have been what is Couch's Creek just above the Fleetwood settlement? Most likely is. (Yes, Samuel Wilcoxen is Benjamin Greer's brother-in-law.)

---September 7, 1778 - Samuel McQueen enters 150 acres on New River near mouth of Mill Creek both sides of the river including camp called Baker's Old Camp.

---December 26, 1778 – Morris Baker 100 acres both sides S fork New River at an island including his improvement.

---January 2, 1779 – William Lenoir 200 acres both sides S fork New River below and including Poison Bottom.

---January 2, 1779 – William Lenoir 200 acres both sides little Elk Creek S fork New River in Osborne's line near head of big meadow.

---January 2, 1779 –Benjamin Cleveland 200 acres S side, S fork New River at foot of hill below Vincent Jones.

---January 2, 1779 – Benjamin Cleveland 200 acres S side, S fork New River where Reubin Stringer and Samuel Collins live. Henry Hardin written in. (The Hardins appear to have become permanent residents since some are buried at old Fleetwood cemetery.)

---August 14, 1779 – Abraham Elledge 50 acres New River drainage near fire springs on path from Timothy Perkins to Cutbirth's cabin on top of mountain. (Today's Hege Greene Creek.)

---August 25, 1779 – John Elledge 50 acres waters of new River near Cutbirth's plantation including the good land both sides of the path leading to the Old Fields of New River. (Today's Hege Greene Creek)

---September 7, 1779 – Alexander Bolton on S fork New River including Bells? Island. James Jackson written in.

---1439-December 29, 1779 – Benjamin Hearndon enters 300 acres on ridge called Deep Gap near an old camp including some headwaters of both Gap and Stony Fork Creeks.

---1525-January 13, 1780 – Benjamin Cutbirth enters 100 acres Deep Gap Creek near the mouth of the little fork below Benjamin Cleveland's entry.

---1000-February 5, 1790 – Thomas Gilbert enters 50 acres on Deep Gap Creek where Stringer's path crosses the creek.

---1661-March 8, 1790 – William McLain and Jonathan Smith 100 acres mouth of Old Fields Creek both sides of the river. Micajah Pennington written in.

---1804-December 6, 1814 – Nathan Horton purchased the Jonathan Lipps property for taxes. (Land Benjamin Greer sold Lipps in preparation to go to Kentucky?).

---December 19, 1814 – David Miller enters 100 acres on Gap Creek begins on John Lipps line and runs S side of Turnpike Road in the Deep Gap of the Blue Ridge.

## Pine Swamp

---June 5, 1778 – Charles Gordon enters 200 acres near head of Pine Swamp on path that leads from the Spanyard's to the Old Fields on the New River some distance below a remarkable spring.

---September 5, 1778 – William Reynolds enters 200 acres on Pine Swamp (Jonathan Tompkins written in.)

---September 5, 1778 – William Reynolds 50 acres on New River at mouth of a small branch.

---June 2, 1779 Benjamin Cleveland 100 acres waters of New River, Little Fork of Pine Swamp including plantation where Church lives. (Cleveland marked out and John Church written in.)

---February 5, 1779 – Sammuel McQueen 100 acres S fork New River below McQueen's improvement. (John Church written in.)

---February 5, 1779 – Sammuel McQueen enters 50 acres on New River.

---November 14, 1800 – Thomas Calloway 50 acres Pine Swamp adjoining Phillip Church where Church now lives.

---August 10, 1801 – Phillip Church enters 50 acres adjoining land he now owns on Pine Swamp.

---May 11, 1802 – Phillip Church enters 50 acres S side S fork of New river on Pine Creek including Robert Cleveland's salt log.

---September 5, 1803 – William Morris enters land adjoining land Church purchased from Greer.

---November 9, 1803 – Phillip Church enters 50 acres on his upper line about the mouth of Bent Creek.

---September 28, 1805 – Jane Morris enters 50 acres including vacant land between James Tatum and Phillip Church.

---November 12, 1805 – Phillip Church enters 100 acres waters of Pine Swamp begins on John Judd's line and runs down creek to include Cleveland's salt log.

---December 15, 1822 – Phillip Church enters 50 acres below his house to James Tatum line.

---September 17, 1822 – Phillip Church enters 50 acres on Laurence's Knob. (This may be ridge between Hardin Road and New River.)

---December 21, 1779 – David McKinney 100 acres N fork Naked Creek of New River at a big crab orchard including all the good land thereabouts.

---April 1, 1780 – Thomas Calloway, Jr. 100 acres S fork New River above mouth of Beaver Creek.

# Boone – Three Forks – Blue Ridge

---April 20, 1778 - Henry Hand enters 320 acres near Coxes Road lower end of great glade called Three Forks. (Henry Hand later marked out and Christopher Mannard put in.)

---July 2, 1778 – Joseph McCorkle enters 250 acres on Blue Ridge between Elk Creek and New River on the path leading to the Three Forks.

---September 21, 1778 – James Tompkins enters 150 acres top of Blue Ridge adjoining Benjamin Cutbeard and John Prophet.

---December 9, 1778 – Peter Ford enters 200 acres near Camp Spring on ridge dividing Yadkin and New River waters.

---January 2, 1779 Benjamin Hearndon 300 acres New River below Three Forks lower end of Cleveland's entry at horse ford. Henry chambers written in.

---March 29, 1779 – Reuben Easter enters 640 acres on ridge north side of Elk on path leading to Three Forks. (William Miller written in.)

## Howard's Creek

---February 18, 1808 – James Bradley enters 200 acres on Howard's Creek both sides of creek beginning on Doe Ridge Fork or creek and including the mill seat (falls of Howard's Creek and the Mulberry Cove). (The mountain side opposite Doe Ridge.)

---June 2, 1778 - William Snoddy enters 300 acres New River drainage head of Howard's Creek. William Snoddy and William Lenoir marked out and Zebulon Beard written in.

---December 8, 1778 – Abner Smally enters 200 acres Howard's Creek marked out. Then Benjamin Hearndon, then John Brown, then Ebenezer Fairchild written in.

---October 7, 1779 – Benjamin Cutbeard 100 acres on Rich Mountain opposite N fork Elk Creek toward N fork New River.

---1532-January 17, 1780 - Menucan Hunt enters 150 acres S side Howard's Creek of New River below path that goes to Camp Creek and the head of the ford of Cove Creek lying between Rich Mountain and Beaver Dams.

---1772- April 20, 1780 – Sammuel Simpson, Jr. 150 acres waters of New River in Gap of Rich Mountain where the path crosses.

---1773-April 20, 1780 – Sammuel Simpson 300 acres on Howard's Creek on ridge including small clearing made by Charles Williams.

---February 9, 1802 – William Eggers enters 200 acres near a little branch that empties into John Norris' sugar camp branch on a ridge dividing Meat Camp and Howard's Creek. Includes Harmon's Knob.

## Meat Camp

---December 22, 1778 – James Jackson enters 100 acres Meat Camp Creek near ledge of rock jutting in from the hills. (Near Tabernacle Church on Castle Ford Rd.?)

---December 22, 1778 – James Jackson 100 acres meat Camp Creek (both sides) near John Brown's line.

---February 5, 1779 – William Snoddy 200 acres both sides Meat Camp Creek above Brown's entry including old cabin.

---June 10, 1779 – Joseph Humphries 200 acres N fork Meat Camp. Humphries then William Miller marked out and Joseph Hagamen written in.

---June 4, 1778 – John Brown enters 640 acres on Meat Camp Creek lower end of the first big crab orchard below an old cabin. Both sides of creek.

---June 26, 1778 – William Lenoir 200 acres W side of Big Bald Mountain between heads of Elk and Long Hope Creek.

---February 1, 1815 – Landrine Eggers and Micajah Pennington enter 200 acres in Meat Camp begins on Pleasant Ridge and includes the ore bank.

# Others of Intertest

---June 26, 1778 – Abel Pennington 100 acres N fork of New River below mouth of Skaggs Creek.

---January 2, 1780 – Benjamin Heardon enters 600 acres on Dogg Creek of New River near Rattlesnake Den including cabins of George Collins and William Harvel. (Was this the location of a snake den on the river told about by Benjamin Cleveland?)

---January 9, 1812 – Shadrack Greer and Micajah Pennington enter land adjoining Greer's previous entry at the end of Yellow Mountain on the headwaters of Watauga River near Wolen's old sang camp. (Greer's previous entry was 200 acres entered August 9, 1810.)

---John Potter's line Hoskins's Fork on Rubing Ridge.

---March 9, 1820 – Re-entered same above?

---March 24, 1822 – Re-entered excerpts joins Landrine Eggers and improvement where Greer now lives. [1]

Unfortunately, the dream of having a secure deed to a homestead did not always materialize under the new state governments. Prominent patriots such as Cleveland would not have anticipated that the process for obtaining their land titles would become corrupted. When it happened, they did not have the education nor the political savvy to deal with it. North Carolina's first secretary of state was to have twenty-two years in a corrupt office. Unwittingly, the state reassumed what it did best, provide settlers for the western lands. Cleveland, who had filed on huge tracts of the best land on both sides of the Blue Ridge, would eventually even lose his beloved home plantation on the Yadkin, Roundabout.

Many of the early New River settlers did not become permanent residents. Many, like the Cutbirths, Wilcoxens and Greers still would follow Boone's footsteps to Kentucky. The move west was likely promoted from high places. First president, George Washington, had promoted a system of land warrants for his veterans. They would receive warrants for western lands, especially Tennessee, Kentucky and Ohio. Washington was a great "Nation Builder" for he expected the colonies to expand to the Mississippi River. As usual, the realtors got involved. Many veterans, for various reasons, did not exercise their claims. Speculators purchased huge tracts of claims for pennies on the dollar. They profited and the country expanded from their resales. Benjamin Greer's purchase of western Kentucky lands was most likely this kind of deal.

Around the turn of the century many of the names associated with the Revolution and the new independent government disappeared from the area. Among them was the old Indian fighter and Boone companion, Acquilla Greer. Like Cleveland, Acquilla and several others would remove to Pendleton County, South Carolina. Unlike Cleveland, the Acquilla Greers would move on to western Kentucky by way of Georgia. Many other locals would follow the road they had helped Boone build. It was not much of a road yet. The road through the Cumberland Gap became a rough wagon road by the early 1790's. Before it did some 75,000 settlers are believed to have found their way through it to settle along the Kentucky and Cumberland watersheds. Among these were the Boones, Calloways, Wilcoxens, Cutbirths and Greers. They would leave family in most cases but knowledge of what happened to them was largely lost for almost two hundred years.

While researching the Greer family history in the beautiful Wilkes County, NC library, I had an unusual experience. My worktable was only a few feet away from the neatly shelved books. My reference materials came from further back in the stacks, but I knew that the shelves mentioned held books about individual families. I began to notice that every time I lifted my eyes to compose my thoughts my eyes would be strangely drawn to one book. It had the family name of "Judd" on it which did not mean anything to me immediately. After about two hours I was ready to leave but could not forget the book that strangely caught my attention. When I took the book off the shelf it almost fell open to a page listing Kentucky settlers Robert and Rachel Greer Judd. (Rachel was Benjamin Greer's eldest daughter said to have married a Judd.) It went on to give some details of Benjamin and Sarah's family and their removal to Kentucky. (Benjamin's second family, daughter Rachel, her husband and children had moved to Kentucky together.) It also had a curious notation concerning Sarah Greer. It listed her name as Sarah Adkins Jones (Cutbirth).

At this time, I have still been unable to determine why the name of Cutbirth was added to Sarah, but I have learned several other things in the search. Benjamin Cutbirth had left an amazing record in Ashe County, NC but it had all but disappeared. He was married to another niece of Daniel Boone, Elizabeth Wilcoxen, sister to Nancy, Benjamin Greer's first wife, but I could find no trace of their burial in our area. Now he reappeared in the Boone family tree in Madison County, Kentucky. The Cutbirth's had moved near grandma, Sarah Boone Wilcoxen. Sarah would later die in the home of a Wilcoxen, daughter Mary, in 1815. Her husband, John Wilcoxen, was killed by Indians in 1782. Sarah had reached the age of ninety-one. She is buried in what became Estill County, Kentucky. Cutbirth's wife Elizabeth also died in 1815.

Another related family had, during the same time frame, been slowly making the journey down the great valley of Virginia and through the southern Appalachians to Kentucky. It, too, had a Pennsylvania Quaker background and had family connections to the Boones. Besides sharing kin, they had kept a loose contact over the years and generations with the Boones. Their family history had been full of hardship and desperate poverty. Into this background would be born a son in Kentucky. They called him Abraham. He would lead his country through the most perilous time of its history.

# 6

## Frontier Life

In a sense they lived off the land. For the early long hunters, it was almost total. They carried little more food than corn meal and hominy with the salt to cook it with and the wild game they found. But the large game was soon depleted. A hunting expedition, the Thomas Walker party, in 1749 found the big game in the Roanoke area already gone. They almost starved until they reached the south fork of the Holston where they found game. (*The Long Hunt* by Ted Franklin Belue) During their six-month hunt they recorded killing 13 buffaloes, 8 elks, 53 bears, 20 deer, 4 wild geese, about 150 turkeys, besides small game. "We might have killed three times as much meat," Walker added, "if we had wanted it."[1]

Daniel Boone first saw the Yadkin Valley about the same time when he and a close friend, Henry Miller, made a long hunt to the Yadkin while still in their teens. The extended Boone family would move to the new Mocksville, NC area soon after. Daniel's father, Squire, is buried there in the old Joppa Cemetery. I have sometimes visited it. Squire would be a grandfather if you go back far enough. Squire gave Daniel and wife Rebecca a farm where they began married life. But farming never gained much interest from Daniel. Morgan in his book, *Boone: A Biography*, reveals Boone the successful hunter. Deer and bear skins could be traded for more lead, powder, and traps. Bear bacon was a favorite of the time. One winter Daniel and a companion hunted Bear Creek, a tributary of the Yadkin. They were said to have killed ninety-one bears. Thirty deer were killed in one day. Deer meat was tough and stringy, and they took only the hides if in the summer. (Deer hides were not good in winter.)

As game grew scarce, Boone and his hunting partners explored the New River valleys. They were not alone. Reuben Stringer and the Judds established hunting camps on its south fork. Benjamin Cutbirth developed a plantation on top of the Blue Ridge above Gap Creek. John and James Ward likely moved down from Virginia. These were adventurous souls. The Wards and Cutbirths sold their furs in New Orleans after a successful trapping season in what would become the state of Tennessee. Many of these early settlers would leave no local families. Only their sites would remain on old deeds as reference. They would move on west when things became crowded. This early history is probably best researched in *The New River Early Settlement* by Patricia Givens Johnson.

Following the long hunter-trappers came the drover and sometimes the makers of maple sugar. Bear meat had been the favorite source of a food rich in protein and fat. Much fat in the diet of those days was necessary to nourish and warm active and often scantily clad bodies. There had been another early source of fat, but it would be gone by this era. Lawson describes the extensive use of fat the Indians rendered from the passenger pigeon.[2] This "pigeon butter" was highly favored but was not available long as the pigeon became extinct. All sources of these high-energy foods had to be replaced as the big game was pushed farther and farther to the west. Herding seemed to come naturally, especially to those with Scottish origins. The need for fat meat in the diet made the ranging of hogs in the chestnut orchards of the New River inevitable. James Fenimore Cooper in his *book, The Chainbearer,* quoted a housewife, "I hold a family to be in a desperate way when the mother can see the bottom of the pork barrel. Give me the children that's raised on good sound pork afore all the game in the country. Game's good as a relish and so's bread; but pork is the staff of life."

Long hunting could be much more profitable than farming. There was a lucrative market for skins and furs and the growing valley populations often depended on hunters for their supplies of meat and tallow. Boone's early hunting career was in the mountains west of the Yadkin. He was not a lone hunter, as a rule, and he was not the first. Christopher Gist, for one, had long been in the area and probably showed Boone many of the mountain trails and the best hunting areas. These early hunters often went on extended hunts and sometimes built shelters. The Meat Camp community in Watauga County is named for one of these camps.

As the game became depleted, Boone and other long hunters moved west of the mountains and hunting became more expensive. Pack horses and oftentimes dogs were required. Powder, lead, traps, and salt for an extended hunt were expensive and financing had to be arranged. Boone's hunts were often plagued by bad luck and he was hounded by creditors. That was part of his motivation for moving west; that and the hopes of reaping a rich harvest from the hunting grounds there.

Boone's first Kentucky excursion was in 1767-68. (Morgan's *Boone: A Biography*) He likely went back up through Fancy Gap, Virginia and made his way through the Virginia mountains to the headwaters of the Big Sandy River. Boone returned to the farm for the summer. It was May of 1769 before Boone could arrange financing for another Kentucky trip. This time his party of six experienced hunters ascended Elk Creek and crossed the Blue Ridge in what became Watauga County, North Carolina. Boone and others had used the route fairly frequently for some years already. Boone had moved his family to Holman's Ford on the Yadkin near this trail in 1766. Though Boone had likely used the trail through horse gap in what later became Ashe County, there is no real evidence that he used the Deep Gap of the Blue Ridge except maybe for local hunts.

Boone had probably used the Cook's Gap trail prior to moving near the Holman's Ford of the upper Yadkin in 1766. A gap through the Brushies had been named Greer's Gap years before. This route reached all the way to what became Trade, Tennessee and beyond. Trade, Tennessee was accessible from many directions and was important in the early trade with the Indians when they were still plentiful in the area. We are sometimes led to believe that this trail became the Wilderness Trail but that is not true.

The early beginnings of the Wilderness Trail connected the Great Wagon Road in Virginia to Castle Woods settlement, later named Saltville, Virginia. This trail was well used by hunters and salt makers long before any serious settlement took place. It is probable that a local trail reached from Saltville, Virginia to now Trade, Tennessee long before Boones time. (Partly due to the salt trade.) Salt was a valuable necessity on the frontier. It was said that a bushel of salt would buy a good cow and her calf. The Boone Trail commissioned by Richard Henderson extended the wilderness west of Saltville, Virginia to the Cumberland Gap and north to now Boonesborough, Kentucky. This route would be used by many thousands traveling by foot or horseback but would not become a wagon road for another twenty years. The Wilderness Road and the Boone Trail are not the same.

Boone's first attempt to move his family to Kentucky was in 1773. As usual he had a partner in the venture. This time it was William Russel, a Virginian who had land interests on the Clinch River. The venture failed when Boone's sixteen-year-old son James was killed by Indians October 9, 1773. The move was not successful until 1775. By then Boone had a new sponsor named Richard Henderson.

The early patterns not only followed the Indian trails but the opened lands they and he big game left. On the heels of the Indians and long-hunter came the cattle herder to take advantage of the lush forage in the mountain valleys and open mountain peaks. The buffalo had been the first to go in these areas. For a short while they had been numerous in the Virginia and Carolina valleys. But there was great demand for their meat, hides and tallow. Early settlers used a lot of leather and the only light at night was the fireplace or candles. The buffalo were easily held at bay by the hunting dogs of that time and then killed by the hunters. The elk population lasted a little longer due to its preference for remote mountain peaks. They left only the names, Buffalo and Elk, scattered through the area.

The demand for meat, hides and tallow did not end with the demise of the buffalo and elk. Plantation owners along the Yadkin were quick to learn how well livestock did in the mountains in the summertime. Benjamin Cleveland, from present day Ronda on the Yadkin, (in fact Ronda is said to be a contraction of the name of his plantation "Roundabout") began to drive cattle to the Old Fields Creek area of Ashe County. He would eventually claim over 300 acres at the present-day West Jefferson, North Carolina, and many other grazing areas. William Lenoir from the upper Yadkin and Fort Defiance in Happy Valley kept detailed records of livestock driven to summer grass along the Blue Ridge. A neighbor and kinsman of Lenoir, Benjamin Howard, ran cattle in the Big Glades of the Three Forks (the Boone Valley). He even built a herder's cabin on present day ASU campus where he kept a black slave as herder. Cattle were unbelievably easy to control under these conditions. Their great appetite for salt assured they would come running for salt when called. The last large-scale activity of this type was Finley's Old Fields Bald in the early 1900's and Fox Brothers. Many location names in the area got their name from this practice (Salt Rock or Salt Log Mountain gap, etc.). West Pine Swamp land entries in present day Ashe County often would give Cleveland's salt log (a hollowed-out log) as a reference point.

Throughout early hunting and herding activities an important part of operations was tanning of hides. This may have been Howard's main justification for keeping a Negro herdsman in the Boone Valley. He lived in a cabin near a spring on the present-day ASU Campus at Boone, North Carolina where Daniel Boone is said to have often shared his shelter. (Sherry Edwards' bronze statue of Boone and his dogs on or near this site.) Cattle in the area likely needed attention for salting and maybe for protection from roving renegades – whites and remaining Indians. But the greatest danger in the high mountains was poisonous

86

plants, which often killed cattle. If someone was available to salvage the hides from dead animals a total loss was avoided.

Besides hunting, trapping, and herding, two other activities usually preceded serious settlement. These gathering activities were "sanging" and sugar making. Throughout the mountains, ginseng gathering for the China market was profitable early. Daniel Boone was often engaged in ginseng gathering big scale. He was said to have lost 1,700 pounds of the root when his boat capsized on the Ohio River on the way up to Fort Pitt. Locally, in what became the Grandfather Community, an Aldridge woman is said to have reared a large family by gathering "sang." She was said to have ranged as far as the headwaters of the Big Sandy River in Kentucky in her efforts. Occasionally an early land entry is located or described as its proximity to someone's "sang" camp.

Look at any topographical map of the area and you will notice that a lot of locations had something to do with sugar: Sugar Camp, Sugar Grove, Sugar Gap, Sugar Creek, Sugar Mountain, Sugar Loaf and the like. The cooler areas of the mountains often contained large groves of sugar maple trees. Likely the Indians, and later the settlers, were involved in making maple sugar. It was the only source of something sweet. (It still is the best tasting.) Honeybees had not been native though they took to the wild and spread rapidly after they were introduced. The molasses of the time was the by-product of sugar making in the Indies. They were imported but not many reached inland. They went to the makers of rum. Sorghum would not be generally known until farming became well developed a few decades before the Civil War.

Sugar making was very important to these early gatherers and the colonies. It was a ready medium of exchange. Early hunters and soldiers used it much as the Indians used it in their travel ration. The settlers made a sweetened mixture of parched corn, bear or pork fat and cracked, parched corn. It was the chocolate bar of the day. It was either praised or vilified. As an occasional snack, it gave quick energy and did not upset the stomach. But eaten over a period of days, it was sure to cause stomach problems and become tiresome.

Popular perceptions of our history rarely give sugar making the place it deserves like early salt making. Our maps indicate an importance that is hard for us to visualize in our day of plenty and low cost.

The men with the axe and plow were really our last settlers. They did not come into trackless wilderness. It had been explored and mapped decades before. The upper Yadkin, New River and Yadkin had been mapped as least by 1750. Bishop Spangenberg carried a map when he came into the area in 1752. This is not to say that there were not hunter's cabins and maybe "axe claims" before land entries were made. Settlers often did not wait until title to the land was available. The colony moved slowly and often with a great deal of inaccuracy and confusion. Many would take a chance on being able to buy or file on their claims when the opportunity came later. If someone else ended up with the property he might sell or at least pay for improvements. If worse came to worst, there might be other land in the area or certainly to the west.

There was no great incentive to settle the mountains early on. There was plenty of land left in the valleys and foothills and the mountains were not very hospitable. It was better for the serious farmer to move to the valley lands of Tennessee or Kentucky. A period of cold weather prior to 1800 made crops chancy. A late spring frost in 1774 sent the few settlers off to the Yadkin to buy corn for the winter. Clearing land was difficult and time consuming and crops were subject to the depredations of wild animals and carrier pigeons. Only when the settler developed a mixture of cropping and living off the land would he survive and prosper.

One livestock industry would overlap cattle grazing and cropping. It was made possible by the huge chestnut orchards of the area. Chestnut trees could provide over a ton of nuts per acre and, unlike corn, the trees required no cultivation. Fat pork was the ideal replacement for the bear meat that was increasingly hard to find. Moreover, there was a good market off the mountain. Plantation owners needed to concentrate on cotton and tobacco rather than food for their slaves.

Hogs and other livestock were usually driven to the off-the-mountain markets. My great grandfather, Henry Miller, and his brother Edmund developed a strategy for moving hogs. They penned them in a large lot where they were fed corn from a wagon. (Hogs ranged in the mountains sometimes had to be taught to eat corn.) They began moving the wagon frequently always rewarding the pigs with a little corn. The herd would soon be ready to move with only a little help to keep stragglers from getting left behind.

The droving of livestock became an elaborate process. John Preston Arthur, in his *Western North Carolina: A History*,[3] describes the operation in the Asheville area where a special stock road was built all the way into Tennessee. Holding pens and lodging facilities were located every eight or ten miles where stock and drovers could be fed and sheltered. The fare was often paid for with lame stock or a problem traveler. One drove of hogs numbered around 2,500. In addition to hogs and cattle, turkeys and even geese were often driven to market.

Farming was extremely difficult on the frontier. Crops had to be protected from wild animals and birds and even the semi-wild livestock of the herders. There would be no fence law for yet another century. The Indians had grown their corn in large community plots. These were guarded at night by women, children, and slaves. Early settlers would have to fence. The materials were there in the form of chestnut trees, but it required a lot of labor. It was not worth the effort if the land was not yet deeded. This was often the case. It was better to harvest the essentials from the woods themselves.

Living off the land required much wild meat, preferably fat meat. Settlers had learned that a diet of fish and lean venison was slow starvation. To keep scantily clad bodies warm and provide energy for the rugged lifestyle, fat meat and large amounts of corn meal were necessary. Before crops became dependable this meant bear meat. Bears became fat in the fall in preparation for hibernation. The hunters turned them into cooking fat and bear bacon. Later the semi-wild "razor-back" hogs took the place of the bears which were becoming harder to find. My ancestor Samuel Greer, his son Riley, son, and grandson of Benjamin Greer, would be noted bear hunters. The last great bear hunter, however, would be Wilburn Waters who lived in the White Top, Virginia area. Both hunting and droving would long shape mountain attitudes toward land ownership.

Mountain society would remain very democratic for generations and generations. So little of the important things depended upon wealth or property. Many items were to be had only by gathering. These only became valuable with the expenditure of labor and the diligence to harvest them. "Sang" was important but probably the best example would be the chestnut. These were gathered by the bushel after the frost opened the burrs. A chestnut storm (a rainy night ending in a chill wind) would bring the gatherers out with lanterns before daylight to beat the hogs and wild animals to the crop. Today it is hard to imagine the importance of this crop. In the first year of its publication (1887) the Watauga Democrat would carry an advertisement for 100 bushels of chestnuts, "wanted by the first day of December." Apparently, chestnuts were in great demand for cooking and for roasting during the Christmas holidays. Chestnuts also fed the droves of half-wild hogs which ranged in the mountains until the fence law came into effect. The nineteenth century mountain economy has been referred to as a "hog economy." There was little difference in bottom land farmers and the hillside farmer. Bottomland farmer's hogs ate corn while the hillside farmer's hogs fattened on chestnuts which the hillside farmer did not even have to gather.

Hogs would continue to range with some fence until my childhood. The chestnut was already gone but hogs also ate a lot of acorns. My Grandmother Miller's hogs still ran in what had been a huge chestnut orchard. One huge chestnut was hollow with an opening near the ground. It was called the "hog chestnut" for it was the perfect place for a sow to have her pigs. This chestnut orchard after the blight became the habitat for several cherry and service berry (sarvis) trees. Brother Elton and I would slip across the nailed-up rail fence to eat to our hearts content. The hogs found that we were there as often as not. We learned early on not to climb the same tree. One could attract the hogs to his tree while the other could run for another tree with the hogs after him. Immediately the other would then drop to the ground and run as far as he could go before the hogs caught up. We jumped downed timber and anything else that would slow the hogs. We always made it to the fence but often not without a fresh crop of briars in our bare feet.

The problem of wide-ranging hogs was not completely solved by the fence law of the late 1890's. Only the demise of the chestnut tree eventually led to hogs being kept in houses or pens. Hogs had been very difficult to fence and were often a point of contention among neighbors. One incident on Meat Camp gives insight to the problem and into mountain character. A sow formed a habit of getting under the garden fence of a neighbor. The owner of the offending sow was warned several times but did nothing much about it. That is until he was told that the sow would be shot the next time it happened. This worked until fall when the garden was mostly harvested, and the sow's owner relaxed his diligence allowing the sow to escape. She was promptly shot. The owner protested, "Why did you shoot my hog when your garden is gone?" "To make my gol darned word good" was the reply.

Mountain families did not feud over land early on. When fencing became, necessary property lines were more visible and often came into dispute. Landowners were often adamant in claiming property as "pap" or "grandpap" had told them even if the crooks in the fence line were obvious. Surveys had often been very informal. Making an elected post of county surveyor did not completely solve the problem. Inaccurate deeds still often exist today and have been a source of wealth for local lawyers.

Even through all the disputes most neighbors felt free to trespass on their neighbor's land to hunt or trap, gather berries or sang, or just to get from one place to another by the numerous paths that crisscrossed the area. Freedom to hunt and fish was a given. Few summer people who came later were ever to understand this. They posted their shirt-tail patches of land with insulting signs. (It made no sense to the native to insult your neighbors and then abandon the property for a large part of the year leaving it without protection.) Mountain folk had had a long history of conflict with absentee owners. Cattle brought into the mountains for summer grazing often ran rough shod over the neighbors. Sometimes cattle were killed. Local courts would never convict the culprits. One group pasturing on the Bald on the Ashe-Watauga border lost cattle but were able to get the case into federal court at Wilkesboro. A conviction was found, and young men eventually left the country over the incident. Mountain people have never trusted federal courts anyway or local courts either for that matter. Native folks no longer resent outsiders as they once did, but the posted signs are still offensive to the free ranging mountaineer. Few summer people can realize the depth of the feeling. "No Trespassing" signs are the worst kind of human pollution to many of them. These days only a few of the old traditions survive. It is still legal to mark and claim a bee tree found on someone else's property so far as I know, but who hunts bee trees these days?

My family has always had a healthy distrust of state and local history as popularly recorded. My Great Aunt Frances Miller had lived to a ripe old age and could recall conversations with family elders much her senior. She could relate a version of much of our entire local history that often differed from the official version. The official version has often been "colored" to fit the political needs of the power structure and to cater to the emotional preferences resulting from a bitter Civil War. Thus, much of what we have accepted as area history may really be largely myth. We are presently experiencing a revival of interest in local histories. Oddly, it is often possible in this information age to document a different history than the one long accepted to be fact. I predict that in the coming decades that much of our history will be examined and may even be given a new look. A look that is more accurate and is fairer and more just to our people.

For the first time in our history it is likely to be written by the sons and daughters of Appalachia themselves. In the meantime, I will attempt to relate here a few of the characteristics so unique to the mountains.

Aunt Frances Miller was a resource beyond measure. She was my great aunt and was already elderly when I was a child. She was one of a kind. She was well educated for her day and lived in a family with a rich history and loved to talk about it. She was different. She wore long dresses all her life and cooked her food in the open hearth because she like it that way. She was a Bible scholar and a devout Methodist. She had an old-fashioned way of talking but could quote Shakespeare when a mind to. Grandma Greer was well read and knew Greer history, but we did not get to see her often for we had no way to travel.

Most mountain families became quite prosperous for their times prior to the Civil War. They were more dependent on grazing livestock than the production of field crops. Even if he could keep his own cattle, hogs, geese, and chickens out of field crops there was still those of his neighbors. A livestock economy gave him more flexibility to plan a work schedule. Time was more easily arranged to trade off the mountain, pursue a trade part-time or even go fishing. But the local resident was really quite ambitious and would find something to either put food on the table or bring in a little cash. It was mostly a barter economy but things like taxes took cash.

Other than livestock operations the sideline that prevailed the longest was probably furs. Some furs would bring a sum equivalent to days or even weeks of work. There is still a business in trapping today although it is not near so profitable as it once was. Co-existing with the fur industry has always been the root and herb business. The collector of furs and herbs rarely got into the big money themselves, but it was an important supplement to many family incomes. These activities cost little to produce and replaced money going out of the local economy at a rate of near one hundred percent. They were ideal economic activities in a cash deficit area.

Some profitable activities have long since faded from the scene and from our awareness. Perhaps the most notable would be the making of tree sugar. This industry began even prior to permanent settlement and continued even into the twentieth century. It was a hot item of trade with the early stores. Whenever a prosperous farmer would sell out to move west or for other reasons, he would often advertise some objects curious to us today. Among various classes of livestock and farm tools often would be kettles, taps and carved white ash sap collection bowls. He might also advertise several barrels of whiskey, another item not always remembered.

The area industry most completely lost in our history, however, was iron making. It was highly promoted by colonial and, later, the state government. The area had small deposits of ore that were frequently worked. Land grants would often make reference to "Ore Banks." They were not hard-rock deposits like those to be found in the north but were deposits that leached into areas that were, or at least had been, swampy. Such deposits would be known as "bog Iron" in New Jersey where they were most important.

The first mention of an iron forge in the area was one on the upper Reddies River on the way across the Blue Ridge. It was on the trail Boone used through Ashe County. It likely had been encouraged by the colonial government. The state would also support iron making and the industry played an important role in early Ashe County to be. Several forges would be built in the northern and westernmost parts of the Ashe area. Thomas Calloway would be one of the first to receive a grant to produce iron. He would be followed by Ballou, Daughtery and others. State grants could consist of ore deposits on yet unclaimed lands but were more likely to consist of thousands of acres of unclaimed timber lands. These lands were to provide timber to burn charcoal for the forge, there being no coal in the area for burning coke. A jury of twelve (the county court?) had to certify that the land was unsuitable for crops. The county court of Ashe in 1807 considered a grant to one James Daughtery for a grant of 3,500 acres. For the grant to become final 5,000 pounds of iron had to be made within three years.

Most of the iron produced probably was for local consumption. Better deposits were opened early on in Virginia and Tennessee, but this did not completely destroy the local business. Demonstrating the enterprise and the mobility of local businessmen prior to the Civil War was innovative marketing developments. Pigs of iron were built with curved, sled-runner type construction and some were skidded to market as far away as Charleston, South Carolina. The Ballou Forge on Helton Creek would remain in business at least until the Civil War when production would go to make rifles for the Confederacy. Today the only thing remaining are some names associated with the iron making process like Pounding Mill, Laurel Bloomery and Eagle Forge.

Other local industries no longer seen but were very important at the time were the local blacksmith shop, local grist mill, local tannery and local saddle and harness shop. All these would remain an important part of the local scene except possibly the centralization of tanning leathers. The tanning operations often fell into local disrepute.

There were several impressive things about this era prior to the Civil War. One was the extent of travel and trade that went on. Locally citizens seemed very capable of coping with the developments over a huge area of our country. Lack of education does not seem to have been a serious handicap. (Possibly many had been educated in more settled areas previously to moving to the mountain.) Opportunity seems to have existed in abundance, otherwise the more discriminating German farm and craftsmen would have stayed in the Catawba Valley.

For whatever the reason, be it outdoor work or nutritious food from the virgin land, the mountain family was huge and generally healthy. Most individuals were vigorous and active. Churches and schools were provided for and, increasingly, the population was content to develop local resources and stay at home. The occasional migrant now was more likely to have the resources to relocate if he chose to. Early on the most notable of those who now chose to move were the

Quakers and others leaving for Indiana and Illinois because of slavery. Later as farm size decreased, and family size increased many would choose to go west. Appalachia would play a huge role in the development of the west and the shaping of a national character.

# 7

---

# The Homestead

The early settlers who crossed the Blue Ridge did not at first live much differently than the hunter-trapper. With the large game already gone, or soon would be, long term survival would depend on turning predominantly wooded land into crop production. This was much more difficult than it appears on the surface. Land had to be cleared and fields fenced. Wild animals still preyed on the crops but now it would include roving livestock. Crops must be fenced as livestock ran loose until the early 1900's when a fence law began to take effect. Even until my childhood gardens would need a chicken proof fence against the farmer's own free ranging stock.

Early settlers would find cropping much different on the New River. Summers were cool and late frosts were common. Crop varieties they bought with them often did not thrive. Fortunately, Indians had long ago adapted varieties that fitted local conditions. Lawson in his book, *A New Voyage to Carolina*, written in 1701 describes an extensive Indian agriculture. The basic crops were corn, beans, and pumpkins but they also did yams, melons, and other edibles. My Grandmother Miller still followed some of the Indian way of growing things. First, she would plant a few grains of corn in widely spaced hills. When the cornstalks got a start, she added cornfield beans which would climb the cornstalks. Last, she would plant pumpkins for they did not need to mature much before cold weather if they were to store for the winter.

Yadkin Valley crops oftentimes were not dependable on the New River. Corn was essential and if it failed, corn would have to be brought from the Yadkin. An Indian corn called "New River Slick" was most dependable. Beans were easier for they were available in many varieties. Lawson called the Indian cornfield bean variety a bushel bean. Some others surviving until my childhood were the Granny Miller bunch bean, greasy cut shorts, the red kidney bean, Kentucky wonder pole beans, old timey butter beans, a little sulfur bean and on and on. Heirloom varieties of everything were super abundant in my youth. German settlers would add Irish potatoes, onions, cabbage, turnips, and rutabagas to the mix. Interestingly, the remaining eastern Indians were not long adapting to the new crops also.

Despite any difficulties settlers poured across the Blue Ridge in the 1770's. The most consistent reason for the western movement was to find good cheap land. Those who settled on the New River in the early 1770's were not able to get good title to their land and oftentimes motivated by other things as well. Many were fleeing their own government after the Battle of Alamance. Others were fleeing creditors, crimes, or even local feuds. A few were just adventurous or would take a chance for something they could call their own. The movement picked up speed when the new government was formed in 1776. One of the first actions was to form land offices. English grants and the land of many loyalists were seized and made available for claims though formal deeds might yet be years away. Veterans of the war were given preference and many of them became land speculators. Loyalists who had lost their land also joined the westward rush. Oddly, they melted into the frontier mix and were usually well accepted.

One Greer family move was unusual. Jesse Greer, a son of ancestor Benjamin, was reared on the south fork of New River. His wife to be, Polly Morris, was reared on the Yadkin. She was only thirteen when she agreed to wed Jesse, who was then twenty-two. Polly's father would not permit the marriage because of Polly's age. He boated Greer back across the river and bid him on his way. The couple had other plans. Later that day Jesse stilted the river gun in hand and took

Polly on his back and stilted back to the safe side. They stayed the night at the home of a nearby acquaintance. Next day they walked across the mountains to what would become Ashe County where they were married by Elijah Calloway. They lived in the Elkland (Todd) community and had seventeen children.[1]

As more land was brought into production patterns of living changed. Land was only cleared of the small stuff. The big trees were only deadened (killed by girding). When I was a child many chestnut trees still stood killed by girding. They were joined by the rest of the of the chestnuts when killed by the blight around 1930. With more land to tend the farmer would need more fence and pastures for livestock but only areas in crops use would be fenced. Fenced property lines would not customarily be fenced for years to come. People and ranging hogs pretty much made use of these unfenced areas unless asked not to by the owner. This worked with the people but not with the hogs.

Work stock could be either horses or steers. (Locally I never heard steers called oxen.) There were advantages to both. Horses were much faster and were more likely to be used for travel and hauling but they required some grain for feed. Steers could get by on some sort of fodder. Not all steers were equal. Some were very docile, and some would even saddle. Women and children would sometimes ride good steers, but many steers were apt to be temperamental. Some would hate hot weather. Cattle did not cool themselves by sweating as did horses. Mature steers were actually stronger and did not panic in wet areas as horses were apt to do.

A temperamental or uncomfortable steer might balk by laying down and refusing to work. My Grandfather Greer had a favorite story about a balking steer owned by a Stony Fork Watson. It seems that their steer could be frightened into getting up and resuming work by a woman flapping her apron or skirt. One day the steer balked near the house and Watson called for his wife to help get the steer up. She was anxious for her cooking and came flapping her apron vigorously and the steer ran away. Watson said, "Now you have played hell, you know you are supposed to sort of shake and sort of not shake." Grandpa Greer never failed to get a big laugh from his own story.

My Grandfather Miller also had a steer story. It seems that he was hauling some cross ties to the railroad at Todd when one of the few early cars came along. It was not at a good place to get his wagon out of the road and the impatient driver honked his horn and used some foul language. Low and behold a few miles further Grandpa Miller found the car firmly stuck in a mud hole. An apologetic car owner pleaded for help, but Grandpa Miller was in a hurry. I never knew my Grandpa Miller but my favorite vision of him is with his steers pulling a short log to break a pathway through the snow so the children could get to school.

I never knew of a cow being used for work stock, but I saw this being done when I was in the army in Germany. A horse and cow were harnessed together to drag firewood out of the forest. We hooked several of their loads to a tank and easily pulled them to their village. It was much appreciated.

The log cabin was the usual habitation. By the second or third generation many homes had become elaborate log houses. They often lasted for generations. A few are still around today. Both my parents were born in log houses.

The usual home of a successful farmer could still be log but was most likely to be frame after a timber industry developed. The normal farmhouse, be it a two-story log or frame structure, was adorned with porches. A long front porch facing the road was considered a necessity. It was here that men of the house reigned supreme. Furniture was usually split log or plank benches with possibly a rocking chair for grandpa. Other interesting items were to be found there, like harness and saddles, for example. There was always a collection of dogs. Above the barking of the dogs, all passersby would be invited to come in and "set a spell." Protocol demanded at least a short conversation and the swapping of news and comparing the time on pocket watches. ("Passing the time of day.") There was no other way yet devised to know what the time was in the community. If it were raining anyone passing the road just had to come in on the porch out of the weather. The front porch welcomed everyone, known or unknown, provided they were male. Inside it was a different matter. Visitors visited only a living room area unless invited elsewhere though girls of the same age group often retreated to a bedroom. A few farmhouses would have a parlor. This was the most restricted area of the house. It had the best furniture in it and was usually kept spotless. Young boys quickly learned that it was for the preacher and other important people, not boys.

The early 1900's was a time of prosperity for farmers. Farm prices of 1914 were long used to calculate support prices through most of the mid twentieth century. Locally burly tobacco would become a cash crop and most communities would have a cheese factory buying surplus milk. Conditions were now right for apple orchards and timber was now being cut and lumber exported. Money was not plentiful but was not rare either. Heating and cooking stoves made life better but not necessarily easier. The faster pace was more demanding especially for women. Increasing demands on men's time and oftentimes irregular hours left the womenfolk to pick up the slack.

One of the worst chores must have been milking and taking care of the milk. This required regular hours and the men were not always available. They likely did not care to be either. A lot claimed that cows preferred to be milked by women and gave more milk. Some claimed to have a cow, or cows, that could only be milked by a woman. (One married man claimed to have looked for such a cow all his life but had failed to find it.) This did, however, open the door for women to have their own money. Butter and eggs became the common medium of exchange at country stores and local hotels. Only a true cheap skate would deny women this money. Women, being women, would usually use their money for family needs.

Dairy operations also called for a more elaborate facility to keep the products cool. Refrigerators were years away yet. Cooling was mostly done by using spring water. A springhouse beside of the home was ideal. If the spring could be piped gravity flow it ran all the time and provided domestic water and a cool drink when needed. If the spring was at a lower level it was usually reached by a path as pumps were not yet available. Women's work gained some conveniences but did not get much easier.

For generations, the most consistent feature of the family farm has been the family milk cow. Usually she was the responsibility of the housewife. But not always. At one time Berea College gave instructions on how to pick a good milk cow as part of the graduation program. At our house, the children became involved at an early age. It was our chore to bring in the cows for milking. Once their calves were weaned, they often lost interest in being milked on time. About 5:00 p.m. grandma would start calling them to the barn to be milked. She would also call a dog if she got no response. I would say "Grandma you don't have a cow dog." Her answer would be "But the cows don't know that." Unfortunately. they did for the grandchildren often had to go find them and bring them in.

Locating cows could be difficult. Pastures were usually wooded and thorny hillsides that were unfit for crops. It helped if at least one cow wore a cowbell. No two cowbells sounded alike. One could identify his or his neighbor's cow by the sound of the bell. On a still, clear morning the tinkling or clanging of the community's cows was almost musical.

Feeding the farm family boiled down to just a few essentials. The family had to grow corn for bread, have a milking cow, grow a garden, and raise a hog. Throw in a flock of chickens and the family was well fed. Hog raising was considered essential for generations. Fall hog killing was one of the most important events of the year. It required all of the family and sometimes neighbors. Preparations often started before dawn. It took a long time to heat the scalding water to loosen the hog hair. It was quicker if the scalding barrel were metal for a fire could be built around it. Steel barrels were not common in my youth, but wooden barrels had been around for centuries. Dad used an Indian method. He heated old plow points and flint rocks in a big fire. When hot they were dipped into the wooden water barrel until cooled and then were put back into the fire. It was not great, but it worked.

The butchering site was away from the house close to a source of water. It was often a duel-purpose site for wash day also used much water and an iron pot for boiling clothes would be handy during butchering also. Homesites almost always had this outdoor laundry site for doing the heavy wash like bedding and the children preferred tending the fire to carrying water to fill the tubs at the house.

Later years would bring big changes to local farming. One was the broiler industry. Chicken was now mass produced. It had once taken months to raise a broiler. Now it was only a matter of weeks. My parents produced hatching eggs for this industry. Unfortunately, what had been a boon to the local economy found greener pastures in Arkansas. Tyson Foods bought out Holly Farms and much of it moved to there. Broiler houses were empty and once common green pastures fertilized with chicken house litter were no longer seen. Just as well for a cowbell was no longer heard in the land either.

# 8

---

# Always Cash Poor

A constant feature of mountain history has long been the shortage of money. It was true even in colonial days and it was a cause of the Regulator Movement and the Battle of Alamance. Tryon's colonial government insisted on cash payment of taxes and quit rents, but the western settler found cash hard to come by. Even a productive farmer likely could not find a cash buyer for his goods. The buyer often wanted to trade his own goods and pay only a portion of the sales price in cash. A system of barter had already developed that survived in some form locally until at least World War II. The "art of the trade" was essential for survival and the mountaineer was usually a master. He might give you the shirt off his back if you needed it, but he would surely take yours in a trade if he could.

Learning trading skills usually began early. Great Grandpa Henry Miller said that his seven boys could trade pocket-knives and sling shots among themselves on a rainy day and each of them feel he had gotten rich. This would serve them well as they would band together to market their produce off the mountain. (They called this "Going down in the country.") They would always keep their sibling rivalry.

The youngest brother, Donald lived on a hardscrabble farm at the far end of the Rainbow Trail. He grew some tobacco for the market and trapped in the winter. He needed a work horse for summer farming and to get in a winter's supply of firewood. But his small operation did not produce enough feed to winter the horse. His solution was to buy a cheap horse in the spring and euthanize it in the fall rather than have it starve. When fall came he took a gun and the horse to a remote spot on the backside of the farm. There he came upon older brother Noah who was squirrel hunting. Uncle Noah did not know why the horse was along, but he liked it. After some trade talk, he gave Uncle Donald ten dollars cash and wrote a promise to pay another fifteen at a later date. Of course, the story was too good to keep. When their sister, Aunt Frances, heard it her good Methodist principles were offended. She could not get Donald to refund the ten dollars cash, but she did get him to tear up the note.

Most trades between individuals usually involved little or no cash. An exchange of property or labor was the norm. This also carried over to the country store where farm goods and roots and herbs were traded for household needs. Here, again, little or no cash would exchange hands. These exchanges often were accomplished with what was called a "Due Bill" which was written to cover any differences in valuation of the goods exchanged. County governments got into the act, also. Credit against local taxes was often given to pay for firewood to heat the courthouse and jail.

Some unusual settlements were sometimes made by barter. The Miller family sometimes talked about a paternity case for example. The court had allowed the family to give a cow as part of the settlement with the new mother's family. The grandmothers later met at the country store. The maternal grandmother complained that the cow kicks so bad that she could hardly be milked. She said, "Don't you think the price allowed for that cow was unfair?" The paternal grandmother replied, "Not considering what it paid for."

Some country stores developed huge businesses in furs and what was called roots and herbs. Ginseng had been a lucrative item for many years. At least four local buyers of roots and herbs became huge. A Greer Root and Herb in

Watauga would relocate to Lenoir and become Greer Chemical. Another Greer store would operate at the mouth of Meadow Creek at Brownwood. It moved to Marion, Virginia to be on the railroad. The old building is now on the historic register and houses a buffet restaurant featuring country cooking. The "Cowles Old Stand" was not far away on Gap Creek. It was a huge operation for years and years. An employee, Grant Wilcox, would learn the business there and start his own at Boone. His Wilcox Drug Company would become the largest and longest lived of them all.

The "Cowles Old Stand" had the most illustrious history. It served the Deep Gap, Pine Swamp, Cranberry Springs, and the territory up and down the south fork of the New River. It was only in existence for a relatively short time from 1869 to about 1900. It was the center of trade during my great grandfather's time and the youth of my Grandfather Greer and possibly my Grandfather Parlier. My Grandfather Greer always fondly referred to it as the "Cowles Old Stand." That has always been its name to me.

The present-day location of the Cowles Old Stand is about three miles from Deep Gap on 221 North toward Jefferson. The old building is barely visible to the right of Idlewild Road. The Cowles home is said to have been located on the present day Idlewild Road right of way. It must have been impressive in itself. It was said to have had five chimneys and a stove in the basement. The store building was also impressive. It was 80 feet long and 30 feet wide on both floors. There was a huge fireplace toward one end and the whole affair had a big generous porch across the front. There seems to have been a cellar for items that needed protection from freezing. It was once said to be the biggest building in Ashe County. Rather than size what really set it off, however, was the rows of large windows in the outside walls. There was no electricity at that time and the Cowles wanted their customers to see all the merchandise easily.[1]

The Cowles Stand began as an offshoot of the huge store and root and herb dealership run by Calvin (C. J.) Cowles in Wilkesboro. The business had prospered there for decades and C. J. had become quite wealthy. His interest in Ashe county, other than roots and herbs, had likely been real estate. He owned as much as 1,800 acres in the Idlewild and Pine Swamp area. He even attempted to mine gold just up the Idlewild Road, though the mine likely yielded more copper than anything else. My dad always said that a dip in the road surface there was due to an old mine shaft caving in.

C. J. Cowles helped son Arthur (A. D.) Cowles begin the huge store as a partnership. Arthur was deeded thirty acres of the huge Cowles holdings. The business flourished for Arthur was an outstanding store manager. He soon became owner of the entire operation. He stocked everything to be had in that day. The young men of the community amused themselves trying to think of something that could not be found at the Cowles Stand. Unless they asked for something like "goose yokes" Arthur was sure to find it. Goods that they advertised were dry goods, hardware, groceries, earthen and glassware, hats, bonnets, shoes, boots, saddles, bridles, harnesses, paints, medicines, books and stationary, tin ware both plain and japanned, candies and raisins, clocks and watches, powder, shot, lead and guns, nails, salt and on and on. The list of materials accepted in trade tells much of that day's society. It began with a huge list of roots and herbs. Wagon loads of these and other materials were being made up all the time to go to Statesville, North Carolina. What is most interesting is the list of farm products also wanted. They were feathers, beeswax, tallow, lard, butter, all kinds of cured meat, chestnuts, dried fruit, tree sugar, wool, spun yarn and thread, hand-woven cloth, furs, dried hides, hog bristles, flaxseed, grain and old copper, pewter, paper and rags. A small note was at the bottom of the advertisement "Cash accepted if offered."

In its later years, the store introduced many new products into the community. As many as eleven store clerks ushered the ladies through the second-floor rooms where they fingered the factory-made dresses. Arthur was much respected over a wide area and he grew quite wealthy. Late in the century his health failed, and he lost most of his wealth. His wife moved the family to the Horton Plantation in Happy Valley. Arthur would die in the state hospital at Morganton, North

Carolina in 1902. During the stores operation it was said that it carried everything from caskets to glass eyes for blind horses. The area had been one of the most active of any west of the mountains with schools, doctors, and post offices. When the store closed much of the life went out of the community. It would live again at another place, however. One of the clerks would move to Boone to start a root and herb business there. His name was Grant Wilcox, father of Charlie Wilcox and founder of the Wilcox Drug Company. (C. J. Cowles was the second largest of owner of slaves at the beginning of the Civil War, but he remained an ardent unionist).

The Millers, Blairs and others developed a wagon trade off the mountain. By the 1920's there was some industrial development and there was a market for mountain goods. Irish potatoes, apples, cabbage, and the still abundant chestnut would find a market at Lenoir, Morganton, Hickory and Statesville.

Good horses were necessary to pull the heavy loads going down in the country. Oxen could do the job but were too slow to be practical. A compromise was reached. The first night on the road was usually spent at a place called Bailey's Camp on the upper Lenoir road south of Blowing Rock. Part of the off the mountain load could be taken there the first day if the ox team started at three or four o'clock in the morning. The Millers would refine this practice even further when they acquired their first truck. The truck had difficulty pulling the mountain all the way up to Blowing Rock. (Most vehicles of that day overheated on the steep grade.) The Millers would deliver produce to Bailey's Camp by wagon. There it was loaded onto the truck to be peddled off the mountain where the truck did best.

A version of this kind of marketing continued even into my childhood. It was a different market then. The destination now was the coal fields in Virginia. Anywhere there were jobs there would likely be money to be had. But local people did not understand that it was not always real money. Mines often paid their miners at least in part with script that was only redeemable at the company store.

A near neighbor did not know this when trying to sell potatoes to a housewife. She wanted the potatoes but said she had no money and could only pay in script. After some sputtering our neighbor said that he had all of that he could use at home

There was also some "up the mountain" trade. Mountain wagoneers usually returned with bartered goods their family and neighbors needed. Enterprising off-the-mountain-farmers also got into the act. It is said that one such trader was trying to strike a deal to barter sweet potatoes to a family in the Dark Ridge community beyond Beech Mountain. The family explained that they had no money. The trader told them that this was no problem that he would trade for poultry. "Too bad," replied the customer, "we had a good crop started but the chickens scratched it up."

The off-the-mountain-traders still visited our area when I was a child. A typical visit would start with someone "helloing the house" from the public road. (No one came to the house unless invited.)

Trader, "Would you like to trade some Irish potatoes for some yams?"

Grandma, "How would you trade?"

Trader, "One for three."

Grandma, "That's too much but let us see them."

Trader, "You don't have mean dogs, do you?"

Grandma, "I have a dog, but he won't bite unless I tell him too."

Another kind of traveling salesman would yet become popular. Regular salespeople for the Raleigh and Watkin's Companies would distribute everything from sewing needles to pie flavorings. Their vans opened in the back to display this variety. Children would likely get the first chewing gum they ever had from the Raleigh man.

The area was to be a cash deficit area until the 1950's. The few banks had some money but if you really needed it you probably could not get it. The only recourse was to borrow from a money person. When Grandpa Miller's place was divided, we desperately need to buy a part of it. Aunt Frances Miller was good enough to lend us the money.

Inspite of these huge businesses, cash money would still be hard to come by for many years. Before any banks were established a few people would have money that they would lend. One of these was Great Grandfather Henry Miller. He probably never had as much money as many believed but the people who bought his house in the 1950's tore it down looking for money. They did not find any. A cousin who lived in the household after being orphaned said that the money was not kept in the house. Grandpa Henry always went somewhere outside to get it.

Other people of some means who might loan money included Chap Proffit and a Captain Critcher. Mr. Proffit was said to be hard of hearing. It was said that a boy seeking a loan once asked, "Uncle Chap will you loan me five dollars?" Mr. Proffit said, "What's that?" "Uncle Chap would you loan me ten dollars?" He replied "Huh, I heard you the first time."

Money must have been still tight when I got out of the service in the late 1950's. I had finished paying the $300.00 I owed Berea College on my education with hard earned army pay. I sent everything else I could spare to my mother for my bank account. When I got out of the army, I got a job teaching. It took all my savings to get a car and pay my first month's rent. Payday was a month away and I would have to borrow to eat until then. The bank was opened until noon on Saturday then. I was ashamed to ask for the $25.00 I probably could have gotten by with, so I asked for $50.00 for thirty days.

I was sure the local bank president would understand for his wife was also a teacher. He pushed a blank note form across to me and said, "Get the signatures of two cosigners with property." Having done my previous banking with his bank I was sorely disappointed. I took it as a reminder of how hard it could be to cross over to the preferred side of the railroad tracks. Dad came up with twenty dollars and I made it do. I have since said that if a town had only one bank it probably did not deserve to have any.

The cash deficit was general for the entire southern Appalachia area. Berea College was located on US Highway 25 which was then a main north-south route. Every weekend we witnessed a huge traffic event. By late Fridays bumper-to-bumper traffic developed going south. On Sundays it reversed going back to the factories. This spoke highly of the mountain work ethic and love of family and home. An often-repeated story was about St. Peter giving a new arrival a tour of heaven. When questioned about a large separate group St. Peter said "That's just a bunch of hillbillies. The weekend is coming, and they think they are supposed to go home."

The South did not begin to provide its own venture capital until the 1950's. The interstate highway system made access to the labor force even in the towns possible. The nation's second largest financial center is now in Charlotte, North Carolina. What a drastic change. It's easier to borrow ten thousand dollars now then borrowing fifty dollars was during my teaching days.

# 9

## Homegrown Medicine

The earliest of settlers were a surprisingly healthy lot. Families were huge. The cabins would not have held them except for that they lived much of their lives outdoors. Foodstuffs gathered from the wild and that grown from virgin soils must have been more nutritious than the foods coming later from depleted soils. There was little immigration into the country during the Revolution or for several years afterwards, yet the population doubled and redoubled.

Another factor contributing to the general good health was the dispersal of the population. Communicable disease was not transmitted well under such condition. This remained the case even until the Civil War. Southern soldiers coming out of rural areas often died of measles, for example. On the other hand, Northern soldiers more likely carried immunity to such diseases for they had them during childhood.

Frontier medicine undoubtedly came largely from the Indians. They had centuries of experience with the native herbs. Some may have been effective, but they had few miracle cures. Diseases that whites lived with decimated the Indian populations. Good health was likely due to coarse but nutritious food, a vigorous lifestyle and isolation from disease. Yet there was a need for medical attention even in a healthy population. This meant midwives, or "granny women." The life was said to be extremely hard on horses and women. Death during childbirth was common among young married women. It would become common again with those having a dozen or more children. These early women's doctors were also the doctors for children and, to a lesser extent, men.

Men often treated themselves or went without treatment rather than reveal their problems to a woman. The communication gap between men and women was due to modesty and the ease at which both could become embarrassed. Men did not use vulgarity or talk of common things in front of women. To use the word "bull," for example, was forbidden. "Gentleman cow" was substituted instead. Well into my lifetime some older gentlemen had problems purchasing their favorite "Bull of the Woods" tobacco from a lady. The Burkett brothers in lower Meat Camp community, for example, would ask for "cow in the bresh", if they could not wait to be waited on by a man. Women would have their "granny women", but men would have to wait for real doctors. These doctors would be men for most of my life.

The most prominent early midwife in our area was Nancy Greer Tugman at the headwaters of Riddles Fork Creek. Centrally located between the Meat Camp and Elkland communities, she delivered many children and treated many sick. Her generous response was legend for decades. She rendered her services out of genuine love of neighbor rather than to make money. Nancy may have been the inspiration for my Great Aunt Frances Miller. Aunt Frances was well educated for her time and "read" medicine from three doctor books she had accumulated from somewhere. (Could have even belonged to Nancy.) In Frances' day medicine would become more critical. Epidemics now frequently made their way into mountain communities. The food and the lifestyles were not so healthy. Diphtheria and Typhoid or Small-Pox frequently wiped out whole families of children. Parents often hoped that their children would have measles, mumps, and whooping cough early for they seemed to kill more teenagers.

113

The early granny women were largely without medicines. Not even an aspirin was available. They relied heavily on herbal teas. Aunt Frances kept the walls of her porch covered with drying pennyroyal, catnip, rabbit tobacco, boneset, red peppers, and the like. Camphor was kept for preparing greasy salves and getting dead bodies ready for the funeral. The woods were always full of roots, barks and leaves believed to have medicinal value. I am sure many were placebos, however, and produced only psychological results. The barks Aunt Frances gave mom to boil for the children's spring tonic I believe were chosen for their bitterness rather than any benefit.

Aunt Frances was an old maid and was free to go after her parents died. I remember hearing her "halo the house" from the field above our house. She refused an invitation to come in saying that she would keep her distance since she might be carrying measles in her clothes. Uncle Smith's folks were down with the measles and she was going prepared to stay. She had the bail of her chamber pot in the crook of one elbow and a finger through the handle of her mysterious brown earthenware jug.

Whiskey was likely the most-commonly used medicine though the children were rarely told that they were taking it. Some neighbor or relative usually made it on the sly. It served its purpose, I suppose, though it was often prescribed for the wrong ailment by the wrong doctor, one's self.

Many noted that most liquid patent medicine contained some whiskey and allowed that there was no use in paying extra for adulterations. My mother saw no good use for it. When she had to quit school at sixteen to see the family through the measles (she had already had them) she put her foot down. She refused to let her uncle off his horse with the jug he had brought. She said she might have to quit school to tend a family with measles, but she darned sure was not going to look after a bunch of drunks.

My Grandmother Miller's approach to medicine was the most simplistic of all. Like her Indian forefathers she was mystified by and respectful of tobacco. She grew her own tobacco, used it and did not discourage children and grandchildren from using it. Tobacco removed the internal parasites that were so prevalent among children of that day. It was soaked in vinegar and bound to bruises and wounds. A good warm chew stuck on a bite or sting was considered beneficial and smoke was even blown into the ears of children suffering from earache. I know of no evidence that any of these uses was beneficial except for its effect on parasites. Snuff enclosed in a head covering would eliminate head lice. As far as worms were concerned my mother had an effective remedy. It consisted of the smelly seed of a plant called tansy. She made it usable by cooking it into taffy candy made from molasses. There can be no doubt that my parents and seven of their eight children became addicted to tobacco at an early age, but all of them quit years ago after tobacco fell from grace.

My Grandmother Miller's second most important medicine was coal oil (kerosene). Kerosene was widely believed to have curative powers. Poured over wounds it reduced soreness and promoted healing. Michael Jordan's grandmother used it on a foot Michael had cut with an axe. He gives her credit for saving his career yet to be. Grandma would even put it on a cloth to be worn around a neck to cure the sore throat. My mother looked on all these remedies with suspicion, however. She firmly believed that good health was closely related to diet. Bringing variety and good nutrition to our diet was her top priority. She always said that it was better, and more enjoyable, to spend money on food than on doctor bills.

By the time of my childhood doctors were becoming available and usually made house calls. Midwives were still common but were losing favor for many women still died in childbirth. My oldest sister was delivered by a midwife but the later seven of us were delivered by a doctor, most of us in the home. My grandmother, and certainly not my mother, ever had great confidence in herbal medicine and used it only as a stopgap measure. The early doctors, however, would not yet be trapped into criticizing the old ways. Grandma Miller taught us to distrust the remedies often passed around whether they were herbal or patent medicine. She once told me that she and grandpa had tried smoking the leaves of jimson weed as a treatment of sinus discomfort. This was decades before pot, etc. was ever heard of. She said she could not say that it would not help but that it would make you "wacky" in the head. Modern day accounts reveal this weed to be very dangerous, often resulting in confinement to a mental institution. I have often wondered if my grandparents' innocent use might have caused the mental problems both of them experienced during their lives.

Family distrust of the usual remedies was bolstered by the outlandish claims made by patent medicines. They seem to be able to cure about everything. If proven to be ineffective they would merely change names or diseases. They were often promoted vigorously on early radio. "Send in your name and address, just a $1.98." Many huge fortunes were made by these promotions. One of these built the famed Grove Park Inn in Asheville, North Carolina. Sickness has long been a profitable business. It still is.

Aunt "Francy" was probably not a "doctor" in the same sense that Nancy Tugman or Salley Winebarger may have been. She was a spinster and was therefore available when no one else was. She would move in, if necessary, and do what she could in sickness. I am not aware that she was ever a midwife. Her information was outdated and might have even been dangerous at times but her help with household chores and with bedfast patients filled a great need.

Not all the family was eager to have her help, however. I remember her spring tonics as being bitter and foul tasting but did not expect them to help or hurt much. Among her remedies for breaking out measles was said to be a tea made from sheep dung. When her nephews Jay and Marvin Miller had the measles Uncle Noah went to great lengths to keep sister Francy from finding out that he also had the ailment. He preferred to pass up Francy's treatment and swore everyone to secrecy.

This was the predicament a lot of sick people of the day found themselves in. We dared not get sick, lest some member of the family would suggest a cure we could not stomach. My dad believed in a frequent dose of castor oil whether you needed it or not. I was careful to appear as healthy as possible. I hated castor oil and got to the place that I would lose my supper when the bottle was brought out. This helped to have the remedy discontinued at our house.

Country doctors of the early twentieth century deserve a lot of research and recognition. Some were better prepared than others, but all filled a gap in early rural society. Most of them brought the best advances in medicine that society would permit them to practice. The idea of surgery for diseased tonsils and appendicitis did not sit easily with the mountaineer. Failures were common because of primitive conditions and because surgery was a last resort and often came too late. Some doctors went to great extremes to succeed. Old Dr. Hagaman took Cecil Miller, more dead than alive, on a long rail trip to John Hopkins in Baltimore, Maryland to treat for a ruptured appendix. With no sulfa drugs and no antibiotics, it is a miracle that he survived. Mr. Miller later moved to Boone and became a prominent merchant.

The early doctors did not often dispute the old remedies. Some even made extensive use of remedies such as camphor salves and teas. Gaining of patient confidence was more important than making a home remedy an issue and it probably did not make any difference one way or the other. These doctors might have limited knowledge of medicine at the time, but they made up for it by doing house calls at inconvenient times and in all kinds of weather. Most treatment was in the home. The first six of the eight children in my family were born at home.

The single largest medical issue of my day was childhood diseases. They were accepted as unavoidable. Most children would survive them though some resulted in lifelong problems. Diphtheria was the most serious. The old Lutheran cemetery on Big Hill is said to have the graves of five children from one family who died only days apart. Diphtheria and smallpox were the only vaccines available by the time I started school. They were given at the school during summer before first grade. Childhood shots were not usually given at doctor's offices then. County health school nurses came out to the schools. By second or third grade a series of three typhoid shots were given. At least one of these was guaranteed to give severe stomach cramps or associated problems. These immunizations were a step in the right direction, but you would still have three kinds of measles, whooping cough, chicken pox and mumps.

There were also communicable conditions in addition to disease, lice, and itch in particular. I do not know how my family missed having lice, but we did have itch on a couple of occasions. It was easy to get. Catching itch was said to be no disgrace but keeping it was. My parents treated our itch with a foul-smelling yellow liquid. I do not remember the name, but it smelled like rotten eggs.

I have said little about the use of whiskey. It was used by many for the treatment of numerous ailments. It was considered the only treatment for milk-sick in both man and beast. Milk-sick was a mysterious and often fatal ailment of the mountains. It killed Abraham Lincoln's mother and, also my Grandma Miller's mother. She died when grandma was only four years old. People and suckling calves died from drinking milk from cows that ate an unidentified poisonous plant. I believe it was snakeroot which was later found to have strong blood pressure lowering qualities. If so, whiskey in significant quantity would have been counterproductive. Grandma believed her mother was given too much and that it contributed to her death. Whiskey was not trusted in my family as a treatment for anything, though it aided in such things as tooth extractions performed in the days before dentists and numbing.

By my youth milk-sick would be rare among humans. The wooded pastures where it occurred had long been noted and were avoided. Non-milking livestock grazing wooded areas still had it on occasion. Such occurrence would set off a search for apple or peach brandy.

My mother had little faith in home remedies. She believed doctors were best even in those days. Even as a teen she was sometimes placed in the position of decision maker for her family. When younger brother, Charlie, developed something similar to appendicitis she gave her approval for an operation. Then young Dr. H. B. Perry operated in the home on the kitchen table with mom as his assistant. The problem was far along, and Dr. Perry did not give it much chance of success. He was right for Charlie lived only a few weeks more. But mom still trusted the doctors. One winter she sent me to see Dr. Perry even though the snow was too deep for cars. I had to ride grandma's horse. But I probably owe my life to one of grandma's old remedies.

One winter when I was only five or six, I had pneumonia. Our house was not then well heated, and I could not get over it. Grandma flatly told mom that unless something was done, I was going to die. Grandma had some Indian blood and she knew what to do. She recommended a hot poultice on my chest to create a sweat. She said that hot mashed potatoes or parsnips would do but onions were far the best. She had made a good crop and she would bring them. With the poultice in place she wrapped me up in quilts and built up the fire in the heating stove. I do not remember much of the night except for trying to get out of the covers to cool off. About four a.m. I heard her tell mom that my fever was broke, and I was going to be alright. I will never forget the smell of those onions. There was no such thing as a mild or sweet onion in those days. Mountain onions were always strong.

The most serious ailment of my time had no known treatment. Polio had occasionally cropped out for generations but became epidemic in the mountains in the summer of 1944. While the allied troops invaded France, a desperate battle was taking place on the home front. Near panic swept the region. Public events were cancelled; pools, libraries and the movies were closed. People were so helpless for no one knew much about the disease. It afflicted rich and poor alike. Some researchers even felt that poor and dirty areas might have a sort of immunity or at least would have mild cases.

Hickory, North Carolina was central to a large affected area. It became known as Polio City. People drove through with their windows rolled up and trains roared through without stopping. The National Polio Foundation and locals developed a risky plan. A makeshift polio hospital would be built on the grounds of a nearby summer camp if victims would be accepted from all-across the state.

Pulitzer prize winning author David M. Oshinsky describes it best in his book, *"Polio: An American Story"*.[1] Essentially, he said "A call went out for volunteers. Hundreds showed up. Merchants donated building materials made scarce by wartime rationing. Carpenters, plumbers, and electricians brought their own tools to the site. Floodlights were installed to allow round-the-clock construction. Families loaned their washing machines and vacuum cleaners. Farmers trucked in meat and vegetables. County convicts cleared brush and dug ditches while watched by shotgun armed guards. The governor paroled thirty-two female prisoners to help with domestic chores."

A hospital was up and running in 54 hours. It was "rough pine board" but it had an admissions center, a kitchen, and a laundry. Not to mention a laboratory, operating room, and isolation wards. Dormitories and a therapy wing followed. Professionals came from all over to help local medical personnel cope. Many of these would be taken into local homes inspite the feared risks. This story is not retold near often enough. Those who may doubt God made man in His own image need to hear it often.

A first cousin, Emma Lou Dollar, was one of those afflicted. She never regained the ability to walk and regained only a limited ability to write. I am not sure if she had learned to write before afflicted but she wrote to me while I was in the service. She wrote beautiful letters. All soldiers look forward to mail call. It was the most important time of the day. She was an inspiration to all, but she died young of pneumonia.

Research on the causes and treatment of polio went on even at the emergency hospital at Hickory but polio remained a mystery for a few more years. A victory was coming though. It would be won a dime at a time.

# 10

## Moonshine

In my parent's world it would have been hard to separate moonshine and medicine. Moonshine was illegal but could not be suppressed; and medicine was legal but often used treatments that should not have been. Prohibition was still in effect in my early years, but repeal was already hotly debated. My parents did not agree on the issue. My mother had the strongest feelings against whiskey but also had the best perspective on how impossible it was to outlaw it. She was for repeal. On the other hand, my father moved easily among drinkers though he was not much of a drinker himself. After his sons came along, he was very concerned with setting an example. Yet he was the one who was strongly in favor of prohibition. So were a lot of drinkers. Will James was quoted as saying that "Baptists would vote against liquor as long as they could stagger to the polls."

Prohibition was not the cause of moonshining. It goes all the way back to the beginning of our country. The constitution exempted the federal government from levying property taxes. Under our first president, George Washington, the government sought a revenue source to pay war debts and finance a government. It resulted in a tax on spirits. Distilling was widely practiced and was especially dear to the Scots and Irish. Interestingly, Washington himself was one of the new nation's largest distillers. On the surface the new tax looked to be minimal and should have little effect on most people. No one seemed to realize that it would not be universally accepted and would be nearly impossible to enforce. Resistance in the western areas would be known as the Whiskey Rebellion. There was violent opposition, especially in western Pennsylvania. Washington was forced to use federal troops to put it down. Locally the upper New River would receive settlers from a new Pennsylvania source. The Potter family on the North Fork of New River is likely the best-known example coming from that state.

The government, it seems, had badly misjudged the very nature of the whiskey business. It had seen the business as a large commercial enterprise. This was not at all the nature of the small family-style operation so much a part of the Scots-Irish culture. A reliable source for kin and friend, to them, was more important than any commercial prospects. With them the tax law was certain to become a heated emotional issue.

The small family-type operation was typical of my day. We knew next to nothing about the large "thunder road" type of operation that made the headlines. My great uncle, Donald Miller, once told me that they did attempt to supply the county's fiddler's convention at one time. They had provided nephew, Tom Woodring, with a white jacket so they could track his movements through the crowd. Tom was only about fourteen at the time and the experience probably did not serve him well. He would later become involved in a commercial operation in West Virginia. They had bought protection from a local deputy sheriff. He was seen approaching the still site and was not expected. Thinking they had been betrayed, both partners shot him at the same time. I once heard Tom say that the palm of a man's hand would cover both bullet holes. Tom served a few years for the killing. His sentence was light because it would have been hard to determine which was the fatal shot. It likely helped that it was a crime among petty criminals on both sides.

All of mom's Miller uncles would at some time be involved in the business. Only one, Uncle Noah, would follow it for a lifetime. He furnished primarily kin and friends and was very careful who he sold to. He was not greedy and only wanted enough money to make the Federal Land Bank payments on his property. Local law enforcement made great efforts to catch him for years but must have eventually decided he was not doing any great harm. He remained careful all his life but did not seem to worry about it in later years.

Aunt Jenny, Noah's wife, was a great help. Uncle Noah was often out and about on his large acreage of mostly rough land. If someone came looking for him Aunt Jenny would yell for him. (This was common with most people before noise pollution made it impractical.) If the visitor was someone Uncle Noah needed to see he would show up soon. If the visitor was suspicious, the yell was different, and he would never show until it was all clear.

A prized part of Uncle Noah's equipment was the copper still cap and distillation coil (called a worm). This copper item was hard to come by but everything else could be improvised. Once the revenuers came at night with a search warrant and the prized equipment was at home. Aunt Jenny took said equipment into her bed. She later said that no law officer in the land would dare search a sick woman's bed.

Uncle Noah called the still worm his "trick ah-ma-do." After the house search, he would hide it in the woods. Dad and one of mom's brothers were once cutting a tall hickory tree for wagon wheel spokes when Uncle Noah appeared, all out of breath, asking where the tree would fall. They pointed out a brush pile down the hill. "Hell's fire boys that will fall on my trick ah-ma-do." They put off falling the tree until the next day. Someone once found and stole the "trick ah-ma-do." Uncle Noah was a great woodsman. He located several area operations before he found the missing article. Of course, he promptly stole it back.

My only close encounter with an illicit operation was while fishing. Brother Elton and I were fishing for native trout on a small trout stream near home. On the upper reaches of the stream it forked. It was getting late and we agreed that he would fish the left fork and I would fish the right and return to the forks in about thirty minutes. I continued to find fish in the small pools but had to crawl through the laurels on hands and knees to reach them. Suddenly, I crawled into a still site. My first thought was that I know who this belongs to and he once was involved in a murder. I did not wait to see if anyone was there, I crawled back down the creek as fast as I could go. As usual Elton had caught our biggest fish while I was gone.

My mother's brothers all tried to carry on the family tradition. I think it was as much for excitement as it was for any hope of making any money. It seems strange now that I knew nothing about it at the time, for I was in and out of grandma's house frequently. Grandma herself was opposed to liquor in any form but could not exercise any complete control over her near grown boys. I would later learn the meaning of suspicious occasions, like when an uncle would suddenly decide to move to another state for a while.

Booze was rarely talked about but was always out there somewhere. What other people did was their own business and there was always the possibility that it might have medical benefits at times. Women would never be involved in any active way in my day. Males could usually recount embarrassing bouts with alcohol in their younger days; but adult alcohol problems seem to have been quite rare though the use was much more common than we knew at the time. Protracted revival church meetings were not excepted as I now understand.

Sister Lena became heavily involved in the fight against legal ABC stores. Both sides had good arguments, but I was never involved in either. The wet's argument of control, however, I found to be a big joke for they claimed to keep alcohol out of the hands of under aged. Their real argument was about abundance and convenience. In my opinion when it came to responsibility the local moonshiner was often as responsible as ABC.

In today's society, local producers have seen a dramatic increase. Local craft beers and other alcoholic products are now common. In the Boone area I have even heard of a product called "Booneshine." It seems ironic that all this is legal now when the practice could have resulted in jail time not long ago. As for the repeal of prohibition, it never had any effect on anything that I knew. On the national scene it may have denied an income source to the gang operations so common then. Some big-time bootleggers, like Papa Joe" Kennedy, had used prohibition to become unbelievably wealthy. My mother thought that repeal would help. It probably did but it was not a cure. There may not be one out there. There never has been.

# 11

## Greer Ancestors

The name Greer is generally conceded to have come from the Scottish Clan McGregor. I have a long list of McGregor ancestors going all the way to the seventh century.

### First Generation

Hugh II was born before 680. He died in 697. Hugh II was a King of Dalriada, ruling in 696 to 697. He was married to Unknown.

### Second Generation

Hugh III was born before 696. He died in 733. Hugh III ruled as King of Dalriada from 726-733. He was married to Unknown.

### Third Generation

Aed Finn King of Dalriada was born before 724. He died in 778. He was crowned in 748. He was married to Unknown.

## Fourth Generation

Hugh "the Poisonous" IV was born before 760. He died in 822. Hugh IV was a King of Dalriada. He was married to Fergusa (daughter of Fergus and Unknown).


## Fifth Generation

Dungal Thane was born before 782. Dungal was the Pictish Thane of Fortrenn. He was married to Unknown. Unknown was born before 825.


## Sixth Generation

Gregor MacAlpine was born before 855. He died in 889 in Dundurn, Strathearn. He was married to Unknown.


## Seventh Generation

Dongallus Prince was born before 880. He died about 900 in Italy. He was married to Spontana Princess (daughter of Unknown and Unknown). Spontana Princess was born before 880 in Ireland.


## Eighth Generation

Constantine was born before 900. He died in 940. He was married to Malvina (daughter of Donald Vi and Unknown). Malvina was born before 920.

# Ninth Generation

Gregor de Bhrattich was born before 940. He died in 961. Gregor was slain by the Danes. He was married to Dorviegilda (or Dorigelda) (daughter of Constantine and Unknown). Dorviegilda (or Dorigelda) was born before 945. Dorviegelda's father was the commander of the army.

# Tenth Generation

Sir John MacGregor was born before 962. He died in 1004, killed in battle. He was married to Alpina (daughter of Angus (or Aenas)). Alpina was born before 990.

# Eleventh Generation

Gregor MacGregor of Glenurchy was born before 1005. Fought under King Duncan I against Normans and Danes. He served in many offices for Malcom II about 1004-1074. Gregor was a Lord of Glenorchy. He was married to daughter Campbell (daughter of Gillespic Campbell Lord of Lochow and Eva). Daughter Campbell was born before 1080.

# Twelfth Generation

Sir John MacGregor Lord of Glenorch was born before 1100. He died about 1113. Sir John MacGregor was a Lord of Glenorchy. He was married to (English beauty) Unknown.

## Thirteenth Generation

Sir Malcom MacGregor of Glenorchy was born before 1113. He died in 1164. Sir Malcolm MacGregor was the 8th Lord MacGregor. He was married to Marjory Lindsay (daughter of William Lord Lindsay). Marjory Lindsay was born before 1150.

## Fourteenth Generation

William, Lord MacGregor was born before 1165. He died in 1238. He flourished during the reigns of William the Lion and King Alexander (1198-1294). William MacGregor was the 9th Lord MacGregor. He was married to Margaret Lindsay (daughter of William Lindsay Lord Crawford and Marjory Galithly). Margaret Lindsay was born before 1225.

## Fifteenth Generation

Gregor MacGregor Lord was born before 1239. He died in 1300. Joined King Alexander about 1248 on an expedition to recover the Western Isles from Haco of Norway. Gregor MacGregor was the 10th Lord MacGregor. He was married to Marion Fileon de Gilchrist (daughter of Gilchrist). Marion Fileon de Gilchrist was born before 1280.

## Sixteenth Generation

Malcom Dominus de MacGregor, Lord MacGregor was born before 1300. He died in 1374. Strongly attached to the immortal Bruce; fought at battle of Bannockburn (1314) under Edward Bruce; wounded at Dunkirk, died at an advanced age in 1374. Malcolm MacGregor was the 11th Lord MacGregor. He was wounded at the Battle of Bannockburn, in service to Robert, and thus was known as the "lame lord." He was married to Mary MacAlpine (daughter of Malise MacAlpine and Unknown). Mary MacAlpine was born before 1340.

## Seventeenth Generation

Gilbert Grierson of Lag was born in 1353 in Dumfriesshire, Scotland. He died after 9 Apr 1425 in Lag, Dumfriesshire, Scotland. He is buried in Old Dunscore Cem, Dumfriesshire, Scotland. The MacGregors were not banned until James in 1603 but the MacGregor name may have fallen from grace already. "The ban was genocide pure and simple." Gilbert was married to Janet Glendening (daughter of Simon Glendening Sir and Mary Douglas Lady) before 1400. Janet Glendening was born before 1383 in Dumfriesshire, Scotland. She died after 1400. Jane Glendening was the great granddaughter of Robert III, descendant of Charlamagne and a signer of the Manga Charta.

I do not know if "Grierson" indicates a Viking ancestry. My DNA is predominantly Northern European. More importantly, a shift from the clan system in Lowland Scotland indicates a mixed blood heritage and a more advanced society. This name change coincided with a land and title grant apparently.

## Eighteenth Generation

Gilbert Grierson of Lag was born about 1397 in Dumfriesshire, Scotland. He died before 20 Dec 1444 in Lag, Dumfriesshire, Scotland. (This Gilbert Grierson was the 2nd Lord of Lag.) He was married to Isabella de Kirkpatrick (daughter of Sir Duncan de Kirkpatrick Lord, Torthorwald and Unknown) on 14 Nov 1412 in Old Dunscore, Dumfriesshire, Scotland. Isabella de Kirkpatrick was born before 1400 in Rock Hall, Dumfriesshire, Scotland. She died in 1472.

# Nineteenth Generation

Vedest Grierson was born about 1415 in Lag, Dumfriesshire, Scotland. He died about 1487. Date of birth based on the marriage date of parents. He is buried at the "old Dunscore Graveyard," several miles southeast of Dunscore. He was married to Margaret Glendonwyn (daughter of William de Dalrymple and Agnes Kennedy).

# Twentieth Generation

Roger Grierson was born about 1439 in Dumfriesshire, Scotland. He died in June 1488 in Sauchieburn, near Sterling, Scotland. He was buried in Lag, Dumfriesshire, Scotland. Roger took up arms against the King, was wounded at the Battle of Sauchieburn, near Sterling, fought on St. Barnabas' Day, 11 June 1488, and died before 26 July 1488. He was married to Isabella Gordoun in 1473 in Dumfriesshire, Scotland. Isabella Gordoun was born before 1460 in Dumfriesshire, Scotland.

# Twenty-first Generation

Roger Grierson was born after 1474 in Dumfriesshire, Scotland. He died on 9 Sep 1513 in Flodden Field, Branxton, Northumberland, England. He was killed at Battle of Flodden Field before he could succeed his brother, Cuthbert, to the Lordship of Lag. His first and second sons also died before becoming Lords of Lag, so his third son became heir to Lag.

He was married to Agnes "Janet" "Jane" Douglas (daughter of James Douglas and Janet Scott). Agnes "Janet" "Jane" Douglas was born about 1467 in Drumlanrig, Dumfriesshire, Scotland. She died after 19 Jan 1519.

## Twenty-second Generation

John Grierson Sir was born about 1490 in Dumfriesshire, Scotland. He died before July 1559 in Dumfriesshire, Scotland. He was married to Egidia Kennedy (daughter of John Kennedy Sir and Jane Stewart) before 20 Aug 1548. Egidia Kennedy was born before 1535 in Cullean, Ayrshire, Scotland. He was also married to Nicolas Herys before 12 Mar 1529. Nicolas Herys was born before 1515.

## Twenty-third Generation

Roger Grierson was born about 1520 in Dumfriesshire, Scotland. He died in Aug 1593 in Scotland. Roger Grierson was the eighth Lord of Lag. He succeeded his half brother William, who had died without heir. He was married to Helen Douglas (daughter of James Douglas and Unknown) on 21 Arp 1566 in Drumlanrig. Helen Douglas was born before 1560 in Dumfriesshire, Scotland. She died in 1578.

## Twenty-fourth Generation

William Grierson Sir was born between 1567 and 1575 in Dumfriesshire, Scotland. He died on 21 Jan 1629 in Lag, Dumfriesshire, Scotland. Sir William Grierson of Lag was Knighted by James VI in 1608. Sir William was a Knight of Lag Castle, Dumfries. He was shot and killed in 1629. From this time on the family called themselves Grier or Greer instead of Grierson. He was married to Nichola Maxwell (daughter of William Maxwell) on 9 May 1593 in Dumfriesshire, Scotland.

Nichola Maxwell was born about 1578 in Scotland.

# Twenty-fifth Generation

James Grier Sir was born about 1604 in Capenoch, Dumfriesshire, Scotland. He died about 1666 in Dumfriesshire, Scotland. In a discharge, dated 1630, James signs Grier and brother Alexander signs Grierson. Died 1666. Married Mary, daughter of the Rev. John Browne, M. A., of Glencairn, first minister after the Reformation; and widow of Thomas Grier of Bargarg Tower, Dumfriesshire.

(Note: The following Scottish ancestors are in the family tree of millions of Americans.)

# Twenty-sixth Generation

James Greer was born about 1627 in Capenoch, Dumfriesshire, Scotland. He died about 1688 in Gunpowder River, Baltimore County, Maryland. Grear, James. Arrived Maryland Nov. 1674 on Batchelor, ex Bristol. Indentured. (Early Settlers Book 18, folio 152)-2112. (A second listing is also shown.) Greer, James. Born probably Dumfriesshire. Son of James Greer and Mary Browne. Settled Joppa, Baltimore County, Maryland, 1675. Married Ann, daughter of Arthur Taylor and wife Margaret, with issue: (1) John, born 1688.

In the Maryland patent Series, Liber 18, page 152, the following passage is found. "A List of Servants Transported by Samuell Gibbons of Bristoll in the Ship Batchellor of Bristoll 1674." This document contains three columns of names; the last name in the lefthand column is "James Grear." The document is dated 2 November 1674 and reads "Then came the within named Samuel Gibbons and proved rights unto four Thousand five hundred acres of Land it being due to him for Transporting the ninety persons herein mentioned – into this province to Inhabit before me (torn) Charles Calvert." The situation was that the various Lords Baltimore offered land in the new colony of Maryland, 50 acres per person, to persons willing to make the journey and to help colonize the province. Also, individuals who paid the transportation costs for another person or persons were, then, entitled to claim that person's acreage as reimbursement.

Many people believe that James Greer was Scots-Irish. (A Scot who lived in Ulster, Ireland.) This is not likely. He was definitely not born there, and his parents did not die there so he likely did not live there as a child. This does not explain why there seems to be no record of his young adulthood in Scotland. If he had a wife and family anywhere, no record has yet been found. Any Scots would have found life difficult with religious persecution everywhere that the English controlled. They also dominated much of the transocean traffic of that day. It would not have been unusual for an English ship to transport Scots emigrants to the English dominated colonies from either England's Bristol Port or from Irish Belfast. There were large numbers of emigrant Scots even in this age though it would not reach flood stage for another fifty years. Then about 1721 they would crowd the dock begging for passage to America. These crowds would include the native Irish and the term "Scots Irish" would come into use to distinguish the Scots from native Irish.

A recent issue of Scotland magazine (May 2019) sheds some light on this era of Scottish history. In 1633 British Monarch Charles I pronounced himself head of the Church of Scotland by divine right. He ordered John Knox's *Book of Discipline* replaced by his own *Book of Common Prayer*. This was considered a breach of faith by the lowland Scots as they had long felt the British had conceded them the right to be Presbyterian. In 1638, a large number of devout members of the Church of Scotland signed a National Covenant of Opposition. This opened fifty years of British religious persecution.

Those who failed to attend government approved churches were fined. Those who attended the out-of-doors churches that sprang up were subject to the death penalty. (It is estimated that over 28,000 were killed.) On November 28, 1666 a bloody battle was fought at a place called Rullion Green. All these events occurred during James Greer's childhood and early adulthood. We do not know anything of his involvement but by 1674 he had made his way to America. The Scottish Church was the reliable source of records for the time and English persecution leaves us with a blank in Scottish records. The English transported some prisoners of this war to America. James Greer seems to fit this category as an indentured emigrant for several reasons besides age and lack of family. Maryland could have also been a destination of choice also for it had declared for "Religious Liberty" some years earlier.

James Greer died before 1714 at which time his widow Ann (nee Taylor) Greer Harriatt "mother of said John Greer" was married to Oliver Harriatt. John Greer, son of James Greer and Ann Taylor, was born about 1688.

## Second Generation

*John Greer, Sr.
Born 1688, Baltimore County, Maryland
Died Augusta County, Virginia (This would become present day
Bedford County.)
Married March 4, 1710, Sarah Day, Baltimore County, Maryland
(Father – Nicholas Day, Sr. and mother, Sarah Day) She was listed as still living in 1743 at Clynomalira, Baltimore County, Maryland. John and Sarah were apparently living apart for John Greer and Cloe Jones were cited at that time for "cohabitating together" unlawfully. It is believed that sometime after this John Sr. moved to Augusta County, Virginia where he lived until his death.

---John Sr. and Sarah Day Greer's children:

*(1) John Greer Jr., born 1712, Baltimore Co., MD, died 1782, Wilkes County, NC
(2) James Greer born 1714, Baltimore Co., MD, died 1742 Baltimore Co., MD
(3) Moses Greer born 1716, Baltimore Co., MD, living 1777, Pittsylvannia Co., MD

(4) Aquilla born 1719, Baltimore Co., MD, died 1790 Green Co., GA

(5) Sarah Greer born February 15, 1721 Baltimore Co., MD – no further information.

(6) Ann Greer born February 15, 1721 Baltimore Co., MD, married John Starkey

(7) Elizabeth Greer born 1723, Baltimore Co., MD, married Jacob Davice

(8) William Greer born 1725, Baltimore Co., MD, died September 19, 1802, Grayson Co., VA

(9) Benjamin Greer born January 6, 1727, Baltimore Co., MD, died 1787, Franklin, VA

(10) Joseph Greer born 1729, Baltimore Co., MD, died 1781, Bedford Co., VA

## Third Generation

*John Greer, Jr. later known as John, in Wilkes, as the Jr. was dropped.

Born 1712, Baltimore County, Maryland

Died July 7, 1782, Moravian Falls (Wilkes County), North Carolina

Married July 1736, Nancy Ann "Nannie" Walker, Wilkes County

(May have moved to NC in 1765, as son Benjamin was already living there.)


---Children


(1) Aquilla Greer born Jan. 29, 1737, died 1818, married a Hannah Riley

(2) John Greer – no information. Some sources do not list a John.

*(3) Benjamin Greer born Feb. 9, 1746, died Oct. 23, 1816 in Green County, Kentucky. Married first Nancy Wilcoxen, second Sarah Adkinson Jones

(4) Joshua Greer died 1796 in Wilkes. Married Sara Davis.

(5) Jesse Greer died 1799 in Wilkes. Married Judith Hampton.

(6) Rachel Greer married James Mitchel.

(7) Sarah Greer married Francis Hargraves.

(8) Hannah Greer born Feb. 3, 1755. Married Lewis Demoss (Wilkes Sheriff).

(9) Ann Greer married a Mitchell.

Early on John Jr. was a citizen of Rowan County, NC with its seat of government at Salisbury. This would change in 1771 when Surry County was formed from the western lands of Rowan. And would change again when Wilkes was formed from Western Surry in 1778. 1778 was a time of upheaval as the state and counties adjusted to being self-governing rather than subjects of the king. John Jr. became a justice of the first Wilkes court and his son Benjamin a constable.

John Greer Jr. was born in 1712 but lived most of his adult life in the Moravian Falls area of Wilkes until he died there July 7, 1782. He appears to have prospered. His will was probated in the Wilkes court in 1782. It provided that his wife Nancy would have the home place.

(1) Jesse – The home place when Nancy died.
(2) Ann (Mitchell) – A Negro girl named Phebe.
(3) Hannah (Demoss) – A Negro girl named Hannah.
   (Hannah's husband was sheriff of Wilkes.)
   Balance of estate divided equally between:
(4) Aquilla
(5) John
(6) Benjamin
(7) Joshua
(8) Rachael (Mitchell)
(9) Sarah (Hargrave)

When the colonies declared their independence July 4, 1776 the functions of colonial government had been very confused to say the least. There was no orderly process remaining for land entries for example. The Granville Grant Owners had ceased making titles about 1767. The North Carolina government acquired the right to vacant lands through the Confiscation Act of 1778. Wilkes County had been formed in 1777 and was ready to accept land entries the first Monday in March of 1778. This led to a flurry of entries because all older entries had to be re-filed. Much confusion existed for several years to come as settlers entered the land they had "squatted" on.

When filing opened for land entries many claims were filed with poor descriptions. Descriptions were given in relation to neighbors, watersheds, fords, gaps, ridges, camps, etc. Real estate had always been a major concern of many prominent citizens. Many of these land speculators filed on land where others had made improvements. The original settlers sometimes prevailed, or maybe received pay or simply filed on other vacant land or even moved on. Tories, especially, may have frequently lost their land. As in colonial days North Carolina again failed to protect deeds and many emigrated only to be confronted with similar situations again and again.

## Fourth Generation

Benjamin Greer –
Born February 9, 1746 Albemarle Co., VA
Died October 23, 1816 Green River, KY
Married Nancy Wilcoxen – Born May 17, 1745 Berks Co., PA. Died October 3, 1790, Ashe Co., NC

Children:

| | | |
|---|---|---|
| (1) Rachel Greer | born March 31, 1768 | Wilkes Co., NC |
| (2) John Greer | born January 14, 1770 | Wilkes Co., NC |
| (3) William Greer | born January 21, 1772 | Wilkes Co., NC |
| (4) Benjamin Greer | born February 14, 1774 | Wilkes Co., NC |
| (5) Nancy Ann Greer | born April 26, 1776 | Wilkes Co., NC |
| (6) Jesse Greer | born November 14, 1778 | Wilkes Co., NC |
| (7) Vincent David Greer | born February 2, 1781 | Ashe Co., NC |
| (8) James Greer | born September 17, 1783 | Ashe Co., NC |
| *(9) Samuel Greer | born November 26, 1785 | Ashe Co., NC |
| (10) Joshua Greer | born April 8, 1788 | Ashe Co., NC |
| (11) Thomas Greer | born October 3, 1790 | Ashe Co., NC |

Married second wife Sarah Adkinson Jones–
    Born _____ Died_____.

Children:

| | |
|---|---|
| (1) Aquilla Greer | Ashe Co., NC |
| (2) Edmund Greer | Ashe Co., NC |
| (3) Sally Greer | Ashe Co., NC |
| (4) Elizabeth Greer | Ashe Co., NC |
| (5) Polly Greer | Ashe Co., NC |

Benjamin Greer was born in Albemarle, Virginia and grew up in Franklin County, Virginia. Soon after obtaining his majority, around 1770, he settled in the area that is now southwest Wilkes County, North Carolina. This was part of Rowan County until 1777. He arrived with other Greers and began clearing land, building cabins and farming, all around the area of Cub Creek (the southwest area of modern Wilkes County). Benjamin, along with brother Aquilla, is found on the tax lists of 1771. By 1772, his father John, brothers Joshua and John, Jr. also appear. Benjamin probably married just before or soon after his arrival in North Carolina. His wife, Nancy Wilcoxson, is of another family which appears to have come from Maryland. In 1781, Benjamin moved to the area that is now Watauga County, entering claims on land tracts on the south fork of the New River in 1781 and 1789. At the first free court of Wilkes County, Benjamin's father, John, qualified as a Justice of the Peace and Benjamin became a constable in Capt. Hargraves district which is said to have been in the area of Moravian Creek. During the Revolutionary War, Benjamin saw various services in the Wilkes County Militia, though documentary record of this is scarce. His most famous exploit was the rescue of his commander, Col. Benjamin Cleveland from the Tories in April 1781 near Meat Camp Creek. (This is a quote from Arthur's of *History of Watauga*.) It was also Ben Greer who fired the shot that killed Col. Ferguson at Kings Mountain. Ben was the participant of the coining of the phrase "Greer Hint." When a fellow soldier stole his tobacco, Ben threatened to whip him for it. When the Col. chastised them to "fight only the enemy," Ben said he'd "give a hint of it to him anyway." When he met the tobacco pilfer, he knocked him down. "Greer's hint" began and was to read "you don't have to knock me down with a hint." Ben and Nancy then settled at "Old Fields" on the west bank of the New River, where Gap Creek enters the South Fork of the New River in Ashe County (4 miles above Cleveland's plantation). In 1890, the old chimney was still standing. Benjamin was a member of the Three Forks Baptist Church from 1790 to 1800 but had to leave the church in 1807 due to intemperance. After his first wife died, Ben married Sarah Atkinson Jones, the widow of Thomas Jones, who died of a wound received during the Revolutionary War. About 1803, after selling tracts of land, Ben and Sarah moved to Green County, Kentucky, (following Daniel Boone), leaving his sons behind. On February 21, 1816, Ben made a will leaving everything to his second wife and their children. To the ten children he had with first wife Nancy, he left to each a single dollar.

TIMELINE: Ashe County was settled in 1773, when the first landowner registered. Acres sold between 5 cents and 5 dollars each. White explorers had been in the area since 1749 when Peter Jefferson and his surveying crew were at Pond Mountain establishing the boundary between NC and Virginia. Ashe was first Anson County, then Rowan County (1753), then Surry County (1771), the Wilkes (1777) and finally Ashe County in 1799. The county was named for Samuel Ashe, a Revolutionary War patriot who serve three terms as a Superior Court Judge and was Governor in 1795, 1796 and 1797. Ashe today covers 427 square miles. When it was established it was 977 square miles. It included present day Alleghany and Watauga Counties.

TIMELINE: From 12/14/1784 until 1789, there was a separatist state on the western border of NC. It was the State of Franklin. Franklin had a population of 25,000+ and included most of Ashe County. (Watauga was still Ashe at that time.) It was a turbulent time for the small state. Because of being isolated, along with political woes, it was decided it would be in the best interests of the people to reunite Franklin with NC. Franklin Governor Sevier was instrumental in this. The territory of Franklin outside of NC became the new state of Tennessee. Governor Sevier became the first Governor of Tennessee and served for six two-year terms.

## Two of Benjamin's many land entries were:

---File #1121 100 acres, Entry #217 January 24, 1781, Grant #1310 July 9, 1794. Oddly, this appears to have been the first entry made by Benjamin. It shows to have been entered Stringer and had improvements including the house where Stringer lived. The original entry day was June 26, 1778. Greer appears to have exercised Stringer's claim. He likely paid Stringer because Stringer enters adjoining 150 acres same and they became neighbors.

---File #1590 100 acres, Entry #268 August 3, 1778, Grant #1881 June 7, 1799. Both sides S. Fork New River.

Of personal interest, my paternal ancestor, Benjamin Greer, listed my maternal ancestor, William Miller's taxes in 1790. (Both ancestors listed 1,000 acres.)

The Benjamin Greer homestead of the south fork is best described as being on the west side of the river across from the mouth of Old Fields Creek. (This would describe the big loop of the river there.) This would have been across the river from where the Perkins Cabin is said to have been. An old chimney is said to have been standing there as late as 1890. Nancy is believed buried at Meadow Creek where they lived prior to Benjamin's move to Kentucky.

Benjamin became a church member by experience at the October meeting of 1792. (There is no mention of Sarah joining then or later. She must have already been a member.) They must have attended fairly regularly for the church of that day would likely have taken them to task if they had not. Three Forks was the earliest church of record. It was established in 1890. It was likely Sarah's home church before Benjamin joined. It was a long way to go to church but others from the area also took the Glades Road across country to Three Forks. Church activities may have even played a part in Benjamin selling out eventually at the mouth of Gap Creek to move further up the river where the church would have been closer. At any rate they did not draw any undue attention that is recorded in the church minutes until 1798.

In 1798 Benjamin was cited for drinking to excess. Apparently, his apologies were well received for he was made a deacon at the June meeting of 1800. He was in trouble for drinking and swearing again by November; apparently, he was reconciled once again. (The charges in all instances were brought by the Wilcoxens. Ironically, they were both neighbors and kin of Benjamin's first wife, Nancy.) In the January of 1801 meeting Benjamin was charged again. At the February meeting it was decided to drop him from the rolls unless he appeared and "made satisfaction." He failed to appear to answer charges and was dropped from the rolls in March of 1801. Sarah may have continued to attend but she most likely was accompanied by the older children.

Quite by accident I learned that Benjamin, Sarah and their five children did not move to Kentucky alone. Benjamin and Nancy's oldest daughter, Rachel, had married John Judd. An examination of the family history of the Kentucky Judds reveals that Benjamin and his second family moved with John and Rachel Judd and their children. The Kentucky Judds seemed to be well aware of ancestor Benjamin and his exploits. The move may have been planned for some time before it actually took place. Both Benjamin and his son-in-law had been disposing of property beginning around 1800. The move would not be made until 1808 but Benjamin may have begun a systematic system for giving an inheritance to his first family who would all become of age during this period. Of course, as some have suggested, it is possible also that Benjamin's drinking had become a problem and he had to raise money to keep everything afloat. I find this unlikely, myself, for his dealings and actions for the remainder of his life are not very much like one who has lost control. The removal to Kentucky bears this out.

Benjamin does appear to have family problems, however. The first census for the new Ashe County in 1890 shows eighteen in his household. Part of these could have been Sarah's children from a previous marriage, though any children by Thomas Jones (the husband killed during the Revolution) would be even older than the youngest of Benjamin and Nancy Wilcoxen's children. We are told that Sarah and Thomas Jones had children, but I have yet to find track of them. There is also the possibility that Sarah had been married a second time in the interval of about ten years between Thomas' death and her marriage to Benjamin. The Judd family history has added Cutbirth to the list of names she had. This is a mystery to me unless she was at some time also married to a Cutbirth. Another explanation for such a large household could have been that Sarah's children by her previous marriage lived with them. One of the earliest deeds recorded in Ashe County is one from Judd to William Greer for fifty acres on the south fork of New River. Ashe records other early Greer family deeds.

---September 1799 Benjamin Greer sells John Lipps 100 acres for 120 pounds. Said land granted in 1794.

---October 17, 1800 Benjamin Greer for sixty pounds deeds Elisabeth Blackburn 100 acres on the New River said lands granted to Greer by the state August 3, 1778.

---August 10, 1803 Benjamin Greer for $300.00 deeds Phillip Church 100 acres where he now lives. Notice that land deals are made both in English pounds for American dollars. The two kinds of money were both commonly used for years after Independence. If Greer lived here, did he move in 1803 to another property? He still has adjoining property and also property four miles upriver. The Meadow Creek property is most likely.

---August 10, 1803 (the same day) Benjamin for 10 pounds deeds Philemon Church 15 acres on the north side of New River in the same general area.

(Elizabeth Blackburn sold for 80 pounds the 100 acres purchased from Greer. She has made 20 pounds on the deal.)

Throughout the years Benjamin disposed of land on the South Fork, he had continued to function in the Wilkes court. After 1799 and the formation of Ashe County it is unclear whether he was ever involved in county government again. It is pretty well definite that he was never involved in a church again.

There has long been much speculation and much misinformation about Benjamin Greer's move to Kentucky. It did come rather late in his life. There is little need for confusion, however, because there is more hardcopy information about him than there is about any Greer before or since. Some have speculated that the move may have come about due to animosities resulting from war-time activities with Benjamin Cleveland; or that he went to claim land offered to his second wife, Sarah Adkinson Jones, the widow of deceased Revolutionary War soldier Thomas Jones. None of these have any foundation in fact. Benjamin continued to live in the area twenty-odd years after the war and was a public official much of that time. Most of the Tories appear to have moved after the war to areas where they were less well known. Those remaining appear to have been readily forgiven. As for the speculation that Greer moved to take up land due his second wife, records from Kentucky indicate otherwise. He paid 100 pounds for the land there as shown in the old deed copy. This money most likely came from Old Fields Creek property which in part was sold to one Jonathan Lipps. This sell is recorded in the Wilkes County, NC records.

Another misconception is that Benjamin might have short-changed the children of his first wife or that the Kentucky land was somehow obligated to the children of his second wife. A copy of his Kentucky will does give that property to those five children, but that does not mean that he had not previously provided for the others. They would have ranged from 18 years old and upward. Some may have received money from land sales. Several of them are known to have lived for many years on other land he had entered in North Carolina.

Why did Benjamin move? He likely had longed to go for many years. The territory of Kentucky was filling with friends and family. In the Barren River area, the land was mostly open and did not require much clearing for crops. The Wilcoxen he purchased land from was likely kin of his first wife, Nancy Wilcoxen Greer. The Aquilla Greer named as an executor of his Kentucky will was most likely his older son by Sarah. He would have been about eighteen but a brother to Benjamin, Aquilla, also lived in Kentucky. At 62 and with young children, Benjamin likely felt young and vigorous enough to start over again.

## The Kentucky Land Deed

(This Indenture) made and agreed upon this 29th day of March, 1808 between Jacob Wilcox and Nancy Wilcox his wife of Green County and the state of Kentucky of the one part and Benjamin Greer of the same county and state aforesaid of the other part, witnesseth that the Jacob Wilcox and Nancy Wilcox his wife forsaid in consideration of the sum of one hundred pounds to them in hand paid hath this day bargained and sold and by these presents doeth make over and confirm unto the said Benjamin Geer his heirs, executors, administrators and assigns, a certain tract or parcel of land lying and being in Green County, and on the waters of Greasy (Grassy?) Creek waters of Little Barren River containing of one hundred and thirty-one acres and 109 poles of land being part of the John A. Davies Survey of six hundred acres surveyed and bounded as follows, towit, Beginning at John A. Davies northwest corner, three black oak trees running thence South thirty nine West ninety nine and one half poles to two dogwood and black oak trees, thence South fifty one East two hundred and twelve poles to three dogwood and black oak trees, thence North thirty minutes East ninety nine and one half poles to two white oak and two black oak trees thence North fifty one West two hundred and twelve poles to he beginning for 131 acres and 109 poles of land more or less to have and to hold the said land and premises there unto the said Benjamin Greer his heirs, executors, administrators and assigns to warrant and defend the aforesaid the 131 acres and 109 poles of land more or less and premises from all persons or person whatever holding any right, title, claim, interest or demands and the said Jacob Wilcox and Nancy Wilcox his wife for themselves, heirs, executors, administrators and assigns will forever warrant the said land and premises with the Revision and Revisions, Remainder and Remainders thereunto belonging to the said Benjamin Greer his heirs and assigns forever against themselves and all and every person or persons free from all incumbrances whatever and will forever warrant and defend the same unto the said Benjamin Greer his heirs and assigns forever. In witness whereof they have set their hands and seal the day of the year first mentioned Signed Sealed and Delivered in the presence of

Jacob Wilcox

Nancy Wilcox

## Benjamin Greer's Will Made in Green Co., Ky. In the Year 1816

In the name of God, Amen. I, Benjamin Greer of the County of Green, State of Kentucky, being through the goodness and mercies of God, though weak in body, yet of sound mind and perfect understanding and memory, do constitute, this my last will and testament and desire it may be recorded as such.

I most humbly bequeath my soul to God who gave it, beseeching (torn and taped) and my body buried like seed in the ground, not to be lost, but here buried to remain till the morning of our Resurrection through Jesus Christ our Lord. As to my burial, I do desire to be interred, at the discretion of the Executors, thereafter named, who, I doubt not will arrange it with prudence.

As to my worldly estate, I will, and positively order, that all my debts be paid. First, I do bequeath to my two youngest sons, Aquilla and Edmund Greer, the two tracts of land I now live on to be equally divided between them; and the reset of my estate to be equally divided between my three daughters: namely Sally, Elizabeth and Polly Greer; but my wife, Sarah Greer, to hold the same in her hands during her life; but the said children to have their equal part as they become of age or marry.

At the discretion of my executors to which I do appoint my wife, Sarah Greer, Aquilla Greer, and Robert Ervin, and do constitute the executors of this my last will and testament and Trustees for my wife and children. In my witness thereof I have hereunto set my hand and seal the twenty-first day of February in the year of our Lord one thousand eight hundred and sixteen.

N. B. and I do will that all my other children, namely, John, Rachel, William, Benjamin, Jesse, David, Samuel, Joshua and James have one dollar each out of my estate. Benjamin Bayly, Christopher Hinker James his X mark Lete (Lile?)

Signed Benjamin X (his mark) Greer

At a County Court begun and held for Green Co. at the Court House in Greensburgh (h is not used now) (zip code 42743, in case you need it) the last Will and Testament of Benjamin Greer, deceased, was produced in Court by the executors therein named and proved by the oath of Christopher Hinker and James Lile to be the act and deed of the said Ben Greer and at the time of executing the same and at the time they believed him to be in his perfect mind and memory and the same with this certificate is truly recorded in my office.

Test. John Bandege

Benjamin's children by Nancy Wilcoxen were left out of his will except for the one dollar. This will should not have been signed with a mark since Benjamin read and wrote well enough to have signed his name. Lack of practice or poor health may have caused him to request a witnessed mark, however. A "witnessed mark" may have seemed more "official" in those days to many. As an early Wilkes County, NC judge of the county court Benjamin was completely familiar with such procedures. As a lister of taxes, Benjamin would also have been required to write though many in such positions did not write well.

Some of the written accounts about Benjamin Greer cannot be accurate. The most flagrant misrepresentation would have been the one concerning the Kentucky land as shown previously. (It should not have happened for no land grant of the day would have awarded land to widows or daughters.) Another would have been the insinuation that Benjamin had become an irresponsible drunk. This is unlikely for he was a magistrate after he moved to Kentucky. (I found that he had performed the marriage ceremony of one of his and Sarah's daughters there.)

What may have been the most unfair accusation was a supposed affair with Sarah Atkinson Jones. Some relate that Benjamin and first wife Nancy were separated. The whole story seems untrue to me:

---Benjamin and Nancy appear to have been a family until her death. She died
        October 3, 1890 on the same date given as the birthdate of their son Thomas.
---On the other hand, any supposed affair with Sarah did not produce children.
        This would have been unusual for the times.
---Benjamin and Sarah were married the following April and did have five children.
---Sarah was a member of the Three Forks Baptist Church. At any hint of an
        affair she would surely have been excluded from membership and the event
        recorded in the church minutes.
---Sarah probably influenced Benjamin to join the church also. She remains a good
        member though he does not.

---When they move to Kentucky Sarah is dismissed by letter, a procedure used to affirm a proper and good standing to another potential church.

## Fifth Generation

*Samuel Greer-

Born November 26, 1785 Ashe County, NC

Died April 20, 1872

Married Sarah "Sallie" Church born about 1789, died May 1, 1860

(Her father John or Phillip Church. Her mother Sarah Hannah Andrews.)

Children:

| | | |
|---|---|---|
| (1) David | born about 1820, died April 20, 1871. Married Ann Watson. |
| (2) Elizabeth | born December 20, 1822, died January 15, 1916. Married Gibson Hendrix. |
| (3) Finley | born March 9, 1823, died October. Married Mary Greer born February 12, 1831. |
| *(4) Riley | born April 23, 1824, died April 1925. Married Frankie Watson in 1849. (His legal name was Raleigh) |
| (5) Louisa | born 1833, died _____. Married Silas Morphew. |
| (6) Emeline | married a Younce. |
| (7) John | died 1869. |
| (8) Lucinda | |

Married second wife Jane (Jenny) Andrews.

Information has been hard to locate on Samuel, but I am sure it will show up yet. He may or may not have been an early clerk of Ashe County. He is hard to track because he moved in and out of Ashe and Watauga counties. He may have lived on or near todays Cooper farm property at Brownwood at times and likely was buried there in the old Greer Cemetery.

---November 16, 1820 – Samuel Greer enters 50 acres on Barnys Branch Waters of Gap Creek, includes vacant land between branch and Jonathan Gipe.

---March 18, 1822 - Samuel Greer enters 50 acres at mouth of Meat Camp Creek on Isaac Greene's line running east to James Jackon line then north.

---May 9, 1835 – Samuel Greer enters 50 acres Gap Creek Township. Mention of land Benjamin Greer sold Philip Church (possibly Samuel's father-in-law).

March 13, 1814 – Benjamin David Greer (Samuel's brother) enters 100 acres north side south fork of New River including Benjamin's old improvement. Begins on white oak near head of little fork of Meadow Creek.

---In 1860 Samuel is living in Gap Creek Township, Watauga County with younger daughter Lucinda and Mary, 13 (probably Lucinda's daughter).

---By 1870 Samuel is in Old Fields Township of Ashe where he is living with son Riley and family. Samuel is listed at 84 years of age at this time. Though he lived to be old, much of Samuel Greer's life is still to be discovered. I can only speculate, but the best evidence I have yet found is that his life followed this course. He likely lived on the remaining 100 acres of land that Benjamin entered at the mouth of Old Fields Creek. Greer descendants are numerous in the area and there are at least two Greer cemeteries in the area. None have marked graves that are any help, however. Samuel lived with a son, "Riley," who lived on Meadow Creek in his old age. I think I can vaguely remember Grandpa Greer saying his grave is on Meadow Creek.

Tradition has it that Samuel was a great hunter. He seems to have preferred to make his living more by hunting than by farming. Bears were still plentiful in the high mountains along the Tennessee line in the Virginia, Mt. Rogers area. Samuel must have been the equal of Wilburn Waters by the accounts passed down and likely was acquainted with Wilburn.

# Sixth Generation

Raleigh "Riley" Greer–
Born April 23, 1824, probably in Ashe County, NC.
Died April 1925, Deep Gap, NC
Married Franky Watson in 1849.
They were the parents of seven children all born in Watauga County.


Children:

(1) Thomas    born February 15, 1859, died March 2, 1951. Married Mary Ray.
(2) Larkin    born September 15, 1861, died June 24, 1940. Married Rhoda Teague.
(3) "Sam"
(4) Rhoda    who married a Green.
(5) Julia    who married a Trivette.
(6) Sarah
*(7) Elijah Calloway, born December 25, 1866, died December 18, 1941.


Married 1- Doane Vannoy, 2- Lula Waters, and 3- Mary Watson.


Riley Greer was born to Samuel and Sarah Church Greer April 23, 1824 probably in Ashe County along the south fork of the New River. He was the fourth of eight children. He lived over 100 years, having died in April of 1925. He is buried at Deep Gap in Watauga County on the hill above the new road behind the fire department.

Raleigh "Riley" Greer appears to have lived most of his life on Meadow Creek and New River in the Brownwood area. His last years were spent with a son, Thomas Greer, at the foot of what became known as Tom Greer Hill on US 421 east of Rutherwood. He was said never to have traveled farther than Statesville, NC, much different than his wandering ancestors. Not much is known about his early life except that he was a great hunter and woodsman. He hunted bears with his father Samuel.

Riley was too old for the Civil War (the Conscription Act went to age 35 and he was 37). But he was active in the Home Guard. My favorite story about him is a story about a Home Guard raid to pick up a "scouter" who was avoiding conscription. This man, named Parker I believe, had come out to cultivate a crop of corn for his wife and children to hoe. One of the guardsmen said, "Watch me shoot him where his suspenders cross as he goes back across the field." Grandpa Riley is said to have replied, "You shoot him, and you will get the next one. All this man is guilty of is trying to keep his family from starving."

Riley lived to be a strong old man. I wrote a letter to the editor of the Jefferson Post asking help in tracing the Greers in Ashe County. An Irene Morphew, retired postmistress of Jefferson or West Jefferson, gave me a call. She said her great grandmother Louisa Greer Morphew was a sister to "Uncle Riley." She and her mother went to see him when she was small. (The place she described was apparently the Uncle Tom Greer place.) She said they did not see him until he came in from the fields from hoeing corn. She thought he was ninety-nine at the time. (Ms. Morphew has since passed away herself. She was 104 years old.)

Riley's 100th birthday party in 1924 was said to have been the largest gathering ever for the area at that time. The Watauga Democrat carried a full-page report and the Winston-Salem Journal and others gave it coverage. Almost 1,000 people gathered to hear many dignitaries speak. Speakers included Dr. I. G. Greer from the college. Much was made of the fact that Riley's life had spanned every administration from John Adams on and every mile of railroad in the country had been built.

Mr. Greer had the unusual distinction of having had all the U. S. Presidents from John Adams to George Bush Sr. alive during his lifetime.

# Seventh Generation

Elijah C. Greer-

Born December 25, 1866, Meadow Creek, Watauga County, NC.

Died December 18, 1941, Greensboro, NC,

Married Doane Vannoy who died in childbirth September 9, 1885;

Married second wife Lula Waters December 8, 1889.

Married third wife Mary Watson, and they moved to Greensboro after 1890.

Elijah C. Greer was born to Riley and Frankie Watson Greer in the Meadow Creek – New River area December 25, 1866. He was the seventh of eight children. He lived in and out of Ashe and Watauga Counties until he moved to Greensboro where he died December 18, 1941. Elijah was married three times. The first two wives died early but all three bore him children. (I found this to be in error. His second wife did not die. She ran away. More later.)

Elijah first married Doane Vannoy who died in childbirth September 9, 1885. The child survived. I do not know who raised him or anything about his early life, but he became a prominent resident of Millers Creek, NC. (Reared by an aunt unknown to me.)

Children:

(1) George Washington Greer married Gertrude Church in 1907. They had nine children.

> In the 1900 census George is living with the Salmonds family on the New River. George married Gertrude Church in 1907. They were residents of Miller's Creek and had nine children.

Elijah married second a Lula Waters December 8, 1889. My Great-Grandmother Lula has long been a mystery which I will attempt to clarify later. Children:

*(1) Ivory Ward Greer

Born September 2, 1891, died May 26, 1972.

Married June 23, 1908 Emma Parlier Born June 1881. Died August 22, 1954.

(2) John Avery Greer

Born April 13, 1891, died March 7, 1972.

Married Nannie Watkins, lived Harlan, KY.


Elijah was married a third time to Mary Watson, and they moved to Greensboro after 1890. His brother, Thomas Greer, kept my grandfather, Ivory Ward Greer, in his teen years. I am not sure who reared John Avery. Most likely his mother. He was just a baby when she left. As a child I remember hearing that she ran away from home. If anyone knew where she went, I never heard. Elijah was granted a divorce later form Lula, but this does not indicate her whereabouts or even if she was still alive. It was likely necessary before he could marry his third wife. The only mention I ever heard Grandpa Ivory make of his mother was that "Some said she was dark." This did not show in either grandpa or his brother. Both were fair skinned, and grandpa had blue eyes. Lula was almost surely part Indian and was a niece of Wilburn Waters the bear hunter. My DNA does not prove or disprove this.


The 1900 census shows Ivory living with Elijah and his third wife and their young children. Ivory is aged 10. If this is accurate, his birthdate is more likely September 2, 1890 rather than 1891 and is more compatible with a December 1889 marriage. This would also make John Avery still a baby or small child when she ran away. I have nothing about John Avery's growing up. Lula most likely took him. On John Avery's death certificate Lula's maiden name is given as Wallace. Is this a mistake or did she become a Wallace later? I do not yet know.

Elijah Greer was a great-grandson of Benjamin Greer and my great-grandfather. I only remember seeing him once. He had moved to Greensboro with his third wife and their children before I was born to take work in a textile mill. As I remember, he was not a big man but was well dressed and personable. (My mother called him a "Dandee.") He was a singer and dancer of some note and had once won the Watauga fiddling championship. Dad wanted him to sing and play for us, but he seemed reluctant. Finally, he did a song or two.

# 12

## Miller Ancestors

There has long been much speculation about the background of the William Miller who left so many area descendants. The most authentic account of William's origins is likely the one provided to the second volume of the *Watauga County Heritage Book* by one Richard E. Miller.[1] William (1735-1820) immigrated to Pennsylvania from Germany about 1750. He was the son of Heinrich Mueller. William came by way of England. This seems common in those days for transatlantic crossings were much more advanced from England than Germany. While arranging passage in England from the port of South Hampton the name was changed from Wilheim Mueller to William Miller. It is believed that William came to America with at least one brother.

William was married to Mary Eldridge, probably after arriving in Pennsylvania. They moved south to the Yadkin valley and settled near Boone's Ford in what was then Rowan County. The move may have involved stops on the way. He may have been active in the Regulator movement. A William Miller is cited in Marjoleine Kar's *Breaking Loose Together* as being involved in a Rowan County court disruption.[2] A William Miller assaulted Justice William McBride of Rowan, cursing him "God damn you, your commission and them that gave it to you." (These officials were appointed by the colonial governor and were expected to use their offices for personal gain.) After the Battle of Alamance those opposed to the colonial government fled in great numbers to the sparsely populated western mountains of NC.

During this time William has moved to Holman's Ford on the upper Yadkin in what was to be Wilkes County, NC. The Rowan County court had earlier commissioned members of the Boone family to survey a route through the lower Brushy Mountains to the upper Yadkin. This route crosses at what is still known today as Boone's Gap. The area of Holman's Ford was important to travel across the Blue Ridge. It was on an Indian trail that reached now to Trade, TN and beyond. It had long been used before Boone used it in his first attempt to move to Kentucky. After the Revolution William Miller, Nathan Horton and Ebenezer Fairchild used it to reach lands west of the Blue Ridge. William would claim a large tract in the Bamboo area of now Watauga County. Fairchild would claim the bottoms of Howard's Creek. Horton's claim was down river from the Three Forks area. Its location was once on a main route to Meat Camp. It even had an early post office. Today it is no longer on any roadway.

Richard Miller seems to credit William with serving under General Wayne during the Revolution. The only record I know of is with Cleveland's Wilkes militia. He seems to have been a procurement officer for Cleveland. There are records of payment to him for goods he bought for the militia. It is for this service that he made the DAR Patriot list as a public official during the war.

In 1783, William crossed the Blue Ridge at Cook's Gap into what is now Watauga County (it was then Wilkes and later Ashe Counties). He entered a claim on a 641-acre tract near Cook's Gap, in the Deerfield-Bamboo area. This claim could have been related to Revolutionary War service. The claim was recognized, and the deed entered into Wilkes County records on May 18, 1789. This land adjoined land claimed by Nathan Horton, another Revolutionary War soldier. Horton moved from Holman's Ford in Wilkes County at the same time. Both tracts had improvements, (hunter's cabins) on them at the time built by

Jonathan Buck and Richard Green. Records indicate that both Horton and Miller paid for these improvements and the four were apparently good friends.

Legend has it that William and Nathan returned to the Yadkin with horses and wagons to buy corn that first winter in the mountains. The newly cleared land was too cold and available varieties too long season to mature in the mountains. Crops such as potatoes, cabbage, beans, and buckwheat did extremely well. While the men were away, the Miller and Horton women had permitted the fires to go out. It was the dead of winter with snow upon the ground. Not knowing how to strike a fire, Elizabeth Horton walked off the mountains to the Lewis homestead on Elk to get coals of fire. She carried a child, and was accompanied by David, William Miller's young son. As they neared the top of the mountain on the return trip, David tripped and doused the coals he was carrying in the snow. It was too late to return to Elk that day, so after crying a while, they went on home, expecting to suffer through a cold night. However, Richard Green, the hunter who built the Horton cabin, had returned and struck a fire. It was the first indication that they had that the cabins on the Miller and Horton property were claimed.

Buck and Green settled their claims with Miller and Horton to the land and cabins as Wilkes County records indicate. Miller and Horton along with William Jackson, Landrine Eggers, and a few others were early members of the Three Forks Baptist Church. Benjamin Greer joined soon after. The church was strict. Both Miller and Greer were "turned out" of the church at one time or another. Greer had attended a horserace and was known to drink. Miller's offense is unclear, but it might have been something minor, possibly poor attendance.

William Miller traded extensively in land in the Lewis Fork and Holman's Ford areas of Wilkes County. He also owned land in the Deep Gap, Elk, New River, and Meat Camp areas of what is now Watauga County. Except for a son, David Miller, most of his family remained below the high mountains. A son, William Miller, Jr., represented Wilkes County in the State Legislature in 1824.

William Miller, Sr. returned to the Holman's Ford property in the 1790's. He was listed in the 1820 Wilkes County Census. He probably died about 1825. Shortly afterwards in 1825, there are Wilkes County records concerning the disposition of his property.

There is a monument for William Miller in the Lewis Fork Baptist Cemetery. His original gravesite is believed to have been destroyed when Highway 421 became a divided highway. When William returned to Lewis Fork to avoid cold winters, son David is believed to have stayed on the new River with the Hortons.

Children of William Miller, Sr. and Mary (Polly) Eldridge Miller were:

1.  Henry Miller, born about 1775
    First married Catherine Lipps in 1787;
    Second married Mary (Polly) McNeil
    Henry moved west to Missouri about 1800.
2.  William Miller, Jr., born _____, died 1825:
    Married Rebecca _____ about 1797.
    William Jr. served in the North Carolina House of Representatives in 1824.
    He died from pneumonia after exposure to cold weather on the way home.
3.  Joseph Miller
    Married Nancy Bingham July 6, 1807;
    They lived on Lewis Fork in Wilkes County, North Carolina.
*4. David Miller – born February 5, 1775, died March 28, 1845;
    Married Elizabeth Norris June 4, 1801.
    Elizabeth was born at a Scott County, Virginia fort during an Indian uprising. Her family apparently was trying to reach Kentucky but decided to stay in North Carolina.
    David is the ancestor of the Meat Camp Millers. He is buried in a cemetery on the ridge east of Green valley School, but his grave is apparently marked with an unlettered field stone.

5.  Mary Miller

    Married John Brown, December 12, 1799.

6.  Virginia (Jenny) Miller

    Thought to have married a McNeil.

7.  Another unidentified son indicated by census records, but possibly died young.

## Second Generation

### David Miller

David Miller, son of William Sr. and father of Jonathan, was one of the most prominent men of his time. He owned hundreds of acres of land, most of it located in the Meat Camp area. He served as Constable and Justice of the Peace for Ashe County, North Carolina. Meat Camp was part of Ashe County at that time. Papers that he possessed indicate that he was well educated and had beautiful handwriting. It is said that he taught all his children to read and write. He also served Ashe County in the North Carolina House of Commons in 1810, 1811 and 1813. David's homeplace was somewhere below the old Green Valley School. Andre Michaux, the French naturalist, stayed with him some while classifying the plant life found in western North Carolina. He described Miller's farm as being one of the most beautiful in the area. Legend has it that David's extravagant daughters ran up a debt at Council's store while he was away serving as representative. As a result, the Riddles Fork farm was sold at a court sale. He is said to have died a pauper. He did lose his homeplace but had already deeded the rest of his property to his many children. David's farm went at public auction to Council's son at only pennies on the dollar. He did not profit by it. He became and alcoholic and never prospered.

David Miller's children probably were also well educated for their time. Two of the four Watauga militia companies were commanded by his sons, William and Jonathan. Jonathan also was a magistrate. David had at least three sons and sixteen grandsons who served the South during the Civil War. At least five grandsons were killed. North Carolina troop records are being updated and revised, and these numbers will probably grow when better records are available.

Children of David and Elizabeth Norris miller were:

1. Lydia Miller, born February 23, 1803.
   Married a Joel Bingham and they moved to Haywood County.
2. Wayne Miller, born May 14, 1804, died April ____, 1904.
   First married Elizabeth Canter.
   Second married Lucretia Marlow.
3. Rebecca Miller, born December 8, 1805, died April 24, 1903.
   Married Bartlett (Battle) Bryan.
   She was the mother of the first mayor of Boone, NC, William Lewis Bryan. He was mayor for twenty (20) years and built the Daniel Boone Marker at Appalachian State University.
4. David Miller, Jr., born August 23, 1807.
   Married Elizabeth Bingham.
5. John Miller, born July 23, 1809, died August 9, 1891.
   Married Nancy Proffitt, daughter of Fillmore Proffitt.
   His son Jonathan B. Miller, rose to 1st Lieutenant in Company I 58th Regiment North Carolina Troops, during the war. The Watauga County Library has a short history of that company's Civil War activities, written by him. J. B. Miller was the grandfather of Colonel Clyde C. Miller.
6. Mary (Polly) Miller, born June 20, 1812, died June 7, 1874.
   Married David Lookabill.
7. William Miller, born November 4, 1814, died March 1, 1908.
   First married Elizabeth Morphew, born on October 3, 1839.
   Second married Elizabeth Jones.
   His first wife died while William was Captain of Company I 58th North Carolina Regiment in Tennessee. He and his second wife later moved to middle Tennessee. Ashe County prior to the separation of Watauga in 1849 appears to have had four militia companies. Brothers Jonathan and William

Miller commanded two of them. These were elected positions and not likely much sought after. The militia does not seem to have been taken seriously at this time. Jonathan was too old for the first call-up and appears to have no longer been an officer. William had previous military service that was greatly in demand. He had served in the Mexican War, and also when the Cherokees were removed to Oklahoma.

8.  Elizabeth Miller, born September 11, 1816;
    Married Jeremiah Ellison in 1843.
9.  Joseph W. Miller born January 11, 1819;
    Married Sarah Blackburn (first)
    Second married Sarah Tatum Canter
    Third married Sarah Church
10. Nancy Miller, born March 23, 1821, died October 27, 1902;
    Married Christian Lewis
11. Ephraim Miller, born November 10, 1823, died March 17, 1874;
    First married Catherine Woodring
    Second married Mary Isaacs
*12. Jonathan Miller, born May 16, 1826, died May 19, 1921;
    Married Rebecca Blackburn, daughter of Levi and Sarah Greer Blackburn.

The descendants of David Miller formed many of the most prominent and progressive families in the county. While they owned much land and apparently had the position and means to own slaves, there is no evidence that any of them ever did. Slavery must had been against their teaching and principles. Nevertheless, they supported their state in the Civil War effort.

## Third Generation

### Jonathan Miller

Great-Great Grandpa Jonathan was the youngest son of David Miller. He lived in the Meat Camp community and was active in civic affairs. He was a captain of the militia though his company likely existed mostly on paper. His position as magistrate was more serious. He is said to have called the first Watauga County court into session after the county was formed in 1849. Legend has it that the first court was held in Henry Hardin's barn near where Hardin Park School is today. The barn was full of fleas. Jonathan is said to have solved the problem by driving a flock of sheep into the barn to capture the fleas in their wool.

Jonathan's Civil War service does not appear in most local history accounts nor in state troop records. The reason being that he enlisted into a Virginia regiment. The 21st Virginia Volunteer Cavalry was formed in 1862 to defend southwestern Virginia from raids by US forces coming out of West Virginia. Wytheville, Virginia and the salt mines at Saltville were essential to Confederate war efforts. The 21st was to be all volunteers who would not already be in the service nor were subject to conscription. They likely had to provide their own horses also. Jonathan fitted this description for he was over thirty-five and not subject to a draft at that time. Legend has it that he rode wife Rebecca's little gray mare off to war. (The mare had been a gift from her parents.) She was often heard to say she hoped that Jonathan would come home soon with her little gray mare. Some speculated that she was most concerned about the mare.

The 21st Virginia Cavalry looked to be good duty not too far from home. Seventy percent of its personnel were Virginians, but most of the rest were North Carolinians with several from the Ashe County vicinity. They would often find themselves far from home. They fought all the way from Cumberland Gap to defending Richmond, Virginia. Other engagements found them in West Virginia and the Shenandoah Valley. The regiment lost a lot of men, including 222 listed as captured. Jonathan was one of those. He is listed as a POW at Morefield, West Virginia August 7, 1864. By October he is being held at Camp Chase in Ohio where he has smallpox. March 18, 1865 he is transferred to Point Lookout, MD for exchange just before the end of the war. He likely took the oath of allegiance as did most exchanged POW's. It was either that or starve to death in prison. He told of boiling elm bark from off the firewood to eat. In his later years he was said to occasionally want corn bread baked with corn cob ashes instead of soda.

In 1908 the state of North Carolina passed a pension provision for Confederate veterans. On July 5, 1909 Jonathan applied. He listed a service-related injury that occurred during the retreat from Knoxville, Tennessee to his right ankle. His horse had fallen on him and he had to be hospitalized. He was disabled for two months. A neighbor, E. J. Norris, witnessed his application. They had not served together but "Lige" Norris at times served as commander of the local CSA Veteran's Post.

Jonathan's service had spanned most of the war. He was one of the three David Miller sons and sixteen grandsons to serve the South. If any served on the other side, I have never heard it. Some people assume that Jonathan had a middle name, David. This is not factual. There are no records giving a middle including military records. There is no middle name or initial on his tombstone. I do not know of any middle name of any of David and Rebecca's children.

Confederate capital, Richmond, VA, fell April 3, 1865 and Lee's surrender at Appomattox, VA followed on April 8. All this happened just days after Jonathan's release at Point Lookout. The war seems to have ended in Virginia then. I do not know how Jonathan got home, but he did not ride Granny Becky's little gray mare.

Jonathan Miller lived most of his life in the Meat Camp area, on Riddle's Fork Creek. He is said to have had a gristmill on a small creek. This mill is said to have ground slowly. One of his patrons is reported to have said "Uncle Jonathan, a jay bird could eat that meal as fast as it is being ground." Johnathan is reported to have replied, "but for how long?" After watching a moment longer, the patron said disgustedly, "I guess until it starved to death." Jonathan moved from this location in 1906 in the Howard's Creek area. He lived there in his old age and is buried with many descendants in the Miller Cemetery at Howard's Creek.

Children of Jonathan and Rebecca Blackburn Miller were:

*1. Henry Miller
   Married Martha Winebarger
2. Edmund Miller, born November 3, 1850, died December 4, 1916.
   Married Jane Holman, born October 8, 1850, died April 29, 1925.
3. Martha Miller
   Married Pat Hodges
4. Caroline Miller
   First married Ben Tugman
   Second married Jonathan Walters
5. Naomi Miller
   Married Marshall Tugman

(Rebecca Miller's obituary says that she had eight children, but apparently only five lived longer than early childhood.)

## Fourth Generation

### Henry C. Miller

Henry Miller was born August 4, 1847, died April 6, 1929. He was married to Martha Winebarger (born February 1, 1851, died September 15, 1935).

Henry Miller was too young to serve in the regular army during the Civil War but is said to have served in the Home Guard. He became a prosperous farmer and was able to leave farms to most of his children. He had many hogs which ranged throughout the mountains around Howard's Creek. The hogs were often a source of trouble with the neighbors. He is said to have brought in the first purebred shorthorn cattle breeding stock. Shorthorns were much in evidence in the family and the community for years.

Great Grandpa Henry married Martha Winebarger, the daughter of Jacob Winebarger and Salome "Sallie" Moretz. Martha was pure German with still warm family connections with the Moretz and Winebarger families. Martha was also a devout Lutheran and had good German business sense. She was too strict and stern with the orphaned children of son McCoy for their liking, however. They much preferred Grandpa Henry who entertained them with stories and involved them in farm activities.

Much of Grandpa Henry's success was due to "Granny Marthy". She likely saw that the children had a better than average education for the times. She also saw that they had the farming and household skills for the times. She kept geese and plucked them to make feather beds. The big new house they built on Howard's Creek had a spring house with running water for milk and butter and a separate loom building for weaving. She sent her wool to the cleaning and spinning mill on Big Wilson Creek at the Mouth of Wilson, Virginia. She received in trade spun wool yarn and other threads for the family weaving projects. Aunt Frances would point out the big loom in later years and relate how she wove 105 yards of cloth one winter.

"Granny Marthy's" bossy ways were usually accepted with good grace and were often valuable. Grandpa Henry once traded for a "springing" heifer and led her home with much difficulty some days later. Granny Martha immediately wanted to know where the new calf was? Grandpa Henry, inspite of his difficulty, had never guessed the calf had been born. Granny's geese were the biggest problem they had though. The geese were messy and would pull up the sprouted crops worse than crows. After one argument over the geese Grandpa Henry fell his large family of boys out one Sunday morning to cut and split chestnut rails to build a goose fence around half the farm for granny and her geese. His anger waned. The logs laid in the woods even until my time and finally rotted without ever being used. Granny kept her geese though. Mom said it was almost impossible to give a nesting goose enough room to avoid getting pinched on the backsides.

Grandpa Henry was very successful for his time, with Martha's help and encouragement, of course. He and the boys hauled huge loads of produce off the mountains claiming kin with Martha's people whenever possible. (Her aunt, father Jacob's sister, married Abner Bolick and lived near the Baily Campground below Blowing Rock.) They also ran hogs in the chestnut orchards in and around the Howard's Creek farmstead. A member of the Blowing Rock Coffey family once told me of walking to the Howard's Creek farm when young to buy pigs to be carried home in a sack. Grandpa Henry himself had the patience to move droves of hogs by dropping a little corn in front of them, so it was claimed.

The couple lived only three or four miles from the courthouse and people having business in the court often spent the night with them. During these periods of time with company there would be much discussion of the Civil War, politics and the Miller holdings of land and cattle. Granny Martha tried in vain to train Grandpa Henry to refer to the properties as "our" properties. After once calling for her to find "our Sunday pants" she was said to have relented somewhat.

The time-period of trade "down in the country" developed into a family tradition of claiming kin with almost everyone. This tradition passed down to later generations. For example, this incident told about Great Uncle Noah. Uncle Noah was always fascinated with water and fishing. In his later years he and his two sons built a wooden boat which they appropriately named "Noah's Ark." There were no large bodies of water in the area, so they decided to take the boat to Lake Hickory. "Noah's Ark" was small for a large body of water, however, and was almost swamped by the wake of a power boat. When they reached shore Uncle Noah took off down shore to give the offending party a "piece of his mind." He was gone some time and the boys were quite worried about him. When he finally returned, he said, "They are really nice folks. In fact, they are some kin to us."

During my younger days, my closest association was with the Miller side of the family, but I am sure that the Greers also had their share of shrewd businessmen. I began to hear of some of these once I got older and could get around more. One of the sharpest was Fred Greer. Just how close kin he was I have not yet figured out for the Greers were not so likely to claim kin as the Millers. Fred had an interest in a real estate development on Winkler's Creek called Leisure Acres. You would not have believed it though. He dressed in overalls but often added a white shirt when meeting a prospect. He played the part of a country bumpkin to the hilt but was really one very sharp individual. Fred once sold a lot to a pair of men from off the mountain who felt they had been taken. (They probably had.) Not ones to despair they bought a very tall bottle and came up the help Fred change his mind. Fred played the game perfectly. The next day the pair found that they had also purchased the adjoining lot.

Henry Miller's immediate descendants were:

1. John Smith Miller, born September 19, 1871, died July 30, 1933;
   Married Laura Hays, born September 15, 1871, died October 17, 1902
2. Carolina Miller, born _____, died _____.
   Married Crittenon Brown, born _____, died _____.
   (They are buried in the Sands Cemetery.)
3. Frances S. Miller, born June 6, 1875, died August 17, 1959.
   (Never married, she was a walking history book, but no one recorded her remarkable recollections.)

> Her versions of happenings sometimes differed from official versions which are often altered to fit "political" needs and desires. She was sent to boarding school in Avery County, at what may now be Lees McRae College. She nursed and doctored with herbs the far-flung family members. Almost every plant had some medicinal value, especially if it would make a bitter tea or tonic. She remained a devout Methodist, although she had to walk far across the country to get to Hopewell Methodist Church. Although she lived alone, she remained indomitable into old age.

She firmly believed that "all things work to the good for them that love the Lord."

Aunt Frances was remarkable for her times. She was said to have many suitors but never married. She wore long skirts all her life regardless of current fashions. When her nieces tried to get her to change, she said that she would keep hers long and someday they would again be the fashion. Aunt Frances cooked her meals on the hearth. She had a stove but used it only for canning. Her grandfather clock kept the standard time for the community for she corrected it using the sun's shadow on the equinox. She was legendary for quoting the Bible and even some Shakespeare.

4.  Inez Miller, born June 19, 1877, died April 15, 1915.
    Married Cornelius Woodring, born January 22, 1870, died June 25, 1958.
5.  McCoy Miller, born November 19, 1879, died June 25, 1957.
    First married to Louella Hefner.
    Second married Alma Jones.
6.  Jacob Miller, born February 2, 1883, died as a child.
7.  Jonathan R. Miller, born April 11, 1884, died September 7, 1946.
    Married Hattie Philyaw, born May 13, 1884, died November 2, 1952
    Children born of the marriage:
    >   (a) Lois Miller Greer
    >   (b) David Miller
    >   (c) Blanche Miller
    >   (d) Blaine Miller
    >   (e) Charlie Miller (died young)
    >   (f) Jake Miller
    >   (g) Calvin Miller
    >   (h) Carolyn Miller Besst
    >   (i) Lillian Miller
    *One other child died in infancy.

(I will not pursue any other line this far. I pick up Grandpa Jont and Hattie Philyaw Miller where mom, Lois Miller, enters the family.)

8. Noah E. Miller, born in 1889 and died in 1960.
    Married Jenny Brown
9. Reuben Miller, born October 12, 1886, died January 31, 1954.
    Married Chessie Graham, born September 1897.
10. McDonald Miller, born _____, died _____.
    Married Docia Barnes, born _____, died _____.

Uncle Donald was the last child and was the last son to die. He sometimes told me stories from his childhood. One was about handling Great Grandpa Henry's ranging hogs. One in particular could not be penned, and would have to be shot on the run as the dogs chased it through the laurel thickets. He was very scared for, as the youngest, he got the poorest gun.

In his last days, I went to him to pin down some less clear events. I caught him at a bad time. He said," My pappy sent Reuben and Frances away to school at Banner's Elk. He didn't send me. I don't know nothing."

## Fourth Generation Uncle

### Edmund Miller

Edmund Miller was born March 31, 1850, died December 4, 1916. He married Jane Holman (born October 8, 1850, died April 29, 1925.)

Edmund Miller did not have a large family, as Miller families go. Lois Miller Greer said jokingly, "Uncle Edmund was away from home trading on land too much to father a large family." Many of the numerous stories about Edmund have to do with his size, (as he was a very tall man), and about his land trades. Aunt Frances Miller told that he once rode to Kentucky carrying gold coins to buy land.

Two suspicious characters took him back into the hills to spend the night in a cabin on the same land they were to look at the next day. Suspecting that they were going to rob him, Edmund was said to have pulled off his boot, preparing to go to bed, and used it to knock the two in the head. They are said to have shot him in the hip, but he picked the bullet out with a horseshoe nail and returned to North Carolina.

## Fourth Generation Aunt

### Martha Miller Hodges

Martha Miller Hodges was born November 13, 1854, died October 22, 1932. Married Pat Hodges (born November 29, 1861, died January 23, 1894).

Martha Miller Hodges was known as "Aunt Matt Hodges" to a multitude of nieces and nephews. She lived at Sands and they saw her often because a store and the post office were located there. She often spent the night with her kin taking enough coffee for a couple of pots and needlework to work on. She was very religious with a "Shouting Methodist" background. When Aunt Matt started looking for safekeeping for her purse; she was feeling the urge to shout, and the meeting was about to warm up. She was born a twin to a sister, who died young with the measles, and who is buried at Hopewell.

## Fourth Generation Aunt

### Caroline Miller Tugman

Caroline is said to have built the old Joe Miller house on Howard's Creek where she probably inherited Miller property. She wrote the obituary for the paper when "Granny Becky" died. Her granddaughter, Lena, married Grover Robbins, Sr. of the Hound's Ear, Beech Mountain, and Tweetsie Railroad Robbins.

Caroline Miller Tugman, born _____, died _____.
First married Ben Tugman, born December 10, 1845, died July 5,
1900. Second married Jonathan Walters, (later separated).

## Fourth Generation Aunt

### Naomi Miller Tugman

Naomi Miller Tugman, born July 18, 1870, died December 26, 1967. Married Marshall Tugman, born July 18, 1865, died August 7, 1931. Naomi and Marshall were married in July 1888.

Naomi Miller Tugman was the youngest of Jonathan Miller's children and was the last one to die, after living to the usual Miller old age. She lived out her later years with her Lookabill descendants. The Lookabill children called her "Granny Omie." She was "Aunt Omie" to a multitude of other Miller descendants. It was said that in her later years, she happened to be in the grocery store with the Lookabill children and was trying to convince them to buy oatmeal because it was good for them. She related that Joe Miller (Howard's Creek Joe) had reared seven boys on it, all but one being six feet or more tall. Caught up in the mood of the conversation, one of the children is reported to have asked, "And what was wrong with him Granny, wouldn't they let him have any oatmeal?"

Many of the dates needed to make this portion of my ancestry complete are now available but are left blank. I no longer live in the mountains and cannot do the research but will add the information if it is available to me.

## Jonathan Miller and Rebecca Blackburn Miller
## About 1910

Jonathan served for most of the Civil War in the 21st VA Volunteer Calvary. The 21st was a unit composed of men too old for conscription. Its original mission was to protect salt makers at Saltville, Virginia, but it ended up fighting anywhere from Knoxville, Tennessee to Richmond, Virginia. He was captured late in 1864 and spent the winter in Ohio's Chase prison, where he had smallpox. He was exchanged at Point Lookout, Maryland only a few days vefore Lee's surrender. Jonathan was the youngest son of David and Elizabeth Norris Miller.

Jonathan Miller with Relatives and Friends
at His Eighty-Ninth Birthday in 1918

Left to right:

Front row- Dave Miller, Lois Miller, Blanche Miller, Carrie Miller, Louise
Hodges, Marshal Tugman.

Second row- Henry Miller, Louella Miller holding Mary Miller, Frances Miller
holding Julia Woodring, Jonathan Miller holding Lily Shore,
Henry Miller, Edmund Miller, Caroline Walters, Martha Hodges,
Naomi Tugman.  (all brothers and sisters)

Third row- McCoy Miller, "Jont" Miller holding Blaine Miller, Hattie Miller
holding Jake Miller, Martha Winebarger Miller, Edd Winebarger,
Floy Walls, Minnie Miller, Arthur Adams holding John Adams,
Lily Adams, Florence Shore, Finn Shore.

Fourth row- Cornelious Woodring, Belle Miller, Tom Woodring, Reuben
Miller, Noah Miller, Charlie Brown, Jonathan Walters, Charlie
Tugman, Tom Tugman holding Billy Tugman.

## Great-Grandpa Henry Miller and His Wife
## Martha Winebarger Miller

He was the youngest son of Jonathan and a grandson of David. Martha was the daughter of Jacob and Sally Moretz Winebarger. They reared a large family of ten children and were successful in farming and business. Both seem to have good farming business judgment. "Granny Marthy" was said to have voiced her opinion whether it was asked for or not.

Grandma Miller and Family

Left to right:

    Back row- Blaine, Grandma Hattie Mae Philyaw
                 Miller standing in back, Lois, Blanche,
                 and Dave.
    Front row- Lillian, Carolyn, Charlie (who died young),
                 and Jake.

They do not stand in the order of their birth. Dave was the oldest. Not pictured is the youngest, Calvin, who had not yet been born. Also not pictured is Grandpa Miller who was likely in the state hospital. He was named Jonathan, after his grandfather, but was always known as "Jont".

Antique Tools

Part of Leonard's Collection Donated to

Appalachian State University

# FRESH GOODS!

We would call the attention of the public to our new

# SUPPLY OF GOODS,

Having bought them in the best market of the States, New York; principally for Cash, and with much care; we confidently say they may and will be sold low. We lay on no extra per cent. to cover bad debts. We have an abundance of the following: DRY GOODS.

## HARDWARE, GROCERIES,

### Earthen and Glassware,

## HATS, BONNETS, SHOES, BOOTS, &c.

Saddles, Bridles, &c., Paints and Medicines, Books and Stationery, Tin Ware, Plain and Japaned, Candies, Raisins, &c., Clocks and Watches, Powder, Shot, Lead and Guns, Leather, Castings, Iron, Nails, Salt, Cotton Yarn, Tobacco, Flaxseed and Fish Oil, &c., &c., &c.

We barter for Feathers, Wax, Tallow, Wool, Butter, Shoe Thread, Cloth, (all sorts,) Pork, Bacon, Lard, Flaxseed, Grain of all kinds, Chesnuts, Tree Sugar, Dried Fruit, Snug, Snake Root, Dry Hides, Fur Skins, (even Cat and Opossum Skins,) Bucks Horns, Bristles, old Copper, old Pewter, Paper Rags, Socks and Stockings

## CASH WOULD NOT BE REFUSED, IF OFFERED.

Our Terms are as heretofore, " Pay down," Thankful for past favors, and asking a continuance, we subscribe ourselves your servants,

### J. & C. J. COWLES,

Elks Month, N. C.

P.S.—We are Agents for the Salt Works, and would like to engage the hauling of Salt on Shares.
Slaves wanting to trade should come as the law directs.

A Pre-Civil War Cowles' Store Handbill

## The Eagle Forge

Old iron forges were once fairly common in the mountains. They were encouraged by the government by issuing land grants, etc. Few of them survived after larger operations came into operations in the North. The one picture here was called, "The Eagle Forge".

## In Honor of
## Rendezvous Mountain Chapter of D.A.R.

Rendezvous Mountain was once a soldiers' training camp. Three long tremendous blasts of a huntsman's horn crashed through the crisp stillness of a morning in the mountains. The hunter, for he appeared to be a veritable giant of a man, took the great horn from his lips and cast his gaze down the valley in the wake of the reverberations. His eyes lighted with pleasure.

From his high vantage point on the top of Rendezvous Mountain he could see the magic of his horn at work. A fawn appeared-two-three-dozen-and in the dim distance scores of men rushed from mountain huts and leaped to their saddles.

The gigantic figure atop the mountains turned slowly, training his horn in a second direction. The mountain slopes become alive with men and horses. In a third direction the immense blast pealed out and echoed, re-echoed and reverberated, finally breaking against Blowing Rock, 30 miles away.

Ten companies of soldiers assembled at Rendezvous Mountain in answer to the blasts. The horn, described as "the greatest ever seen," was used by Colonel Ben Cleveland when he was a comparatively small man of only 300 pounds. He later weighed 450 pounds. He was almost worshipped by his mountain soldiers of the Revolutionary period for his prodigious strength and daring. He trained them on the flat top of the mountain and later led them, a regiment of sharpshooters, against the British at King's Mountain.

The mountain and the men have become inextricably merged in the traditions which have existed on the hills and in the valleys in the "State of Wilkes" for generations. The mountain's name, "Rendezvous," comes from the mere fact that Cleveland's men gathered there in answer to his powerful blasts.

The story of the man is seductive to the romantic instincts, and that of the mountain is no less so. On its great green flanks are the rhododendron, the laurel, the azalea and sturdy primeval forests. Its ice-like springs gush with crystal water, its amphi-theatre was apparently scooped by the hand of some beneficient and bedecked with shrubs by the fairies. And from its summit are views that invite the eyes to sweeps of entrancing beauty.

Rendezvous Mountain is at the tip of a spur of the Blue Ridge chain which reached to a point nine miles from Wilkesboro.

# 13

---

# The Civil War

My account of the Civil War will not be one of battles and military actions. Those things have been done well by numerous authors. I will attempt to cover the war as it affected my family. I was fortunate to have my Great Aunt Frances' stories as far as they went. She knew a lot more than she told. She could tell you that a forty-four-year-old Norris and his sixteen-year-old son were both killed on the same day at the second battle of Bull Run, but she was usually silent about local atrocities. There seems to have been a general agreement that those things were best not talked about, and they were not. I find this was also true in Ashe County where so many horrific things took place. In *Neighbor to Neighbor* by Ballard and Weinstein there seems to have been a very deliberate effort to gloss over the past. (Carolyn Greer Wilson carefully avoids antagonizing the neighbors possibly involved in the murder of her husband Isaac Wilson for example.)

North Carolina (the mountain area in particular) was not overjoyed at the prospects of secession. Some prominent citizens, like the Cowles and the Banners, opposed secession even though they owned slaves. Secession was strongly promoted by the usual vocal eastern power structure. But when they had their way, the vast majority of the people would be loyal to their state though support for secession was not really popular early on. A vote to call a state convention to consider secession failed to pass statewide. In Ashe County it was opposed by 84 percent.[1] It is remarkable that the area and the state continued to support military efforts at great sacrifice yet opposed the states secessionist government. That government was replaced in 1862 when Zebulon B. Vance was elected governor with 72 percent of the vote statewide. In Ashe Vance won 98 percent of the vote with his opponent getting only 15 votes.[2]

Though opposed to a secessionist government, locals seemed to have little choice but to support the war. Opposition expressed at the polls was mostly drowned out by the more vocal and dedicated rebels. (It would even be repeated when the eastern power structure recaptured control after Reconstruction.) This had been noted in the North during the war. Northern armies were usually instructed not to conduct the kind of destruction in North Carolina that they had caused in Georgia and South Carolina. Opposition to secession and the war was largely silent though desertions from the southern cause were common.

Opposing viewpoints were ridiculed and suppressed early in the war and would resume when the old power structure regained control of the government after Reconstruction. Even in my high school days no one would dare to suggest that there might be another side to that point in history. In recent years that has begun to change. The book "Cold Mountain" for example.

The Greer side of my family could not probably be considered reliable rebels even though there was not much way to avoid confederate service. Great-Great-Grandpa "Riley" Greer was too old to serve in the early years and was a member of the Home Guard late in the war. One story about that service still survives though little else of importance in known. The Home Guard was detailed to pick up "Scouter" by the name of Parker on the South Fork of the New River. This man was found cultivating his cornfield for the wife and children to hoe while he hid out. One of the guard members said, "Watch me shoot him right where his suspenders cross." Grandpa Riley said, "If you shoot him you will get the next one. The only thing he is guilty of is trying to keep his family from starving." Wartime loyalties were never discussed in my hearing by the Greers, but I knew that many Greers slipped into Tennessee and fought for the Union.

Some years ago, I noticed a place called Greer Hollow just over the Tennessee line. I drove over one Sunday afternoon to see the place. The Greer name was on most mailboxes and there was a Greer cemetery. I saw no one until I reached the end of the road. An older man there admitted to being a Greer. I asked him if he knew where the local Greers came from, "North Carolina, I believe", was his reply. (This was a logical conclusion.) I then asked him if they might be descendants of my ancestor Benjamin Greer. He said, "I wouldn't know, but my name is Ben." I told him it would be interesting to know which side his Greers took in the Civil War. His voice grew shrill as he said, "I can tell ye that, they fit for the Republican side."

On my Miller family side, it was common knowledge that Great-Great-Grandpa Jonathan was a Confederate veteran and his son Henry was in the Home Guard at age sixteen. There was always something mysterious about that service. A neighbor once told me that Grandpa Jonathan and his Confederate ancestor were once both Democrats and had ridden to vote together until the Millers became Republican.

Civil War sympathies did not always determine one's politics. Many had changed during the nation's deep recession and Cleveland's administration of the 1890's. This was especially true of what was considered the middle class because they were hurt the most by the economic collapse. Even so, many die-hard Southerners considered them disloyal. (The feeling still prevailed during my youth.) The state elected the first Republican governor since Reconstruction. Most would return to the party, but these Millers remained Republican and were great supporters of Teddy Roosevelt.

It was always acknowledged that Jonathan was a Confederate veteran, but local details are lacking in works of local history. Michael C. Hardy and others have done great local histories, but Jonathan's war service is not found in NC records. He enlisted in the 21ˢᵗ Volunteer Calvary of Virginia and served for most of the war. (I give more detail elsewhere.) He was a Union prisoner during the winter before the war ended.

The Civil War is probably the most traumatic and lasting event of our history. Though it continues to draw a great audience among our people, it is not my purpose to add another history to the many already in print. Only as it affected the lives of local people both then and now, will I endeavor to add anything to what has already been said. Unfortunately, my understanding of those events does not always agree with the now accepted versions of our history.

To begin with, I doubt there was ever any great support for slavery in our area. A few of our people, especially in Ashe County, point with pride to that kind of past, but I believe that it did not play a lead role in the everyday lives of most local people. The more common and more realistic scenario is of mountain families who did their own work and tended to their own business. The war itself was the best example of a "rich man's war but a poor man's fight." Neither does there appear to have been an all-consuming hatred of the black race locally. Many of the homeless elderly or otherwise destitute blacks must have found shelter in white households after the war. Not infrequently are they found to have been buried in white family plots in the old family cemeteries of the area. It seems likely that real racial division did not appear until the blacks were hounded out of the election process by those who were later to achieve a strangle hold on government in ours and other southern states. Fear between the races was used to preserve that strangle hold for over a century. The rhetoric used by politicians and their cronies is offensive by today's standards. Moreover, both races suffered from it. This poor government is not evident in our "official" history but is evident in the oral history found in the mountains.

Support for the Union in our area was more common than we have often been told. The problems growing out of the difference of opinion have been deep. That is not to say that the area did not fight for the South with vigor. Most citizens remained loyal to their state regardless of reservations arising out of principle. But, in my opinion, there were two things wrong with the war. One, it should never have been fought in the first place and, except for a lot of extremely loud-mouth politicians, it probably would not have been. Second, it has lasted far too long and has cost far more than we have been aware. We complain about what we endured from the North during and after the war, but it pales in comparison to what we have done to ourselves. I know that is not popular and will win me no friends but, if I cannot shed a new and better light on this segment of our history, I probably should not say anything.

Nevertheless, the South made a heroic effort. Never mind that the principles southerners fought for faded and were largely destroyed in the war effort. It is highly unlikely that the new nation (CSA) would have ever been able to re-establish those principles it fought for. In fact, the best chance for southern ideals of liberty to survive may very well could have depended upon a Union victory. (But that is another, much longer, story.)

The local soldier, as always, fought with great distinction regardless of any philosophical differences he may have had. The North Carolina 26th Infantry Regiment is one of the best examples. This regiment already had a reputation from Front Royal, VA, and other actions before Gettysburg. (A great painting exists of a proud NC 26th on the move through a Virginia town. I am sorry I cannot remember the artist.) This same NC 26th made the furthest advance into Yankee guns at Gettysburg made on the last of three days of fighting. There was great loss of life, especially among those from Ashe County and the surrounding area. When Lee withdrew, his ambulance wagons stretched for seventeen miles. The army of northern Virginia was very vulnerable at the time, but the North failed to pursue, and Lincoln fired another general. Though its ranks were depleted, the NC 26th was still with Lee at the surrender. (So was the 21st VA Volunteer Calvary.)

The thing that amazes me most, when I compare those great military actions to my own army experience, is the endurance of the soldier of that time. They often marched thirty to forty miles and then engaged the enemy for a battle that might last three days. (The infantry sometimes referred to itself as "foot cavalry.") They did this on poor rations and often without decent shoes. Sure, some could not keep up and fell out. This was especially true after a bout of sickness with little or no medical attention. But they rejoined their friends, kin, and neighbors at the front when they were able for the most part.

All the soldier's sacrifices would be in vain after Gettysburg. In fact, this was true even before the battle, otherwise the slaughter could not have been justified. Lee had concluded that the North was growing stronger and the South could not win a prolonged war. He believed a large battle, even a costly one, was the only way to drive the North out of the war. He probably also realized that the South was beginning to lose the war on the home front.

The peoples of New River entered into the Civil War with great enthusiasm. They had not wanted secession nor had they great interest in having slaves. But they did feel, with some justification, that the state had a right to secede. In all fairness, nothing in our previous history would have taught them otherwise. Volunteers came to the service faster than they could be trained and outfitted. When conscription came in it only went to 35 but a lot of men up to 50 and beyond had already volunteered and were in the war. There was still a lot of Union sympathy along the western borders but a lot of them allowed themselves to be conscripted by the state. Of course, a few were publicly opposed from the very beginning, but they were not vocal in their descent.

It was the struggle between the local officials, Home Guard and these Unionist elements that tore the local populace apart in the most horrific of ways. As scarcities grew those enemies of the Confederacy were sometimes denied the critical ration of salt. (A small war was fought in Madison County over salt, for example.) Government promises to "look after the folks at home" often meant stealing the bare essentials from suspected unionists whenever it could be done. There was precious little left toward the end of the war. Even the outlaw bands now hiding out in the mountains were pushed to find enough to steal to get by.

In this atmosphere atrocities were bound to happen. In Ashe County the Price family is an example. Even today we are often led to believe that the Union sympathizers were little better than "poor white trash." But the Price clan farmed 2,000 acres and had lots of hogs in particular. In his mid-fifties at the time of his death, Jesse Price headed a large family of ten. Price became a Union martyr when asked if he had any final words before hanging. He said, "Doctor, I have done nothing to be hanged for. I am old – not even subject to military duty. I have committed no crime. I have only been loyal to my country, and if it is for this you intend to murder me, I will go to eternity as I am. I want no rebel to pray for me." Later the same day they also hanged all but the youngest of Jesses sons. (One of them did survive hanging and lived at Wytheville, VA.)

Of course, there were atrocities on both sides. A Tennessee born Thomas Stout was suspected of killing Isaac Wilson who was home on leave from the Confederate army. Stout was not trash either for he farmed 500 acres. To simplify a story long complicated by partisan hindsight, Stout's father Thomas was arrested, and a detail appointed to see him to a military stockade at the Confederate Camp at Morganton, NC. His captors took him along the Junaluska Turnpike to a place on the Rich Mountain. There they decided to go no further. They twisted a withe from hickory bark and hanged him. Then they threw the body into a hole under some logs and covered it with brush. Stout's gray hair and bones were discovered later. E. B. Miller, my mother's uncle Edmund, told of seeing Stout's wife at the site on her hands and knees sobbing while picking up his bones and placing them in her apron. Some of the participants in this gruesome episode were shot down in the field as they gathered Isaac Wilson's corn that fall. One who was not killed soon went blind.

From Arthur's *Watauga County, NC: A History*[3] – Thomas Stout, elderly father of the Stout boy or boys thought to have been involved in the killing of "Little Isaac Wilson," was captured by the Confederate Home Guard in the spring of 1864. Big Isaac Wilson, a cousin to the slain man, Jay Howington and Gilbert Norris left with Stout the next day supposedly to take him to the Confederate Camp below Morganton, NC. (This camp was the local confederate army induction center. It seems unlikely that this elderly man was being conscripted.) Stout's escort was instructed to take him the "nigh way." Two months later James H. Presnell found a shoe while hunting cattle on Rich Mountain and reported this to his brother W. W. Presnell when he got back to Brushy Fork. The next day the two found Stout's bones under the trunk of a fallen tree. The hickory bark thong used as a hangman's rope was still hanging from a nearby tree. (Tradition has it that this stands on an old cart road to the Junaluska Turnpike on Rich Mountain. My brother Johnny Greer once developed a Christmas tree farm on this property.)

This account differs from the account given by the Wilson family who seem to think that the Stout family was notified where to find the body the next day.[4] But Arthur also quotes Edmund Miller of Meat Camp saying that on the 10th of April 1864 he was near the little summit of Rich Mountain. Hearing someone sobbing, he went to where the sound came from. There at the roots of the tree stood Stout's wife with the bones of her husband in her apron crying as if her heart would break.

The Wilson family seems to have gone to great lengths to gloss over their difficulties with their neighbors during the war. Largely to their efforts they achieved a sort of peace that was remarkable. Arthur's version seems to be most correct . . . .

---There is little reason to think that Stout's hangmen would be so kind as to notify the next of kin.
---Edmund Miller's discovery was near one year after so only bones and hair survived.

---The Miller's owned land and likely pastured in the area.

---There is no reason to think Uncle Edmund was lying.


As the war dragged on people in their right minds wanted an end to it. There were exceptions. An Ashe County slave owner was quoted as saying to this effect, "You can forget about all that stuff about Liberty, I'm fighting for forty niggers." He was losing support every day in the last years of the war. Most mountain soldiers were poor and homesick. They were also war weary. Often many of them slipped away home to plant or harvest crops. Possibly with the encouragement of the Home Guard, the vast majority would return to their outfits to fight again.


The war did not last long after Stoneman's Raid. It still amazes me that as Stoneman's Cavalry worked their way over Stone Mountain before daylight, lighted fires marked the trail. Where sight of one grew dim, another would appear on up the winding trail. It was as if the wretched populace would bear any sort of humiliation to see an end to their misery. Much of the Home Guard was in Yankee prison in far away Ohio by now. They had been taken prisoner during and after the controversial surrender of Camp Mast. A few desperate men were meeting at Watauga's county seat of Boone to form a defense against guerillas. Mistaking Stoneman's men for local raiders they fired on his lead elements. They were quickly charged by the cavalry and several locals were killed. Elijah Norris was home on convalescent leave. He recognized what they were up against. He shouted, "They're Regulars, run boys run." It was too late for Elijah's father Ephram. He was killed.


The divisions of the war were deep in Ashe and Watauga Counties. They were even worse in Wilkes. Wilkes raised entire units of soldiers for the north. Many others tried to avoid the war altogether. The Home Guard pursued these diligently. Boys were supposed to be sixteen years old to serve, but boys as young as twelve in Union families were often conscripted before they could go over to the other side.

Only a few southern atrocities made the pages of history books. They were only whispered in small family groups with a Union background. Most were lost for it was not wise or profitable to talk about such things. One story concerned a Blackburn in Ashe who was shot at his own table while eating breakfast. In Wilkes a fourteen-year-old boy was hanged by the Home Guard for being overheard singing the following ditty:

"One tenth our grain the Rebels exact,
They say we must bring it if we have it to pack.
They know very well we've no horses to haul,
For they were the rogues who stole them last fall.
And it's hard, hard times."

In some ways Wilkes suffered more than Ashe or Watauga for it was a richer source of grains and livestock for the war effort. Horses and mules were in great demand for the armies and were often confiscated. So were cattle for they were a mobile food source. Some commanding officers forbade the taking of trained work oxen for without them a new crop could not be made. It was hard to keep hungry foraging soldiers form taking essentials from the farmers. One local confederate hero was said not to have received wounds in battle. Instead, he was said to have been digging sweet potatoes from a woman's garden.

Great Aunt Frances Miller often told a story about those times. It was about an occasion when the men were away at night. The women were home alone and more than a little afraid. Their worst fears were realized when they heard noises and mumbled talking on the porch. Someone tested the door which had been locked. They were very afraid but not to the point of inaction. Granny Becky got Grandpa Jonathan's old saber, one of the daughters got the fireplace poker, another an axe from the chimney corner, the other two selected clubs from the wood box. One of the daughters, Caroline I believe, had a rather husky voice. She immediately began a two-sided conversation with herself that sounded like two men talking with each other. The others waited breathlessly until the strangers retreated and were gone.

Civil War letter from my Great-Great Grandfather Parlier

January 11, 1865
Camp Near Petersburg, VA

"Dear Brother. It is threw the kind hand of Providence I am bless with the opportunity of dropping you a few lines to let you no that I am well as common. Truly hoping this note will find you all well and hearty. N. B. I want to see you all very bad and I can inform you that I received your very kind letter dated the 5th of Sept. which gave me much satisfaction to (hear) from all, ya must excuse me for not writing to you sooner for I have bin at the hospital parte of the time and had a ball cut out of my hand it was lodged against the bones in he back of my haind. It nearly made me twist my tale when the doctors was cutting it out but it is nearly healed up. I can sorty rit that is all that I do. I don't do any duty at all. I haint done any since I came back nor shut my hand no never Expect to again. I think this cussed war will end soon and in the way I have though all the time. N. B. the time is heard here and I want you to send me nother ham bone. Please help Phoebe to ficks my another and send it to me for I don't get only half enough to eat. Rit soon and often.

Yours J. W. Parlier. Truly farewell to N. B. Parlier".

The average mountaineer could not really be forced to fight for the confederacy. He did it out of a sense of duty to his state even though he felt betrayed by a system that exempted slave owners and allowed hiring of substitutes. It had truly become a "poor man's war." Yet he had not been wholly a citizen of his nation. His loyalty was first to his state. After his family of course. He usually was willing to go and help out when he could. He often responded to family sickness and the planting and harvesting of crops by returning home as he felt the need. His high desertion rate is misleading however, because he usually returned to the fight when it became possible to do so. (At least a long as he was permitted to do so.) Not understanding this way of thinking his so-called leaders eventually began ordering deserters before a firing squad. "Lige" Norris, an old Confederate veteran in our community, once lamented that it was the beginning of the end for the South. They never won a major battle after adopting such a despicable practice.

Mr. Norris was said to have drawn duty on a firing squad. Of six or more riflemen one would have a rifle loaded without a bullet. This rifle would have slightly less recoil when fired. Mr. Norris thought he fired the blank. (Every other man probably thought so also.) Mr. Norris had apparently been touched by the experience beyond what one might expect for one who had become hardened to war at an early age. (He was also quoted as saying that "Shooting the enemy takes no more effort than shooting a rabbit or squirrel.") The difficulty might be laid in part to the fact that most units were taken from a single community. Soldiers had likely known each other from childhood.

Given the mountaineer's priorities during the war, it becomes evident that those who were in it form the start to the finish were only boys who had limited family responsibilities. (Is not this true for all wars?) Among these boys were a goodly number who felt allegiance to the "Old United States." Without property or wives and children it was easier for them to pass through the lines to Kentucky and the Union. They never guessed, however, the atrocities that would be heaped upon their parents and other kin, like the Price father and Thomas Stout.

In recent years, a rapidly expanding proportion of the population of the South is finding itself able to make an objective analysis of our Civil War heritage. This has always been true with a few mountaineers who felt no solid ties to the "down-the-country" Cotton Snobs or Bourbon Democrats. The occasional mountaineer who spoke out at one time found himself drowned out and laced with ridicule.

But things have changed. A recent article in *US News and World Report* titled "Who Really Won the Civil War?" scarcely drew fire. This would have been unheard of in my youth.

This recent article raises the question what did the North win other than a brief military victory? The South has long bemoaned the fact that the region suffered greatly during Reconstruction. The facts are that the great losses of wealth and manpower would have been felt even without Reconstruction. The same ruling class quickly re-established control. We were given "Jim Crow" to replace slavery and a hatred of carpetbaggers. Had we looked closely we would have found that those who pursued carpet bag activities were largely a homegrown product. We were our own worst enemies.

## Lost Confederate Gold

Many, if not most of local Civil War stories now seem to have to have long been forgotten. Others are remembered only vaguely but will not quite go away.

One in particular I heard as a teen was from a Mr. Ellison, who lived on Meat Camp Creek near Boone. Mr. Ellison appeared to be unlettered but had a keen mind. When he heard that I was interested I the Long Hope Creek area, he related a Civil War story.

It said that when it became evident that Richmond would probably fall, plans were made to relocate the Confederate Capitol to Alabama. A considerable gold and silver treasure would need to be re-located also. Plans to move it by rail through Tennessee became impossible and a wagon route through the Ashe-Watauga County areas of Western North Carolina became an alternate plan. It also proved too late by the time the wagon arrived in the area. The Federals had fortified the gap of Rich Mountain to protect the flank of troops entering North Carolina through the Boone area. A last-ditch effort was made to take the wagon across the mountain in the Long Hope area. This too failed as there was no safe way into Tennessee. Not wanting the Confederate treasure to fall into Yankee hands, it was said to have been taken to the top of a water fall on Long Hope Creek.

There it was dumped over the falls into what was said to be a bottomless pool below. Mr. Ellison made no opinion on the matter but said he had heard this story many, many years before.

# 14

## The World Wars

The two great world wars were so close together and so interconnected that they both can be considered together. I limit myself to local impact and cannot claim any expertise in individual battle actions. World War I mimicked the Civil War in at least two respects. First, the great loss of soldiers to disease. Second, the practice of putting soldiers on the attack in numbers greater than they could be gunned down. Both would influence some needed changes. The army would get involved in medical research. (Search for a polio vaccine was done under army contract, for example.) The army would also become more mobile although not so great as Germany under Hitler.

World War I was not universally popular. France was a long way from home and the war there was horrible. A lottery system was devised to select draftees. The lottery was to be administered locally and that was not the advantage it was expected to be.

Early in World War I Ashe County was to find itself in a situation that begins to remind us of the late days of the Civil War. Young men were refusing to accept service in the army when ordered to report by the local draft board. This was a rare occurrence in the country. They were joined by a few deserters. Much to Ashe County's embarrassment the situation had gotten out of hand. On

July 24, 1918, chairman of the Ashe Draft Board, W. E. McNeil, wired governor Bickett to the effect "There are about forty deserters now roaming Ashe County. One civilian has been killed trying to arrest a deserter. Request troops to handle the situation as local authorities either cannot or will not." Governor Bickett immediately requested that State Adjutant General, General Lawrence W. Young, to investigate and report. General Young had been in Jefferson less than an hour when he wired, "Situation here appears acute. I consider outside force necessary. Reported about thirty deserters hiding out. Sheriff reported sympathetic to deserters and will not help. I am convinced the only solution is outside force. Please advise."

General Young did not get his troops. Instead the governor ordered him to arrange a car to meet the train at Wilkesboro and to spread the word that the governor would speak at the Ashe Courthouse at 3:00 p.m. on Saturday afternoon. The governor was known to be a great orator. The courthouse overflowed with the crowd. He waxed long and hot on the Selective Service law. He felt the current situation to be because of ignorance of the law and could be corrected if the guilty parties reported for duty. But the governor nowhere compromised the law. He promised to do everything in his power to see that everyone would be "given his fair chance to die for his country." It worked. They took him at his word. The local board worked hard to clean up its act. Ashe County's final desertion rate proved to be among the lowest in the state.

Ashe County has worked hard to live this record down. But has it covered up rather than addressed root causes? As it was late in the Civil War, many people seemed to have felt they were getting into another "rich man's war but a poor man's fight." The Civil War had really changed very little in the Ashe government. The same wealthy, former slave-owning crowd ran everything. They also looked down their noses a little at their poor neighbors. They felt some areas of the county only occupied by "low lifes." They must have contributed to the situation by exercising their authority to order draftees to report without ever explaining the law or the lottery system in effect. The draft evaders must have had the support of the sheriff for some good reason. The point is that many in Ashe County felt alienated from their government and did not trust it. One old patriarch was heard to say, "My boys will go when old "Slicky" Miller's boys go." Doesn't this speak volumes?

Nationally, World War I was better accepted "as the war to end all wars." An Appalachian mountain boy, Sgt. Alvin C. York, became the country's hero. He was awarded the Congressional Medal of Honor. The "York Character" had great impact on the national character. Americans would hate war and would go to great lengths to avoid it; but, if forced to fight, they would fight like hell to win. Woodrow Wilson's League of Nations did not end all wars either, but it did influence to some extent how they were to be fought.

During this era of national history, the country began being influenced by Appalachian values and culture. President Wilson was of the opinion, that in the Appalachian South the country had a great reservoir of strength and character that would serve the country well in times of great need. He had a close connection to the area. Wife Edith was from Wytheville, Virginia. She is said by some to have been the country's first woman president. Wilson was ill for months and she kept him isolated. She carried important work into him, but many believe that the work she carried out was more hers than his. She was born in a second-floor apartment on main street Wytheville over what has long been Skeeter's World Famous Hotdogs.

World War I brought a tremendous slaughter of American troops over a short period of time. The Yanks broke the German lines and brought an end to the war but at great costs. Not all the costs were left in France. The surviving veterans seemed different somehow. The ordinary cares of life no longer seemed to be important to them.

Much of what I have to say about World War II is the same as what I wrote for Pat Beaver and her Appalachian Studies' book *Voices, From the Headwaters*.[1] We first learned of Pearl Harbor at that Sunday's night at church prayer service. No details were yet available, but everyone was sure that we were now at war. Another meeting was scheduled for Monday night for few had radios and those who did were to report to the rest then. They would have little more to tell except that President Roosevelt was calling for a Declaration of War. War with both Germany and Japan was now expected. If anything, war with Germany was most feared. Hitler was promising new weapons often. All too often he was delivering. Time was of the essence and we were ill-prepared to say the least.

Manpower for the services was not an early problem. Unemployed but able-bodied men of draft age were made immediately eligible. Early on the services had more men than they could arm. The mobilization of a huge civilian and military war effort is one of the most remarkable stories of our times. The country would eventually put twelve million citizens into uniform. Women and children would help the old and the infirm pick up the slack.

The home front responded to the challenge. Rationing of nearly everything came in early on. This did not affect my family much because we were allowed more than we had ever been able to buy anyway. Besides, much of what we ate came from the family garden and livestock. Eventually the country would supply not only itself but would ship vast quantities to Britain and Russia. The children would help to tend and harvest the crops. Many older men would work in the shipyards at Norfolk, Virginia. Locally, many young women would make the long bus trip to Ohio to man the defense plants. Appalachian State University Professor Cratis Williams was a frequent passenger on these buses up through West Virginia. He marveled at their optimism and spirit. He called them "Columbus Girls." A near neighbor moved his entire family to Ohio for the duration of the war

Most boys watched the war closely and were afraid for it to last but were also afraid it would end before they could go. The big day came on June 6, 1944. The long-awaited Normandy invasion was on. Near everyone had a personal interest.

Mom's brother, Jake Miller, went ashore with the 4th Infantry on Utah Beach, first wave. Many of our kin were in the service all over the world; but only two participants in the Normandy invasion can be included here. One is my Uncle Jake Miller and the other is Darrell Hicks who married a cousin.

The greatness of the American people in the twentieth century was best illustrated during World War II. I have already written a little about the country's response. I believe we owe a debt of gratitude to Tom Brokaw who coined the title phrase of "The Greatest Generation". Hopefully, others will follow his example and the stories of that war's unassuming soldiers will be recorded before it is too late.

It has not been my purpose to do war histories though war stories have drawn my interest since I followed the progress of World War II as a boy. I would like to do an account of two or three area soldiers who have family connections. One is my late Uncle Jake Miller and the other is the late Darrell Hicks who married a cousin. Jake was in the 4th Infantry Division and Darrell was in the 101st Airborne Division. They were both great examples of the kind of fighting men that this country produces in its citizen soldiers.

Jake was drafted early on in our preparation for war. The early call-ups were for single men from about twenty-seven to thirty-four. The whole 4th Division followed this pattern except for Cadre which might be even older. The average age and potential expendability of the division was high. They would be even older by the time they reached the shores of Normandy. (A lot of these soldiers would be married by the time they went overseas. Jake was one of them. His first son would die shortly after birth while Jake was in Europe.) By that time, they would have survived training and conditions that many doctors felt beyond human limitation. Theirs was Utah Beach on Normandy. We do not hear as much about Utah, possibly because the Navy missed it and they went ashore two miles further down than planned. That was OK. Their commander said, "We will begin the war here." Under the direction of German General Rommel, the "Atlantic Wall" had been built from Spain to Norway. It was not a real wall but was a line of reinforced concrete positions along the coast. They used an amount of concrete similar to that used in our interstate highway system, I have heard. The Germans hoped it was impenetrable. Even without a lot of artillery on the position the 4th assaulted, it held them up for only twenty minutes. The men moved off the beach double time. They did not stop until their lead elements were four miles inland. As a result, they avoided being pinned down and lost only about 200 men of their twenty thousand on the beaches. They were the first to contact airborne units. They continued to force the issue with the enemy until the break-out at St. Lo. (The 101st Airborne had dropped to pave the way for the 4th.)

Much of the fighting was bitter hedgerow warfare. Jake lasted longer than many others. On D-Day plus 8 he was wounded in a German counterattack. His outfit fell back without him. They did leave him well armed with two Browning automatic rifles and plenty of ammunition. He covered their retreat and fought off the Germans single-handedly until his outfit was able to retake his position which was surrounded by dead Germans. He was evacuated to a hospital in England and was awarded his first Silver Star for gallantry. The following article was released to the Watauga Democrat sometime later.

Boone Soldier Gets Silver Star for Gallantry

"With the 4th Infantry Division in France, Private First Class John J. H. Miller, son of Hattie M. Miller, Route 2, Boone, who served as an automatic rifleman with the Fourth Infantry in France has been awarded the Silver Star for Gallantry in Action and given the following citation.

Pfc. Miller was a member of a company that was subjected to heavy artillery fire preceding an enemy counterattack. The enemy attack caused confusion among our troops and they began to withdraw. At this critical time Pfc. Miller moved to a position that afforded good fields of fire. Here he succeeded in holding back the German advance until his comrades could affect an orderly withdrawal. Pfc. Miller suffered wounds but undoubtedly saved many lives. His company was able to reorganize quickly and repel the counterattack. Pfc. Miller's courage and aggressiveness under fire are worthy of the highest standards of military service."

Jake would recover and return to his division by fall. The fourth would suffer 122% causalities during the war. Many, like Jake, would be wounded more than once and return to their outfits. But the worst was yet to come. A lot of us have never heard of the Huertgen Forest, but those who were there would give anything to be able to forget it. Evergreen forests in Europe are cold, ten to twenty degrees colder than anywhere else. Even perimeter fields are much warmer in comparison. The fourth spent the coldest part of the winter pinned down by German artillery and repelling counter attacks. The conditions can only be described as cruel. The cold, lack of sleep and constant harassing fire pushed them to the limit. They often did not even find the energy to pull their dead out of the jeep supply trails. Some were so weary that they no longer even retuned fire. The fourth was supposed to be resting when the Germans broke the American lines and drove a bulge into Belgium. The weary veterans were thrown in to help stem the tide. But when the breakout came in later winter the indomitable human spirit was to shine forth once more.

Jake was to continue to receive decorations. He was wounded once again and given time to recover. He remained in Europe to help ship armored equipment to the Pacific Theater. Ironically, his age, service time, wounds and decorations gave him such a high point total that he was exempted from seeing combat against the Japanese. He lived a quiet life and only his family and a few friends marked his passing. He was one of the county's most decorated World War II soldiers, but few people had noticed. John Jacob Henry Miller's discharge shows that the received a Silver Star (second only to the Medal of Honor), two Bronze Stars, one Bronze Arrowhead and two Purple Hearts.

As stated earlier it is not my purpose to give a real history of any war. But we cannot ignore the large part war has played in the history of the upper New River valley and the rest of our nation. All our wars have been fought in the name of liberty. Even the Civil War where both sides fought for its perception of liberty. We have been enormously successful. Only when the definition of liberty has become confused, have we had problems. This happened late in the Civil War in the mountains, but it did not keep the soldiers from performing what they saw as "duty."

"Gone for to be a soldier" is a phrase that is part of our heritage. It is unfortunate that war has been so much a part of our history and it is often hard for us to realize that so much of the world marches to a different drum. Hard-won freedom has to be won and re-won. Our soldiers have not always understood all the reasons for their military service, but through the misery of heat, cold, hunger, loss of sleep and weariness they have always understood "Liberty." An amazingly high number have, when the moment came, been able to overcome unspeakable fear and fatigue to do their duty.

My second example I also consider to be family. Darrell Hicks comes from some of the oldest families in the county. He married Lena Tugman Hicks, a descendant of both my Greer and Miller families. Darrell's son Wayne and wife Sandra Wilson Hicks attend Bethelview United Methodist Church where my wife and myself also attend. We have long enjoyed their friendship. Watching their sons, Marshall and Ben, take part in our church has been one of the notable joys of our lives. Wayne and Sandy agreed to furnish information on "Pawpaw" Darrell. I felt the way it came to me was just too good to change. They gave me permission to reprint or edit. (This was written about 2004.)

## Wartime Service of Darrell Hicks

Arlie "Darrell" Hicks went into the army March 13, 1942, barely three months after Pearl Harbor. He was twenty-six years old at the time. (The army considered then twenty-seven to be the ideal age for maturity was considered as well as physical development. By late in the war before the draft age was lowered to eighteen and one-half. Over twelve million men and women would eventually serve in the conflict.) Darrell reported to Fort Bragg, NC for basic and then was ordered to Fort Claiborn, LA. When the army formed the 101st Airborne Division he volunteered. He said that "Not only did paratroopers get $50.00 more per month, they were promised a free ride to the battlefield," as opposed to marching. Jump school was at Fort Benning, GA. Darrell later related that he made seventeen jumps before he ever had occasion to land in a plane. Then he found himself scared half to death.

The first action the 101st saw was in the Normandy invasion. The division dropped inland from the beaches prior to "H Hour." (Darrell once told me that most people in the landing counted their landing in "H" plus hours or "H" plus days. He counted his landing in "H" minus hours.) The Normandy drop was nothing but confusing. They were dropped off course, too high and too fast. They fought for days before they could regroup. Many attached themselves to the infantry units that finally caught up with them and continued the fight. The troopers lived for a chance to get back to England and find the pilots that had brought them. (When Hicks did get back to England, he found that their plane and crew had not made it.)

The 101st next jumped with British and Polish paratroopers in operation Market Garden. (This jump was an attempt to free the low country from German occupation. It was a Field Marshall Montgomery scheme. He needed to redeem himself after sitting on his hands immediately after the invasion of Normandy. His inaction had allowed the Germans to set up in the hedgerows where the Americans had to fight for days before they could begin reaching most of the paratroopers dropped during the invasion.) The Market Garden Operation was told in story and film in "A Bridge Too Far." Again, the British moved too slowly with their armor to relieve the paratroopers. The German defenses were greater than expected and tanks blocked the roads through the marshy countryside whenever they were hit. The Americans moved in armor but the troopers holding key bridges were hard pressed to survive until the armor could relieve them.

After Market Garden the battered troopers looked forward to a long rest in England. It was not to happen. The Battle of the Bulge intervened, and all resting troops were thrown back into action. The 101st soon found itself surrounded at Bastogne along with others. The Germans showered them with leaflets demanding their surrender. The soldiers used them for toilet paper. The official reply to the Germans was the now famous term "nuts." During the time they were cut off they nearly ran out of everything. Darrell had some c-ration cheese that someone offered him $30.00 for on Christmas Day. He thought about it and then ate it himself. Shortly after Christmas the weather cleared. The allies put everything in the air that could fly. It deeply impressed both the Americans and Germans at Bastogne. When Patton's tanks broke through to relieve them soon after, Darrell's brother Ray was with them serving as a medic. They were both unaware of each other's presence, however. That is the kind of war it was.

Hicks went on to be wounded by a mortar round in July or August of 1944. He was placed in a private hospital where he was expected to die. (His mother was notified that he was believed dead because they had lost track of him. He survived however and returned to service with the 101st when they took Hitler's stronghold, the "Eagle's Nest" at Bertesgarten.

Darrell's mother would not know him when he got home. He had been through a lot. But he never lost his sense of humor. Once a family discussion centered around his war experiences and noted that a chocolate bar would buy some unusual items. When youngest daughter Diane asked if she had any brothers or sisters left in Europe, Darrell replied, "Hell no. I ate every chocolate bar I ever got hold of."

Darrell Hicks was in the service for about three and one-half years. He received a Purple Heart and four Bronze Stars during his service. These are only two of thousands of area veterans of World War II. As of this writing they have no national monument and the stories of many are largely forgotten. I had expected to write some accounts of the Pacific theater but, like most others, I waited too late to contact my best prospect. Glenn Miller, neighbor and cousin, passed away unexpectedly, and I will have to look elsewhere for Iwo Jima.

Among those fighting in the Pacific were two local brothers. They were Glenn and Ralph Miller, sons of Joe and Clemmie Miller who lived near Boone. Glenn would be on Iwo Jima when the flag was raised on Mt. Suribachi. It was visible to most of the troops in the fight and was a source of encouragement at a trying time. Ralph landed on Okinawa and fought there.

The privations and hardships of the World War II soldiers were not publicized during or after the war. They were never as well armed or equipped as we were led to believe. The winter of 1944-45 was miserable beyond belief. Eighteen and nineteen-year olds were rushed into the war the less than ideal training. The war had to end quickly for who knew what Hitler would come up with? He was already using V-2 rockets against Britain and would adapt them to tactical use at big targets on the continent.[2]

The nation was forever changed. It had found muscles it did not know it had. New industries like aircraft assembly, once located in fields, would move inside and become permanent. The home front had performed heroically. The much-prized P-51 fighter plane had gone from drawing board to test flight in just 119 days. It was an excellent British design but he American firm that built it had never made a plane before. Tom Brokaw got it right. It truly was a magnificent generation.

The surprise of the Pearl Harbor attack was questioned at the time and still is. It probably should have been anticipated. We were already at war in a way. We were heavily involved helping the Chinese fight the Japanese. A neighbor, Joe Hardin, was "flying the hump" in India to deliver war supplies behind the line in

China. After much controversy we had finally stopped selling scrap iron to the Japanese. The Japanese were "oil poor" and the U. S. had an abundance which it now refused to sell them. It seems that the Pearl Harbor attack was to buy time until they could consolidate a hold on Indonesian oil and tin. Perhaps they hoped the U. S. would find interests in the Philippines and the South Pacific too costly to pursue. At any rate, no military prepares for the possibility of defeat.

# 15

---

# My Grandparents' Day

The story of my grandparents is largely about two strong grandmothers. It also involves numerous aunts and uncles. My father and mother were the oldest child in each of their families and both left siblings at home who were not much older than their own children would be.

Grandpa Ivory Greer was considered to be a good worker, but he had almost no education. He was born to Elijah and Lula Waters Greer in Ashe County September 2, 1890. He had one full-brother, John Avery Greer, born the following year. While John Avery was still a baby, Lula took him and ran away. She was never located that I ever heard though the two brothers would make contact in their later years. Little is known about Ivory's younger years though he is listed in the 1900 census as being a ten-year-old living with his father and his third wife Frankie Watson Greer. Soon afterwards Elijah and his third family would move to Greensboro to find work. Ivory would remain behind with his uncle, Tom Greer. I once held Uncle Tom responsible for grandpa's lack of an education; but his father, Elijah, must have neglected it at the most critical age when Ivory still lived in his father's household. Grandma "Emmy" would try to teach him after they were married but by then it was too late.

Grandpa Ivory followed cutting timber most of his life, but he worked for the railroad and lived at Fleetwood when my dad was school age. They had expected to stay there permanently for they bought a building site. Grandpa was a section foreman responsible for keeping the tracks open in the White Top area. He gave up that job after a particularly hard winter.

While at Fleetwood they lived through two huge area events. First was the 1916 flood. The second was the 1918 flu epidemic. The flu was really bad with so many people sick that there were hardly enough well people to do the burying. Grandpa went from house to house tending to people and their livestock. He wore an asifidia bag around his neck which he believed prevented sickness. Whatever the reason, neither he nor the family got sick.

Grandpa was always at his best during disasters. During the 1940 flood he left home to help flooding and landslide victims in nearby Stoney Fork. He helped carry out people who needed to be in a hospital and to search for missing victims. Three days later he came home, his clothes in rags and his shoes near off his feet. He ate, slept a few hours, got more shoes and clothes, and went out again. Though he was a never-do-well and not a responsible family man he had great feeling for anyone needing help.

In his later years it became my lot to sit with him when he was in the hospital and occasionally provide transportation. I sometimes picked up his surplus food allotment for him. I found him to be down-to-earth honest and I liked him. He made no excuses and there was nothing pretentious about him.

Grandma Greer was the anchor that held the family together. She was born Mary Emeline Parlier June 18, 1881 in Watauga County, NC. She died August 11, 1954 and is buried in Laurel Springs Cemetery, also in Watauga County. She married Ivory Ward Greer June 23, 1908. They reared seven children.

As children we lived probably fourteen miles from Grandma Greer. Since we had no way of our own to travel, we were likely to visit her home at Deep Gap once or twice a year. She and some of her unmarried daughters would visit us even more rarely. Nevertheless, we knew quite a bit about her, and she became a very special person to us.

Grandma's life was a hard one. As a young woman I understand that she left home to work in a textile mill in Rhodhiss, NC. It was the custom at the time for the mills to furnish employment for young unmarried women. Hours were long and pay was not great. They usually worked ten hours per day for six days of the week. They were furnished their food and were boarded in a company barracks. Bible study and prayer services were required, and the young ladies were strictly supervised. They were expected to save their meager wages to build a dowry against the time that they would be married. I believe that Grandma Greer began to acquire the work habits and skills that she would use much of her life while there. She "tatted," or made lace, and tied fringe all her life for small amounts of money to help the family finances.

Grandma "Emmy" and Grandpa Ivory were a mismatch almost from the beginning. Though he was a good worker, he was not as dependable and steady as she was. She was the rock upon which the family was built, and their children would take the best attributes of each of them. They were married June 23, 1908, when she was twenty-seven. He was only nineteen at the time. They made heroic efforts to farm, usually on other people's land and with borrowed money. But it was a hardscrabble existence that found them moving often. My dad said that they lived at seventeen different places before he was twenty-one. I am sure they had many good times together, but grandpa's tendency to wander and to drink sometime did not sit well with grandma's values. Their problems finally came to divorce and he remarried. She was left with the younger children to rear but this was not a great deal different from their later years together.

Grandma Greer was probably better than average educated for her time. I was amazed at her knowledge of plants. She seemed to know the habits and names of about everything that grew. I had learned to distrust the accuracy of plant names given by neighbors, but I have never found her to be wrong. Her knowledge must have been self-taught which says a lot about her curiosity about the world around her.

Grandma was a strongly built woman who rarely asked anyone to cut her firewood. One time, however, her neighbor Hamp Blackburn offered her several piles of logs and poles if she would have them cut into firewood and move them. She wrote dad and he took my brother Elton and myself to cut them for her. Elton and I were only 10 or 12 but we had already been sawing firewood for several years. It took us several days to complete the project. It was tiresome work, but we ended each day by catching trout behind her Deep Gap house.

Dad sharpened her saw and axe for her before we left. He was good at it and was in great demand to sharpen tools for neighbors and fellow workers. Grandma's axe was never very dull, and it was never rained on. It stayed in her woodshed or in her kitchen firebox if there were children around.

Once during the depression, we were visiting but all the men of the family were gone. A man came to the door about 2:00 p.m. begging for food. He was trying to get across the mountains to Tennessee where he said he had people. He offered to cut wood, but grandma did not need any. She set a table for him and watched from her kitchen door as he ate in the dining room. When he finished, she told him he would have to move on. My mother said she would have been afraid to let a stranger in the house with my teenage aunts and the children. Still standing in the kitchen door grandma allowed she was not afraid. She brought out her shiny, sharp axe where she had held it in her hand all the time.

Some of the other times we visited grandpa and grandma were real fun times. Unless grandpa was away working, he could be a lot of fun. He was always talking to people and loved a good story. They were typically short and to the point. Once during the depression, he had a real nice ham bone with some meat left on it. They had cooked it with pinto beans, and they were very good. They next tried it with potatoes, and they were good. Feeling sorry for the neighbors, they loaned it out on occasion. They and the neighbors enjoyed ham flavored beans and potatoes until someone cooked it with blackberries and ruined it. He loved to tell us this.

On rare occasions Grandma Greer would bring dad's younger sisters and visit us for a few days. On one occasion I remember that the girls came by themselves. Grandma had written that the girls had a box camera and wanted to get a of picture of me fishing. I could hardly wait until they got there so we could go fishing. They took me down to our small branch to a nice pool but not large enough for fish. There they tied a rock on my line so I could appear to be fishing. I was mad for months.

After grandpa and grandma finally divorced, he remarried Omie Chester and they had three children, Lonnie, Geneva, and Joyce.

## Miller Grandparents

### "Jonathan" Robert Miller

"Jont" Miller, as he was commonly known, was my mother's father. He was born April 11, 1884 in Watauga but died at the state hospital in Morganton, NC September 7, 1946. Although his grandchildren never knew him personally, his influence on our lives was far from being blank. We saw his presence in the large house he built for his large family on his Howard's Creek farm and the stories we heard about him were numerous and complimentary. I will not list his children here as that is done in information given on his wife, Hattie Mae Philyaw Miller.

Grandpa Jont was apparently an intelligent and progressive man. He and his several brothers were engaged in various farm activities in order to make a living for their large families. They pooled teams and wagons to market Irish potatoes, cabbage, apples, chestnuts, and various other items off the mountains in the fall. Their markets were usually in Lenoir, Morganton, and Hickory, but occasionally they would go as far as Gastonia or Statesville. These trips were referred to as going "down in the country." Their purpose was to market mountain produce and return manufactured goods to the mountains. Teams of oxen, locally referred to as steers, slowly pulled the heavily loaded wagons to Bailey's Camp below Blowing Rock. There, during the first night out, the goods would be reloaded to the faster horse drawn wagons which operated off the mountains. Later one of the brothers, Coy who had been in the Spanish American War, would modernize the operation. He acquired a truck, which like all trucks of the time, would pull the mountain only with difficulty and frequent watering stops. The horse drawn wagons would now be used to meet the truck which did quite well in the flat lands. More about this subject in a later article.

It was grandpa's practice to go off the mountain to the Globe and Blackberry communities to purchase cattle in the spring to put on pasture for the summer. He moved the livestock with only the help of a shep dog. Once the dog returned home his first or second night out. Needless-to-say, grandma was very worried about him until he returned with his cattle several days later. It was his custom to spend the night with bare acquaintances wherever night caught him. He had spent a night at the home of a preacher he knew but who came in late from a revival meeting. The preacher did not recognize the cow dog and chased it away. It came home and left grandpa with a difficult drive home with the cattle.

Grandpa Miller's interest in business, family and community affairs often kept him away from home. Oftentimes weather that was balmy and sunny turned cold and blustery before he returned. Always with small children, Grandma Miller could fend for herself and the children in good weather but not if it turned bad for any length of time. The old log house they lived in early on was in poor repair and was almost impossible to heat. (Even in their new home there would be no provisions for heating the bedrooms. Heated bedrooms were believed to be unhealthy.) Charlie Brown, a nephew, often knew just when to show up. Once he cut an ash tree near the house so the firewood would be handy to the house. When grandpa returned, he was exasperated. He said, "Charlie, I wouldn't have had that tree cut for five dollars." Charlie replied, "Well Uncle Jont, it is cut, and it didn't cost you a thing." Charlie was "different" but was a lot brighter than given credit for. He marched to a "different drummer" pursuing only those things which interested him. (He once cut a huge chestnut in Grandpa Henry's barn lot to see how big it was. He was disappointed when the stump measured only fifty-six inches.)

In off seasons cross ties were cut, hewed, and hauled to the railroad terminal at Elkland (later named Todd) NC. Grandpa usually did the hauling with steers. They handled heavy loads and were not bothered by the mud as much as horses. On one trip it is told that one of the area's first cars caught up with him. Its driver grew impatient before grandpa found a place where he could leave the road with his load. He honked his horn and cursed. Later in the day grandpa would overtake the car stuck in a mudhole. It is said that he ignored the pleas of the car's driver to pull the car out with the steers. He said that he was in a hurry to get to Elkland so he could feed the steers at their usual feeding time.

The railroad had reached Elkland about 1915. The result was a thriving market community far larger than Boone at the time. It took a day to get there with steers. When business was done a camp would be made near the Episcopal Church until the return trip the following day. Elkland and the railroad introduced a new world to the area. On one trip grandpa bought a new product called oatmeal. He liked it so well that he would later buy a whole case to divide among family and friends for trial. It was at Elkland that he bought the seeds for the garden. He had a policy of planting something new every year.

As mentioned earlier, grandpa was frequently away at night, sometimes for several days at a time. Once while he was away a strange voice "haloed" the house and asked about a bed for the night. The children were horrified when grandma told the strange sounding man to stable his horse and come on to the house. With the children becoming more upset by the minute she finally told them that he was their father who had changed his voice. The young couple often had company to share their meager means. Once grandma asked grandpa what kind of bread he wanted for breakfast. He quickly caught on and said cornbread, an unusual choice. There was not a cup of flour in the house. Wheat flour was much harder to have than corn meal though a roller mill would be put in at the Crit Norris mill far down Howard's Creek, later-on. Wheat bread for breakfast was expected in most homes unless money was desperately scarce. In, *The People of New River* by the Coopers, I learned of an acceptable alternative. In an interview Ruby Trivette tells of egg cornbread. It was made with eggs and a mixture of corn meal and wheat flour and was an acceptable breakfast bread.[1]

Grandpa had a presence in the huge house that he built though the only time he was there, in my memory, was for his funeral. The organ that his daughters played was used by the church youth choir to practice on Sunday afternoons. My interest, however, was in the many books and magazines that he had left when he went to the state hospital. His interest in farming magazines and books on scientific developments was far ahead of his time. My grandparents had lived an active and interesting life there. The old place burned a few years ago after it passed from family hands.

## My Grandmother
### "Hattie" Mae Philyaw Miller

Hattie Mae Philyaw Miller was my grandmother on my mother's side of the family. She was born in Watauga County May 13, 1884 and died November 2, 1952. She married Jonathan (Jont) Robert Miller (born April 11, 1884 and died September 7, 1946). As children my brothers, sisters and myself lived on the Jont Miller place almost in sight of grandma's house in the Howard's Creek community near Boone, NC. We were close to Grandma Miller and her children, our aunts, and uncles.

In order of their birth they were:

| | |
|---|---|
| (1) Annie <u>Lois</u> Greer | born January 22, 1907, married Roscoe Greer. |
| (2) <u>David</u> Patterson Miller | born May 14, 1908, married Bina Greene. |
| (3) <u>Blanche</u> Elizabeth Miller | born May 19, 1910. Never married. |
| (4) Joseph <u>Blaine</u> Miller | born January 13, 1913, married Goldie Jones. |
| (5) John <u>Jacob</u> Henry Miller | born March 21, 1915, married Margaret Miller. |
| (6) <u>Charles</u> Evans Miller | born July 11, 1917. Died July 2, 1925. |
| (7) Harding <u>Calvin</u> Miller | born February 7, 1920, married Laverne _____. |
| (8) Viesta <u>Caroline</u> Miller | born May 25, 1922, married Earnest Besst (changed name to Carolyn V. Besst). |
| (9) <u>Lillian</u> Lucille Miller | born April 12, 1924. Never married. |

*An unnamed female was stillborn.

Grandma Miller's father was John Philyaw, a son of Gideon Philyaw. Her mother was Fannie Lane Philyaw. She had an uncle who lived on present day Rainbow Trail Road near Boone, NC named Govan Lane. I do not yet know who their parents were. Grandma Hattie was said to be one-fourth Indian and her appearance verified it. I suspect the Indian blood came from the Philyaws rather than the Lanes because of the Philyaw appearance. Hattie's mother died of a malady called "milk-sick" when Hattie was about four. She had numerous relatives most of whom lived in West Virginia and mined coal. They came visiting about as often as the miners went out on strike. Their North Carolina relatives were strong "right-to-work" advocates and felt they were inadvertently supporting Unionism if their West Virginia kin happened to stay too long.

Milk-sick was an often-fatal ailment caused by drinking poisonous milk from a cow that ate a poisonous weed. The weed could have been Turtle Head but was most likely White Snake Root, which was later learned to lower blood pressure drastically. Non-milking stock including the calves were poisoned but a milking cow might not show any symptoms. The only remedy for a man or beast was brandy or white liquor. The treatment probably did more harm than good since it also contributed to lowered blood pressure temporarily. Certain areas frequently produced milk-sick while it was unknown in others. The ailment was widespread in the mountains especially when summers were dry, and cattle browsed the weeds and herbs of the woods. As grazing and living habits changed, the ailment became less and less frequent. It disappeared before any veterinarians or medical doctors were able to determine for certain the identity.

Grandma Miller was not brought up by her blood kin who had mostly moved to the coal fields to find work. She was adopted by John and Bessie Barnes who had no children of the own. Grandma Miller called them Grandpa and Grandma Barnes. Census records reveal that they had adopted Grandma Miller's mother, Fannie Lane, when she was young. I have never learned the circumstances of that adoption nor a lot about the early Lanes though her family claimed kin with Govan's children. Grandma inherited ten acres from the Barnes remote Doe ridge farm. They reared at least two other adopted children, Joe Church who married Samtha Lane and Mary Greene, who married Tilden Foster and moved to Ohio. Grandma Miller looked upon these two and their adoptive parents as her real family and she kept in touch with them throughout her life. Her birth father, John Philyaw, remarried Elizabeth "Liz" Doneho and they had eight children.

Bessie who married a Coffey
Roy
Stella who married a Greer
Cecil
Cuba
Felix
Lonnie
Oma who married an Archer

Both Grandma and Grandpa Miller suffered from periods of violent insanity. It would likely be treated as a chemical imbalance today but at that time confinement in the state mental hospital at Morganton until it passed was the only solution. Grandma usually returned home after a few months, but grandpa spent the last 16 or 17 years of his life there. I never saw him alive. The children on occasion were left to fend for themselves. My mother, being oldest, felt the burden most. But the family always managed to stay together and refused to be separated from each other for long.

Grandma was a hard worker and a pretty good manager. She grew plenty of food and kept horses, cows, hogs, sheep, and chickens. Cabbage and potatoes were buried to prevent freezing and molasses were made for the winter. Apples and walnuts were gathered and stored if the crop escaped the frequent last spring frosts. Her pride and joy, however, was her dryer-smoke house. She smoked the meat to keep the skippers out. But she had designed the building and its rock furnace so as to dry vegetables. Shuck beans, or leather britches as they were often called, was a big item. So were dried apples. She even sliced and dried sweet potatoes. (She had a hard time keeping her grandchildren from eating the dried sweet potatoes before winter however.)

Being the oldest grandchild, I was said to have been her pet. I probably owe my life to her in more ways than one. I took pneumonia when about four years old. It was winter and our house could not be heated well. I grew progressively worse until grandma took charge. She flatly told my mother that I was going to die unless something was done. Her Indian blood must have told her that I needed a "sweat" to break the fever. She recommended hot poultices on my chest and back. She said that boiled and mashed potatoes or parsnips would do, but that baked onions were best, and she had plenty of them. On top of everything else I was wrapped in layers of quilts. I do not remember much of the night except trying to get out of the covers and grandma putting me back. She woke mom about 4:00 a.m. the next morning to say I was better, and she was going home. At daybreak I was the best I had been in days.

Grandma Miller held all her family as close to her world as she could. She did her best to talk me out of going away to college. She would die of a heart attack before I was ever to return home, but the memories of the visits to her house while growing up are precious. On cool, rainy days we amused ourselves by baking potatoes in the ashes of the fireplace and popping home grown popcorn over its coals. If we were lucky enough to spend the night, we would awaken to the sounds of the breakfast fire being laid in the kitchen stove. The smell of roasting coffee beans would soon follow. When those beans were being ground in the wall-mounted grinder it was time to get up. Breakfast would begin with all the buckwheat pancakes and homemade butter and molasses that you could eat, often followed by ham and eggs with biscuits and gravy. I will never forget the time I drank from the glass of kerosene that grandma kept to start her cooking fires, thinking it was water she had poured for me. It was not as bad as you might think, but very laxative. Or the use we put to the coffee grinder after it was retired to the grainary. We used it to grind the stems grandma pulled from the tobacco she made into twists for her use and the use of her family. Our idea at the time was to make our own brand of snuff.

For many years I have known very little about my Grandmother Miller's mother. I knew that she was named Fannie Lane and that she married John Philyaw and that she died when grandma was about four years old. She had an uncle, Govan Lane, who lived on what is now Rainbow Trail north of Boone. (This road had no respectable name that I know of until Patty Hodges, later Marion, named it when we rode its curves on the school bus in the late 1940's.) Govan's house was a nice white frame house that stood where the ASU water reservoir is now.

Grandma's father, John Philyaw, likely had come from Caldwell County to Watauga County but I do not yet have a lot of information on them. They show in the Boone Township, Watauga County census in 1870. (John's occupation was listed as chairmaker.)

The census of 1870 also reveals some interesting information about Fannie Lane. In 1870 the Lane family shows in Boone Township as a family of eight.

Earlier they had shown as the only Lanes in Watauga County. Fannie Lane Philyaw died July 8, 1888 of milk poison. I believe Grandma Miller thought they lived in what we called the Cornelious house on the road from Doe Fork to Doe Ridge. Fannie had lived with John and Bessie Barnes as a teenager at least. The 1880 census gives this information. John and Bessie would take Fannie's child, my grandmother, and rear her. She would always consider them her real parents although they were also the only grandparents she would ever know.

Our house and grandma's were only a few hundred yards apart. We children kept a well-worn footpath between them. We kids went barefoot even when picking blackberries. We made frequent trips to grandma's to have briars and thorns picked out of our feet with darning needles. Mom's teenage sisters still at home competed for the opportunity. We had our favorites because some of them had a steadier hand than the others. They would scrub the dirt off our feet so the suspicious places would show. Deep and difficult ones needed a few days for infection to develop. This made removal much easier. In the meantime, it was best to walk without a limp unless you were ready for the darning needle.

Mom's teenage sisters could be rather finicky. They sometimes thought we carried fleas into the house. They insisted that grandma look us for fleas before we could come inside. This grandma did. She would lift our collars and other places fleas liked. She sometimes found a flea, or at least she said she did.

We could not have been reared without their help.

Note:  The Find A Grave website wrongly gives Grandma Miller's maiden name as Phillips. Husband and children are correct, but she never had any connection to the Phillips family listed in Ashe County. This is a classic example of the misinformation that ends up on the internet. Internet info can provide leads but must be confirmed by reliable sources to be of dependable value. They had the picture of the right tombstone, but little else.[2]

# 16

---

# My Parents' Day

My parents began married life at one of the most difficult times in recent history. They began with almost no worldly resources and their families could not be of much help though the meager help from Grandma Miller and her family would come at critical times. Though barely in their twenties they both already had become mostly self-sufficient. Dad had held various jobs and mom worked in the dining hall of Appalachian state Teacher's college. Both would have an almost unexplainable inner strength.

My father's name was Jacob <u>Roscoe</u> Greer. Friends and kin alike called him Ross from a childhood nickname. He usually signed his name as J. Roscoe or just J. R. Greer. He was born on May 27, 1909 in Ashe County, NC at Bowie, NC (now called Fleetwood). He was married June 14, 1930 to Lois Miller, daughter of Jonathan R. and Hattie Philyaw Miller. They had eight children, all of whom lived to adulthood. I will list them by name and birth date only as their statistics are more detailed in a chapter to follow.

Their names are:

(1) <u>Lena</u> Elizabeth Greer Norris      born 1931

(2) James <u>Leonard</u> Greer      born 1932

(3) Robert <u>Elton</u> Greer      born 1934

(4) <u>Emma Mae</u> Greer Kultgen      born 1935

(5) <u>Jack</u> Norman Greer      born 1936

(6) Kenneth <u>Grant</u> Greer      born 1939

(7) <u>Johnny</u> Roscoe Greer      born 1943

(8) Patricia <u>Gail</u> Greer Hayes      born 1948

## My Father
### <u>Jacob "Roscoe" Greer</u>

Dad spent his early years at Bowie (now Fleetwood) where Grandpa Ivory was section foreman on the "Virginia Creeper" railroad that ran from Abingdon, VA to Todd, NC. Dad said it was the best job grandpa was ever to have but grandpa could not see it at the time.

Dad began school at what became Fleetwood school and worked his first job there. He skidded blocks of ice to shore after they were cut out of the river. They were then loaded on the train and hauled somewhere to be stored in icehouses for the following summer. (This was in the days before refrigeration.)

After grandpa quit the railroad, they began a pattern of frequent relocations. By the time dad is in the third or fourth grades they are living on Pine Run Creek and he is going to the Rutherwood School. Grandpa seems to have taken the three boys out of school about age twelve or earlier. He had no education himself and could not see that it would benefit them any. The only jobs were hard manual labor and he needed them to help him cut timber. Dad, the eldest, left school in the fifth grade and I presume that Uncles Roy and Isadore did not go much longer. What a fifth-grade education could do in those days. Dad eventually did carpenter work and Uncle Roy ran his own building business. The youngest, Uncle Isadore, left home at sixteen and eventually did well for himself with Baltimore Gas and Electric in Maryland.

All the children rose above the desperate times of their childhood. Grandpa was a good worker and he passed that trait along to his children, but it was Grandma Greer who steadied the course and gave them aspirations for the future. Dad was a very highly principled person in-spite-of a less than ideal childhood. Grandma was part of the reason but there were others. Dad became a "Lone Scout" because there were no Scout Troops nearby. He received his manuals and materials through the mails. He kept those boyhood treasures in his trunk for years after he was married.

All three boys loved guns and hunting and fishing. Their boyhood activities and their adult get-togethers frequently revolved around these activities. The day the youngest brother, Isadore, was sixteen, dad killed sixteen squirrels for him to carry home. Wash Norris, once a neighbor, soon learned to take the boy's shells and count them. He allowed only the shells for squirrels he was willing to part with when they asked him to hunt in his woods

Dad stayed at home the longest of any of the three boys. Usually any wages he earned went to help keep the family fed. During their teen years all the boys helped cut timber and farm. They made some money working on the farms of Walter and Murray Brown. Mack, Murray's son, says they weren't paid much but were fed one and sometimes two meals a day. Mack tells that grandpa would tell the boys to "eat hearty" that "their pay wasn't ever going to amount to much." Dad was working and living on the Walter Brown place on the river when he got married. He and mom moved into a place on the Wildcat Road until he could build their house on Grandma Miller's place at Howard's Creek. He had learned his lesson at a young and tender age. It was the only move he ever made as a married man.

The house dad built is a story in-itself. He cut a huge chestnut tree given to the young couple by Grandma Miller. Dad cut it down cut it to lengths and quartered the larger logs. This was necessary before a big team owned by Ira Brown could pull them a short distance to Wilby Brown's mill. The one tree cut enough lumber to build the house with some to sell to pay on the roofing metal. The house was small and drafty at first but was improved some about every year until it held the eight kids whenever it had to. Children lived outside a lot of the time in those days.

Living was hard during the depression. Farming was about the only work. Dad was young and strong and was sought after to cradle and thresh grain. Cradling grain was a killing job, but dad was good at it. He usually received two men's pay for that kind of work. As the depression wore on, there began to be a market for timber in the furniture plants. Dad and some friends went off the mountain to Buffalo Cove on the Yadkin to cut huge tulip poplars for veneering blocks used in the furniture plants. They would cook and sleep in a sawmill shack all week and make their way home for the weekend. The day before Christmas in 1938 or 39 found them on their way home during an ice storm. The resulting events are almost too much like Walton's Mountain to be believed.

They left early Christmas Eve morning walking out through Happy Valley to US Hwy. 321 planning to catch the bus up the mountain to Blowing Rock and Boone. It had been cold for days, but the weather had warmed up and it began raining. Almost immediately things began to ice up, but they kept going. By the time they reached US 321 the ice was so bad that neither the bus nor anything else was running. They turned up the mountain hoping that the weather would warm, and traffic would resume. They passed through Blowing Rock late in the afternoon. It was now snowing. They still had about thirteen miles to go and it was icier than ever. There was nothing the four could do but trudge on. I believe they were dad, uncle Jake Miller, cousins Jesse Brown and Earnest Lane. They made it home well after dark and the ice as being covered now by a heavy snowstorm. Dad had walked all the way in a pair of knee-high rubber boots. They said it was twenty-six miles, but it still measures over thirty for me today in a car. As it turned out that was only the beginning of the story.

Mom was glad to see dad, of course, but she had expected him to get to Boone in time to buy food for Christmas day. She had some flour left and decided that we would have biscuits and gravy with some fruit she had canned for breakfast and add potatoes to it for Christmas dinner. Like most kids we were up early Christmas morning. Santa had been there leaving mostly homemade things. Dad was still in bed. Something unusual for him. It had snowed about eight inches but there was already a bright but cold and sunny sky. We kids noticed some large birds in the trees across the small stream in front of the house. In those days before wild grapes had black rot heavy tags of grapes would freeze dry on the vines. Grouse would feed on them all winter and sometimes become intoxicated on grapes fermenting in their craws. These birds were sitting in the sparkling ice-covered branches and vines without a care in the world. We called dad and he soon confirmed that these birds were ruffled grouse or pheasants as we called them then. He struggled into the same boots he had worn home and went out the back door with his shotgun. We watched through the window as he crept up the streambed within range. He fired twice and killed two grouse. Our border collie pinned a third against the bank of the steam. Mom added the three grouse with heaps of dumplings to our Christmas dinner. We never talked much about it, but I am sure it was a Christmas the older kids will never forget. The way it came about was forever special.

With the beginnings of the war in Europe the economy began to improve a little. Dad was able to find timber cutting and sawmill work. Most loggers liked to have him on their crew because he was considered to be one of the best saw filers around. He continued to work in timbering through the war years. He switched to carpentering with the building boom following the war. The kids did most of the farm work. He would promise to take us fishing on Saturday if our work was done by the end of the week. It was a promise he was glad to keep for he loved to fish. The sight of him with five boys following him as we walked two or three miles to the river is still legend in the community. He always knew where his boys were. They were with him. They would return to see him most weekends as long as he lived.

On one very memorable occasion dad had taken all the boys big enough to walk to the river fishing. In the afternoon we made our way to another location down the river where we often fished briefly off a riverbank in the edge of a small pasture. While we fished the cattle came to investigate. This time though there was a bull with them, and he was looking for a fight. Going off the high bank into the water was not an option since my brothers and myself were still pretty small and did not yet know how to swim. The bull was tearing up the ground something fierce and seemed determined to have a fight. Dad made a quick search of the riverbank and came up with a locust fence post that had rotted off at the ground. It was otherwise solid. He at least was armed although not very well. The boys were advised to watch and to take to the river only in absolute necessity.

Dad did not wait for the bull to attack. He charged putting the post end ways into the bull's forehead. The bull was charging also and was not stopped. Dad sidestepped and brought his club down across the back of the bull's head with all his might. The bull went to his knees but was up in an instant. Before he could get under way again dad brought his club down on the bull's head again. This time he turned tail and as he left; he was measured full length along his back with the fence post. Dad chased him and threw the post after him as he raced for safer pastures. Sometimes the best defense is a good offense and it pays to pursue it with everything you have in you.

Some years later we made another trip fishing to a place where dad had lived and worked as a young man. This place was cut off by the river and at the time of our fishing trip was used for pasture. (I was later to learn that this place in the bend of the river where Old Sixty bent to meet it was the "Great Bent" of New River that would appear so often in early records time.) In dad's youth they had often lived near here and he often talked of "setting people across the river" there in a boat who were on their way to the old Fairview Methodist church. In dad's time it was owned and farmed by Walter Brown. Dad worked on the farm there before he was married. Today it is forested with white pines. At the neck of the "Bent" you could throw a rock into the river on both sides though the river flowed probably a mile on the way around. An older man lived there alone at this time and looked after the cattle. There seemed little to do but salt the cattle, fish, and shoot ground hogs. He asked me if I would like to come and help him. He may not have even been serious, but it sounded interesting to me. I especially wanted to shoot the .22 Hornet that he used. He was missing a left hand but cradled the rifle in the crook of his arm and shot with great accuracy. Of course, dad said "no" and I guess I knew that kind of job was too good to be true.

The lesson I learned had to do with the herder and his missing hand. It seems that his number had been drawn in the lottery for service in World War I. He did not want to go and pulled a big drunk. While intoxicated he had laid his left wrist across the muzzle of a shotgun and pulled the trigger. Three days later the war was over and his call to report for training was cancelled. My dad told me this and advised that there are no just ways to prevent or shortcut the hard facts of life. If we try, we only make things worse for ourselves.

Dad never owned a car after he was married. He would walk miles to work if necessary. People respected him and would often drive out of their way to give him a ride or bring him home. He said that he never wanted to have to choose between gas for a car or food for his family. That was the kind of man that he was.

During early married life dad never had much in the way of tools. He had bought a few things from his Uncle Larkin Greer's estate sale. (Larkin had been a noted local carpenter.) With these few tools and a lot of improvising he made do with what he had.

One particularly cold winter he and mom were worried that their small children needed a warm place to sleep. They moved their bed into the living room where a homemade oil drum heater was in place. Dad made two trundle beds for the children. (These were small beds with wheels.) These beds were rolled out until the children were asleep in them and then rolled under the big bed for the night.

Mom made quilts for these trundle beds. Dad made quilting frames from chestnut boards he salvaged from a nearby sawmill. He had no small bit to bore the holes used to adjust the size; so, he made one from a twenty-penny nail. I still have these frames today.

In his later years as a carpenter dad would accumulate a good selection of hand tools. It was some time after he died before I could bring myself to open his toolbox. When I did, I found everything sharp and ready to go to the job.

His had been a busy life other than the job also. He had barbering tools and he cut hair for all of us. This would take at least a half of a day. When we got new shoes for school, he stood each of us against a wall and marked the length of each right foot on the floor and added one half inch. He then cut a measuring stick for each one's new shoes. He did this shopping himself.

## My Mother
### "Lois" Miller Greer

My mother was born to Jonathan R. and Hattie Philyaw Miller on January 22, 1907. She was their first child. They lived at an old mill site downstream from the falls of Howard's Creek. Grandma Miller operated the mill when someone had grain to grind. The last evidence of the mill and much of the creek bottom there disappeared during the 1940 flood. Much of the side of Doe Ridge slid off knocking the old log house into the creek. (Wellborn Greene's family lived there at the time. His wife and two boys lost their lives. Their baby girl was spared when a tub overturned over her protecting her during the collapse of the building.)

Times were hard for nearly everyone then. Mom recalled being awakened during the night by the popping of her mother's jars of fruit, which were freezing and bursting in her bedroom. One late winter and spring they were reduced to eating little more than turnips and cornbread. After the turnips sprouted tops in the hole they were buried in, they ate turnips cooked tops and all. Mom grew up tough and she was going to need that toughness much of her later life. She learned to chop the heads off of turtles that were getting her baby ducks at a tender age. Along with her brother Dave they attempted to break goats to pull a small cart. She often said years later that those were among the best years of her life.

Before mom and Uncle Dave were old enough to work, they were called on to do things that would be unthinkable today. Her Uncle Reubin had bought a larger farm on the river near present day Todd. One year he needed the family mules as soon as the planting on the home place was done. In the middle of the week mom and Dave were placed on the backs of the mules to take them to Uncle Reubin some ten or twelve miles away. They were given explicit instructions of where to make their turns and who to ask if something did not seem right. They would ford the river at the Tatum place and would be to Uncle Reubins shortly after. Grandpa and grandma would not know even if they got there until Uncle Reubin brought them home on Sunday.

Sometime after mom got big enough to do some work the family moved to another old log house about a mile away on some acreage that great grandpa deeded them. It was a small place, but grandpa and grandma bought an adjoining thirty acres. This old house seems to have held bad memories for mom. Grandpa and grandma both were subject to periods of insanity. When mom was fourteen both parents were placed in the state asylum for some time. The baby at the time was given temporarily to Uncle Donald and his wife Docia who were childless. The rest mom was determined to keep together at all costs, and she did it. Neighbors were not much help. They apparently thought that any help would only delay the inevitable. Only Ira Brown offered them a bushel of corn to make meal if they would walk across the mountain to get it.

Mom loved school. A cousin with no immediate family, Charlie Brown, would buy her school papers and pencils and encourage her. When the snow was deep grandpa would hook his steers to a short log of good diameter and pull it to break a path through the snow. Mom went to a one-room school about a mile away called "Growling Rock." (How it got its name is a story best left for another time.) When mom entered high school, she went to live with Henry and Grace Hardin and his mother. Grace was a teacher and mom called her Miss Grace. Grandma Hardin was always referred to as Granny Hardin. Mom helped to care for the two Hardin children, Joe and Martha, to pay for her keep. Joe was to become a pilot and would fly "the hump" in India and China with the Flying Tigers during World War II. Mom always regretted that her education ended in the tenth grade when she had to return home to help the family through a long bout with measles.

Mom moved onto the campus of Appalachian State College during the late twenties to work in that school's dining hall. She was quite proud of the football boys that she helped to feed. She followed their progress even after she left work. They not only won every game in 1938 but were also unscored upon for the season. Mom made many friends on staff that she would keep in touch with all her life. While there she would also meet another young person, who would become our father.

Mom's life could not have been easy. She was pregnant or had small children to tend to much of her life. Besides household duties she often labored in the fields, milked a cow if we were lucky enough to have one at the time, and grew a huge garden. She canned and preserved huge stores of food for the winters. She was a very strong person who never gave in to discouragement for very long. She always said the "The best days of our lives are now."

Mom operated on three major fronts. First were her children. She weathered crisis after crisis determined to better feed and clothe her family and improve her home. She joined the Home Demonstration Club to learn more about food variety and good diet. She said that it was better to spend money on food than to spend it on medicine. She supported her children in efforts to get an education. She often walked the four miles to the high school for athletic and other events her children were involved in. Secondly, mom made sure her children learned to work by doing the garden and her flowers. It took a lot of work and imagination to take care of everything for she was always trying something new. All her children would be able to grow a garden and would like flowers. Most of all they would know, and like, work. She would tell us that unless we found something that she had not found we would always have to work, and we might as well learn to like it. She reared a bunch of workaholics. At a family gathering she once said, "I taught all my children to work." Her daughters-in-law all nodded in agreement and allowed that she just might have overdone it a little bit. Thirdly, mom took great interest in sewing and needlework. Early on, winter days were used to make patchwork quilts. As her children began to move away, she sewed, knitted, and crocheted for children and grandchildren. It was good to see her involved in projects she so enjoyed. Dad managed for her to get a portion of the Social Security money so she could pursue her hobbies with some independence.

Mom became diabetic and lost most of her vision to glaucoma in her eighties. She had to have the help of others, a situation she had never been used to and which she despised. It became my privilege to help her though she had to depend on my sisters for most of her personal needs. Later, no sons were ever better to come and care for a mother than her sons, my brothers. She never complained and wanted nothing better than not to be any trouble to anyone. Those who helped her most were the most blessed.

Mom seemed worried in her later years because I had never married. She seemed to think that she had failed me in some way. Finally, nearing sixty-three, I met and married Martha (Marny) Cox Cole. We were married June 4, 1995. I still stayed with mom some nights and my brothers and sisters were good enough to stay the others. Mom was pleased with the arrangement and my marriage. I do not think she ever thought I could care for myself without the help of another good woman.

It fell my lot to be with mom the morning she fell and broke her hip. She had tried to use her potty chair without help because she did not want to bother me while I was doing breakfast. We learned of the break after an ambulance took her to the hospital for x-rays. The doctor recommended an operation to pin the hip in- spite of her age (ninety) and heart condition. Otherwise she would likely suffer for months and was not likely to ever learn to walk again. Since I had power of attorney, it was up to me to decide. I hesitated only a moment. I felt she had already made the decision herself by the way she had lived. She had made it easy for me.

The operation was a success, but she began to have heart problems that night. By the next day it became apparent that she was not likely to make it and the family gathered in. At 3:00 that night she ceased breathing for about two minutes and then came back. Brother Johnny said that "she couldn't bring herself to leave at that time of night because it might inconvenience somebody." About seven a.m. Marny and I went home to get our medications and maybe a bite of breakfast. We were called soon after we got home to tell us we should get back as soon as we could. They said later that mom held on until we got back into the family circle. She died a few minutes later. As Marny and I held and consoled each other I could almost hear her say, "Didn't I tell you the best times we will ever know are now." Two days later we laid her to rest beside our father. They were two of the most courageous and caring people that I ever expect to know.

Both dad and mom came from close families. Without their help a hard life would have been even harder. Mom's family lived nearby, and we saw them most often. During our early years, dad farmed and worked timber with mom's brothers. Her oldest brother, Dave, was dad's frequent partner in such ventures. He was very talented and could build water wheels and harness waterpower to do a lot of household chores. He could also be a lot of fun. He hunted and fished with the family even after they no longer worked together. Grandma Miller and her daughters were an even bigger part of our lives.

232

Dad's family lived further away but did visit once or twice a year. Uncle Roy came frequently during his teen years. We especially looked forward to a visit from Uncle Isadore who lived in Maryland. His first three children were girls which we thought was a shame for we thought he would be an ideal father for a boy. I think he was and the fourth was a boy.

The Miller and Greer families joined on another front when mom's cousin married dad's sister Ina. They lived near us during their early married life. They frequently spent the night with us and were favorites with all the children. They farmed an adjoining cornfield and Aunt Ina often gave me a biscuit filled with brown sugar and butter from their lunch pail. They caught two baby ground squirrels (chipmunks) and kept them as pets. The called them Joe and Moe. One of them, I could never tell them apart, ran up my pants leg. Everyone was yelling "Don't squeeze," but some things are not possible. Whichever one it was only lived a few days afterwards.

Roscoe and Lois Greer
On Their Wedding Day
June 14, 1930

## Roscoe Greer Family Summer of 1943

Left to right:

Back row- Mom holding Johnny (the youngest at that time, Gail had not been born) and Dad.

Middle row- Emma Mae, Elton, Leonard, and Lena.

Front row- Jack and Grant.

(Please note how young Mom looks.)

A Growing Family at a Family Celebration

(Birthday or Anniversary)

Grandpa Ivory Greer

Grandpa was still cutting timber the old hard way during World War II. This picture was when he was working for a timber operation in Maryland, which was run by a Greene, who was from nearby Stoney Fork.

## Grandpa Ivory and Grandma "Emmy" Greer

This is the only picture I have of their family. Grandpa Ivory is holding Roscoe, my father, and Grandma is holding Uncle Roy. If the rest of the family was ever photographed, I am not aware of it. There are not any good pictures that exist of Grandma, that I know of.

## Emma Lou Dollar

First cousin Emma Lou Dollar in her wheelchair after she graduated from an iron-lung; not even polio could stop that smile. She would never walk again but continued to educate herself and learn to write even with crippled hands. Her letters were beautifully done. Pneumonia took her at age nineteen.

## The Old School House
## (Howards Creek School)

Seven of the eight Greer children began their education at this school. It closed before Gail, the youngest, began school. The grounds were once worn but now able to grow grass and trees.

The Governor's Inaugural Committee

requests the honour of your presence

at the Inauguration

of

James E. Holshouser, Jr.

as

Governor of North Carolina

Friday, the fifth of January

Nineteen hundred and seventy-three

at twelve o'clock

The Capitol

Raleigh, North Carolina

## Invitation to the Holshouser Inauguration

My short journey into big-time politics.

# 17

## A Family of Ten

As children we had no way of going anywhere and were not often visited by anyone except Grandma Miller and her younger daughters, our aunts. They lived less than a quarter mile away. Dad had built our house on the Miller farm from the lumber of a huge chestnut tree donated by Grandma Miller. The house was small, but we lived out of doors much of the time anyway.

We children developed a language of our own complete with other names. I was "Bud," Elton was "Pert", and Grandma was "Gonie." None of us recalls the origin of these names. We often did not complete our sentences. There was no need if we understood each other without it. Grandma Miller saw this would be a problem when we started school, so she insisted that we learn a more correct way of talking. We rarely went anywhere, but I do remember visiting mom's Aunt Frances Miller while Great-Grandma Martha Winebarger Miller was still living. There we met a cousin, Clint Tester, who lived nearby. We both were proud owners of pocketknives though neither of us were school age yet. Aunt Frances kept honeybees. It was Clint's idea that we could cut the bees heads off as they came out of the hive and then get some honey. There were too many of them. I learned two things – not to mess with beehives and that I could not outrun cousin, Clint.

"Granny Marthy" did not live long after that. Mom's sister, Aunt Blanche, came to offer to take the children to the funeral since few children ever knew a great grandparent. (Mom was expecting again at the time.) Mom said we were too young to remember except maybe for Lena, the oldest. This led to a new game and I believe Lena must have remembered every detail. She insisted that we act out every detail of a game called "Funeral." She was the preacher, Elton and I were the singers, and Emma Mae was a flower girl complete with flowers. At first Elton and I insisted that we did not know the songs, but Lena would stomp her foot and insist that we were just being stubborn. Finally, Emma Mae led off with a mournful sound but no words. We joined in and made a noise appropriate for the occasion. Mom came to the door to see what was wrong.

As we grew older, we made frequent trips to grandma's. We went barefoot and we frequently went to have briars, thorns, etc. picked from our feet. Mom's teenaged sisters enjoyed doing this for us. First, they would wash the dirt form the soles of our feet and then press suspicious spots until we yelled. Then came out the darning needles. Blanche and Carolyn had steady hands, but we tried to avoid Lillian who was nervous. These visits included another ritual insisted upon by our aunts. The briar picking took place on the outside porch. Before we could be let inside grandma must search us for fleas. She would look in our hair and under shirt collars. She sometimes found one, or at least she said she did. We would have never been reared without their help.

Our visits to grandma's were near perfect but not quite. They had a Rhode Island Red rooster that would fight. They did not know this as he was a sneaky coward. He only attacked children and dogs when no one was looking. He soon learned to make the trip to our house when looking for a fight. Granted, we gave him some cause. We could crow almost as good as any rooster and we mocked him to no end. He would hang around looking for a chance to hit us from behind or get in the last crow. He seemed to grow meaner every day but soon learned to keep his distance. We all chewed grandma's homemade tobacco and Elton was a champion spitter. He could put tobacco juice in the offending rooster's eye at twenty-five feet or even more.

This rooster was a part of our lives for several years. He seemed to have a charmed life. He once caught me in the back while I was taking an armload of firewood into the house. He ran off about fifty feet and stretched his neck to crow. I threw a stick of firewood and it looked on target by the time it left my hand. It seemed to be in slow motion as it took him on the near side of the head, the other end rotating around to take him again on the other side. He fell over with rumpled feathers and did not move. I gathered my firewood and took it inside wondering how I could explain. When I came back out, I could see he was beginning to move a little. It was near thirty minutes before he could stagger back home. I was so relieved that I did not send him off with a victorious crow.

Mr. Rooster went on to live a charmed life. He once challenged some dogs and they pulled out most of his feathers. He was so ashamed that he hid in the weeds until he could grow a new crop. We would search him out just to make fun of him. When he recovered, he was meaner than ever. We were not through with him yet. One Sunday afternoon we had been fishing and stopped by grandma's for we were thirsty. No one was home but we helped ourselves to water anyway. The rooster spied a still baited hook and swallowed it whole. We could not get it back up so we cut off a length of line. We did not expect him to survive so we put him under a washtub near the door so they could prepare him for cooking if they desired. By the time they got home Mr. Rooster had swallowed the line and they could see nothing wrong with him, so they turned him loose. Digesting a fishhook did not improve his disposition. An aunt and uncle wanted him at their new home sometime later and he did not visit anymore. I am sure that he lived to a ripe old age. He was indestructible.

Elton and I were near the same size and some people sometimes took us to be twins. We were constant companions. As we grew older, we spent more and more time away from the house and in the woods. The wooded pasture where Grandma

Miller's hogs ranged was one of our favorite areas. There were cherry and service berry trees there that needed our picking. We had to improvise some precautions. The hogs oftentimes came to our tree and free-ranging hogs could be dangerous. We learned not to be caught in the same tree. When we were ready to leave the one without the hogs would drop down from his tree and get the hogs attention. When they chased him, he would race for the fence. If caught he would climb another tree temporarily. Meanwhile the other would leave his tree and race for the fence by a slightly different route. This process was repeated as needed until both of us were safely across the fence.

Our free-ranging lifestyle was more limited as we became old enough to work. Dad worked outside the home, but mom was a tough task master. I wrote the following in Pat Beaver and Sandra Ballard's, *Voices From the Headwaters*.

Like most women of our day, our mother bore most of the responsibility of seeing the family fed. Grandma Greer sometimes suggested that mom could cook less, and we would not really suffer from it. This would infuriate our mom. She was firmly convinced that inadequate diet caused doctor bills and she believed it to be more prudent to spend the money on food. There was never much to spend so she developed other methods.

We always had a large vegetable garden. All of us learned to garden whether pulling weeds or by the handle of a hoe. But it did not stop there. She belonged to the first Home Demonstration Club and studied diet and nutrition. She tried a new vegetable every year and learned to prepare fruits and vegetables in the most nutritious way.

Before home freezers were available, a freezer locker plant was built in Boone to provide individual locker space for rental. Mom took advantage of the service, not for fruits and vegetables, but for home-grown meats. In the spring she would buy 100 chicks to be grown out for the table. Those not used at home made the trip to the freezer locker about ten at a time.

Our dad was a hard worker. Grandpa Greer was a timber cutter and he took dad out of school after fifth grade because he needed someone else on the other end of the saw. What a fifth-grade education. He would eventually become an accomplished carpenter after building jobs came available. Before that he took anything-else he could find. He was big and strong and could handle the man killing job of cradling grain. He was often-times paid double wages for this. In fact, most of his life he would make a little better than the going pay for one of his education.

Dad also did some farming off the job, but he did not like it to interfere with his love of fishing. He would promise to take us fishing if we took care of any crops before Saturday. We tried hard not to let him down. He and all his boys were often seen walking one behind the other the three miles or so to the river. We carried no rain gear nor food and were often late at night getting home. (We knew every apple tree and berry patch on the trail.) We did not have much and we walked everywhere we went but we were sometimes envied by boys who were much better off.

These later years it has given me great pleasure to watch son John parenting his three boys. While there is no blood relation to me or my father, it brings back pleasant memories. John has carried it a step further. He finds individual time for each boy. Time with dad was mostly a group thing.

I was born at home on Howard's Creek, Watauga County, NC to Roscoe and Lois Miller Greer July 22, 1932. I was the second of eight children. I will ty to relate an abbreviated story of my brothers and sisters and myself in hopes of doing a more expansive writing with their participation at some later date. The children are listed below with brief notes.

## "Lena" Elizabeth born 1931

She was first born and was pushed into adult responsibilities far too early. She sometimes responded to situations beyond her control with frustration or even hysteria. I often wonder that if she had had less responsibility as a child, she might have learned to handle life with less wear and tear on herself. Thankfully, her later years have been much easier on her.

## James "Leonard" born 1932

As my Grandmother Miller's first grandson, I was much spoiled early on. I became quite a tyrant. It was rare that I could go all week without a whipping and only then if I missed some that I deserved. As the eldest son I was expected to see that the chores were done and done right.

Dad usually left for work at daybreak and did not return until night. When I was twelve, he told me that if anything happened to him and mom. We were to make it on our own. This scared me near half to death. I used my considerable talents as tyrant to coerce the others into doing the wood, water, etc. before dark. They sometimes cried to go in out of the cold to warm, but I was hard hearted. I knew that if they went in, I probably would not be able to get them out again and I would catch it when dad got home.

## Robert "Elton" born 1934

Elton was about the same size as me and not all that much younger. We were inseparable playmates and work mates. He was not only my brother; he was the best friend I ever had. We were very close. We cut most of the mountains of firewood needed together with a short two-man saw sent to us by Uncle Calvin who was in Idaho. I wanted Elton to have that saw and I suppose his family still has it. He once chopped off a toe while splitting wood. Fortunately, it has never bothered him much. Elton had a great sense of humor. When splitting firewood, I would usually divide the chore equally with him although he was younger. Once my pile of wood to be split was taking too long. I discovered he was adding to my pile from his own while I was busy. I had already split most of the wood myself by the time I figured it out.

## "Emma Mae" born 1935

Emma Mae's strongest trait was loyalty to family and tradition. She supported her family members always, even when they were wrong. She broke with family tradition somewhat by joining the Women's Marine Corps after high school. There was nothing else she could do of interest locally in those days. She was basically a gentle soul. She left around twenty cats when she reported to duty. I think she made a good Marine. Years later a fellow worker of mine, a retired Marine, could get a little obnoxious. I would tell him that it was true that my brothers and myself were army veterans but that we have a sister who was a Marine.

Once when I needed help very badly Emma Mae came to the rescue. Our family had made a good crop of molasses the fall before and the excess had been kept in a small wooden barrel on the back porch. It was near empty in the spring and it was decided to leave the cover off so grandma's bees could finish it off. I decided the bees had a good thing and that I could reach far enough to swipe and lick my fingers. I went in head-first and only held my face out of the molasses with my trembling arms. I screamed as loud as I could but doubted if the sound got far from the barrel. I feared I would be remembered as the one that died head down in a molasses barrel. Emma Mae, who was only three or four, heard and yelled for mom. Mom finally came and lifted me out by the heels. She said that she couldn't see why the molasses in the bottom of the barrel would be better than the jar on the dining room table.

## "Jack" Norman born 1936

I believe Jack was the last of the eight to be born at home. Only Grant, Johnny and Gail would be born in a hospital if I am correct. Jack was very independent in thought. He came quickly to common sense decisions and did not seem to look back. He rarely needed to. Being too young to follow his older brothers did not keep him from trying. It sometimes got him into trouble. I once caught a polecat in a trap set for ground hogs. I pulled it by a long chain and stick to the woodshed above the house. This did not make much sense, but I hoped dad would let me shoot it when he got home. I would not dare to touch his always loaded rifle without his permission. Curious Jack got too close and got his eyes filed with the liquid scent. He told mom "I'll never be able to see again." Later he would even the score to some degree. I had placed about a dozen strange eggs found during late plowing in a bucket in the woodshed. I thought they were snake eggs but wanted them to hatch so I could be sure. Jack found the newly hatched snakes before I did. He did not care to risk my deciding to keep them. He chopped everyone into pieces about one inch long with a hoe.

## Kenneth "Grant" born 1939

Grant could not pass high school English unless they changed the teacher and maybe not then. He was the only one of the eight not to graduate. He would later acquire a GED. Grant's talents lay in mechanical fields. He collected and studied flashlights, clocks, motors, and most kinds of junk. He would eventually be recognized by Governor Hunt as a state employee of the year for his work in mechanical maintenance at the Western Carolina Center at Morganton. His collecting became more disciplined and is now limited to antiques, most of the time.

Grant was the only one of the eight not to get at least a high school diploma. He failed English twice and did not feel it worthwhile to try it a third time under the same teacher. Sometime afterwards he decided to go for a GED. The day he went they were testing those who had just finished the course. They asked him to take the test to determine his need for remedial studies. He did well and they issued him a diploma without any further work. (He even passed English.)

## "Johnny" Roscoe born 1943

Johnny was the youngest son of the family. He became the most frequent companion of our dad in dad's later years. Their principles are so similar in many ways. They loved hunting and fishing so much. Only Johnny's self-imposed limits controlled the squirrels and rabbits he could bring in. After the first day of squirrel season he often limited himself to taking only those squirrels that could be shot in the head with his rifle. The squirrel population still suffered.

## Patricia "Gail" born 1948

Gail was the last born. Simply said, she was bright and pretty. She was prone to big ideas; big for anyone except herself. She married soon after high school but went back to earn a RN in nursing.

We all went to school in a one teacher school at Howard's Creek. Early on there had been two teachers and maybe 40-50 students. In later years one teacher, Miss Maggie Moretz, would teach most of the Greer children in small classes. Miss Moretz did a lot of spanking. Grant even managed to get a spanking while visiting before he was old enough to start school. We carried our lunches to be eaten cold at school. We were ashamed of our biscuits filled with country ham or strawberry jam. Some others had store bought bread. (How things have changed.) Later on Miss Maggie would cook a rich vegetable soup on top of the pot-bellied stove that heated the classroom. Once while she had the lid of the pot off a paper airplane sailed into the pot without her knowledge. Unfortunately, the used lesson sheet had Elton's name on it. The first dollar I ever earned came from Miss Maggie. She paid me a nickel a day to come early and build up a fire in the big stove before time for school.

The school only existed for a short twenty-five years. Miss Moretz taught most of them. Those years spanned the years of World War II. Early on there had

250

been even a feeling of uncertainty about the war. Hitler was promising new and better secret weapons every few weeks. All too often he was making good on his promises. We learned early on that the Japanese fought a cruel and fanatical war that most of us found hard to believe. The country was far behind in war efforts, but we set out to remedy that situation as quickly as possible.

We carried our scrap metal to a collection point below the old schoolhouse and bought ten-cent war stamps to go into our savings book. (Miss Moretz bought our scrap metal from us, probably out of her own pocket.) It was all part of a war effort that reached from mom's kitchen to the front lines.

The early months were desperate with the outcome sometimes doubtful. I remember the first time I felt we were going to win for sure. A large flight of planes passed over pulling gliders. They were probably on their way from Fort Campbell, KY to Fort Bragg, NC. We were all outside planting more garden. Somehow, we realized that those gliders meant an offensive war that would carry the war to the enemy's homeland. We all waved and cheered. Even my no-nonsense mother led the cheering. Cratis Williams wrote in one of his books of the same feeling but in a different setting. Unknown to most of us, Cratis had left a tubercular wife in a Huntington, WV sanatorium when he came to Boone. During the early war years, he traveled to visit her as often as he could. The buses wound their way up through West Virginia overloaded and sometimes breaking down. The buses were loaded with young mountain girls making their way to the defense plants in Ohio. (Cratis would call them Columbus girls.) They rarely stopped talking and laughing and rarely slept. The first money they earned would buy red or white three-quarter length coats and new shoes if they could find them. Observing them, Cratis seems to have concluded that there was no way that we were going to lose this war. (Our aunt, Carolyn Miller, was one of these girls.)

Our war production surprised even the most optimistic. On the farms the women, the young and the old and infirm produced record amounts of food and fiber, all the while giving up their best to the armed forces and the defense plants.

Aircraft plants had been set up in fields of the warm south and southwest. There was not time to build buildings to house them. Industry met its challenges well. The British contracted for a new fighter plane with a Long Island firm that had never built a plane. It went from design to test flight in just 119 days. It took off and landed on wooden wheels because the metal ones were not yet ready. But did it ever fly. It flew 450 miles per hour, the fastest of any production plane used in the war. They called it the P51 Mustang. Needless-to-say, our own pilots wanted it as soon as the British would let us have the expanding production, and they did. Several versions of the Mustang were produced. Rolls-Royce engines made them even faster and extra fuel capacity allowed them to escort the bombers all the way to Berlin. By the invasion of France on June 6, 1944 we would pretty much control the skies over Europe. All too soon jet fighters would make the Mustang obsolete, but it is still rated the number one military aircraft of all time.

On June 6, 1944, the invasion of Normandy began. A quiet came over the land. The whole country seemed to hold its breath. In the days ahead mail carriers, like Mr. Clyde Winebarger, would often retrace portions of their routes in the evenings so letters from the wounded and the survivors would reach their families a day earlier. It was a hard time to be a parent. It would be even worse for those with loved ones in the Pacific Theater. There one invasion following another was the normal procedure.

It is well and good that we refer to this generation as the "Great Generation." It was not yet done with war, for the Cold War would last for forty years. But war was far from being its only achievement. Veterans set about building the world's strongest economy and the world's strongest government. We put a man on the moon, but this was probably insignificant compared to our other achievements. Polio, for example, had become epidemic. Those that it did not kill were sometimes left with fates worse than death. Space trips cannot compare with the Salk vaccine.

Those of us who came to school at Howard's Creek learned the importance of the church to our society. We co-existed with the church next door and often took part in programs there. But much of the world was disillusioned by the war. Church people warred with each other, even built concentration camps. We began to change our society through the mechanism of our government. With some difficulty, civil rights became the law of the land. The rights of criminals even became protected. While all this was going on, we forgave our enemies, the Germans and Japanese. We helped the world to rebuild and become prosperous.

The threat of war remained with us. Our nuclear power and armed forces defended the free world. At long last the Germans themselves would tear down the Berlin Wall. We were within sight of our victory only to discover something we had not thought of. The world was far more impressed with our ability to produce cheap and abundant food and our progress in medical fields than with our military might. This generation truly was the heroes of those times. It asked little but gave much just by doing what Americans do best, "being Americans."

Mom was always looking for ways to better feed her family. She grew chicks by hatching them the old-fashioned way under a broody hen. (In later years she would order them through the mail.) She preferred Barred Plymouth Rocks, or dominickers; because the hens laid pretty-well, and the roosters were good for frying. Freezer locker rentals became available long before home freezers became available, and she had learned about such things when she worked at the college. It was the custom to prepare maybe a dozen roosters at the same time and take them to her freezer locker. The kids got to catch the semi-wild chickens and chop their heads off. I did the chopping though it took both hands to handle the axe. They would later get to help pluck the chickens, but mom took over from there. We kids knew better than to try to outsmart these farm reared chickens. When the chickens became confused in the wild action of the process any kid worth his salt could run down a chicken in one hundred yards or less. Emma Mae was too small yet to chase chickens, but she could carry them to the chopping block by the legs and hold them for their heads to be chopped off. She was a little afraid of the axe. When I used it, she did have a tendency to turn loose of the chicken legs before the axe got there. Once she turned loose too quickly and only the beak of the chicken was cut off. Though in no pain it was now running loose again. She was almost in tears, but I told her that we still had chickens to go and we would be sure to catch it again and do the job right. Neither of us would have known what a chicken's beak was back then. Emma Mae rushed about to tell all the chicken chasers to be sure and catch the one with its pecker cut off. What had been a normal barnyard rodeo turned into a riot.

Dogs were usually a part of our life. Early on dad had owned a border collie named Nell. She was very smart. She was a big help to mom. She and her pups would hold to our clothes to keep us from slipping away to grandma's house. They would bark to get mom's attention if we got ourselves into a dangerous situation. We were probably the only children ever reared by a family of dogs. After dad had to do away with them because of an incurable mange, he was never interested in having dogs anymore. Fate, however, often plays a hand. Glenn and Alma Beach lived on the mountain above us. Alma was mom's cousin and she almost adopted our family of children. When she and Glenn moved away to a defense plant during World War II, they left a female rat terrier with three puppies for us to either keep or dispose of. Dad was not yet interested in having a dog, but Emma Mae especially liked one of them and it gradually was to become a part of the family for about eighteen years. Of all things, she called it Junior. At first the boys could hardly tolerate Junior. She would not allow him to go hunting. She said she was afraid we would lose him in a groundhog den. Gradually she overcame this fear and Junior was accepted by all the family.

Junior learned to like to sleep with some of the boys. Our folks did not allow indoor cats or dogs, but we learned that he might slip through the open back door when the first risers began stirring and slip up the stairs to warm up with the late sleepers. He later learned to bump the back door for it sometimes was not latched well and would come open. If he woke anybody downstairs, he would be returned to the out-of-doors. So, he learned to slip quietly up the stairs to avoid waking anyone. This could be scary until you learned to expect it. Once the girls were feeling ambitious and changed the location of the beds around. Junior managed to get the door open and slipped up the stairs in the dark. He paused at the usual place and then leaped high, only to come crashing down where the bed was supposed to be. I was awake at the time, I thought it was very funny. We woke the whole household and Junior had to be put outside again.

The next dogs in our lives were Johnny's beagles. He had started with one female that he named Sputnik. Sputnik was not allowed to have puppies often, but she usually obliged, with six puppies per litter. These happy little hounds helped keep rabbit on the table for several years. The pack was only allowed to die out after our area began to develop. There were household pets about everywhere you took them. I do not know why so many people want huge German Shepherds and large hunting breed dogs for pets. They can make short work of any beagle who dares to chase a rabbit into their territory.

We have a lot of good memories as a family. But there were also some trying times. Dad was sick the summer that there was to be five of us in high school. In Miss Maggie's one room school Elton had been held back a year and Jack made two years in one to join Emma Mae in the third grade. (This allowed the teacher to teach only third grade and drop second and fourth.) Lena and I were three years ahead already and in the same grade. Welfare was not an option though we were probably well-qualified for it. Neither was dropping out of school. The neighbors kept us busy all summer helping in their crops and by the time school started we kids were able to buy our clothes and pay our fees. The high school had long had a practice of accepting homegrown foodstuff in return for lunch fees. We had canned all our surplus snap beans in the community cannery at the school for this purpose. A local grocery run by Farthing Hayes and Boyd Cook delivered those things we had to have on credit. We owed a huge sum, over eight hundred dollars, when dad was able to return to work in the fall. He only worked a few days at a time at first. Each week we got only what groceries we had to have and paid a little on what we owed. They just do not make merchants like Farthing Hayes and Boyd Cook anymore.

Where we lived there was always plenty to do even before the family got to be large. Knowing that "idle minds are the devil's workshop" our parents saw to it that we had chores to do from the time we were small. The first chore I remember having was carrying the household water from the spring. The spring was not too far from the house, but it was down a steep bank. It required both Lena and me to carry any amount of water up the bank in the peck-sized water bucket. The two of us could only manage about a third of the bucket full without spilling it. Needless-to-say, we were a long time making enough trips to furnish us for a day. We watched with dismay as our meager load disappeared into kettles, wash pans and the spare water bucket. Fortunately for us, mom had an outdoor wash place near the spring where she washed if the weather was right. We kids kept the fire going to heat the water and had a good time in general.

Once, soon after Lena and I started carrying water, we had an experience that we still disagree on. Dad had fixed the spring, so the water collected in a large tub. I liked to look over into the tub before we got our water. Once I happened to fall in, but Lena was ready for the occasion. She pulled me out so quickly that I almost missed getting wet. To this day she insists that she saved my life. I still think I would have never fallen in if she had not nudged me.

Lena waited until she was seven to start school so there would be two of us walking to school together. Elton and the others would not be far behind us. We would soon be the largest family in Miss Maggie Moretz's school. The school enrollment would eventually dwindle to thirteen. Seven of these would come from the Greer family. The options for closing the small school were not good. The schools at Boone were severely overcrowded and efforts to meet the needs were not forthcoming until the state forced a response by firing the entire local Board of Education and the locally appointed School Superintendent on July 8, 1955.[1]

Finishing high school in our day was quite an accomplishment. It required a huge family effort. It was especially hard on my parents for Lena and I graduated together. It only got worse, for Elton, Emma Mae and Jack would all graduate in the same class. We never thought of quitting for my parents never gave us any other option.

After graduation in 1951 Lena and I were accepted to Berea College. It was only the beginning of the dispersion of the family. For most of us it began with the military. Elton was first to go into the army. He served in Japan. I followed him after college and served in the reactivated 3rd Armored Division when it moved to Germany. Jack was in the army before I came home. He would serve in a Nike missile unit in Connecticut defending the New York metropolitan area. During the same era Emma Mae served in the Marine Corps where she met and married Elmer Kultgen, a Marine Corp Sergeant. Johnny, the youngest son, was last to serve. He was in the army and served in my old outfit, the 3rd Armored, in Germany. Our parents furnished five of their eight children to serve in the country's military.

### Descendants of Jacob Roscoe and Lois Miller Greer, at this time:

1. Lena Greer was born in Watauga County and lives in Boone, NC. She married (1) Ronnie Boulanger, (2) Glenn Norris.

   Children of Lena Greer and Ronnie Boulanger are:

   (1)  Bruce Boulanger
   (2)  Jimmy Boulanger

2. James Leonard Greer was born in Watauga County and lives in Clayton, NC. At the age of 62 he married Martha Cox Cole.

3. Elton Greer was born in Watauga County and lived in Lenoir, NC. He married Shirley Norris (both now deceased).

Children are:

(1)   Robert Greer
(2)   Elizabeth Ann Greer
(3)   Virginia Gail Greer

4.  Emma Mae Greer was born in Watauga County and lived in Sheboygan, Wisconsin. She married Elmer Kultgen (both now deceased).

Children are:

(1)   Michael Kultgen (deceased)
(2)   Joseph Kultgen
(3)   Teresa Kultgen
(4)   Jeffrey Kultgen
(5)   Dennis Kultgen
(6)   Dorothy Kultgen

5.  Jack Greer was born in Watauga County, NC (now deceased). He lived near Boone, NC. He married Betty Moretz.

Children are:

(1)   Norman Greer
(2)   Nelson Greer
(3)   Stephen Greer

6.  Kenneth Grant Greer was born in Watauga County and lives in Morganton, NC. He married Ethel Canter.

Children are:

(1)  Larry Greer (deceased)
(2)  David Greer
(3)  Dawn Greer

7.  Johnny Roscoe Greer was born in Watauga County and lives in Boone, NC. He married Doris Trivette.

Children are:

(1)  Brenda Greer
(2)  Alan Greer

8.  Patricia Gail Greer was born in Watauga County and lives in Elk Creek, VA. She married David Hayes.

Children are:

(1)  Nancy Hayes
(2)  Nathan Hayes

# 18

---

# Days of My Youth

My formal education began in 1938 at the Howard's Creek Elementary School. It was not quite one-half mile from our house. Older sister Lena and I began school together. She had been held back until age seven so she would not have to walk to school alone. She would be a year behind her age group. Most of the eight of our family would soon be also. The teacher, together with more influential neighbors, decided that first graders would be allowed to miss school in bad weather and would be taught a "primer" for no credit the first year. The reasoning being that we would finish the classes offered before the age of fourteen when we could legally drop out. Our neighbors were certain that their boys would not want to "get above their raising" by going on to school in town. Not much was expected from my family. There would be exceptions to the primer rule. Those first graders living near or having dependable transportation (including some picked up by the teacher on the way to school) were allowed to finish first grade on schedule.

The above situation was to complicate my family's efforts at schooling even further in years to come. Our school became a one teacher school offering one through sixth grades. Emma Mae was in the third grade, when the teacher realized that by combining Elton, Emma Mae, and Jack into third grade she would not have a second or fourth grade to teach that year. It worked fine for Jack, for he was a bright kid and could easily skip a grade, but it complicated things for Elton. He would be ruled too old to play football in his senior year of high school.

School days were hard. Much of the country was said to be recovering from the depression though recovery had not yet reached us. In fact, the new schools, all built in the western part of the county, negatively impacted our school. The new recovery project schools had indoor plumbing and steam heat which could not be allowed to freeze. Our coal stove was taken out and a wood stove put in and parents were expected to furnish the firewood. This presented problems. A parent visited the school and suggested that the teacher write a note to some parents who were suspected of voting for Hoover (now some ten years earlier) that they were expected to provide the firewood. It was getting pretty cold when the matter was resolved but not before there were threats to make Republican children sit farthest from the fire. My dad and others began dropping by the school to see where their children were being seated. Wood cutting became a community project in the end. At a tender age it became my job to build the fires early before school. The teacher paid me five cents a day and it was the first dollar I ever earned.

Fire building at the school could be hard. School could not be called off for weather. There were no phones nor radios to cancel classes. If I was lucky there would be a few coals left from the day before. Mondays following a weekend freeze were hardest. The fire would die out and the building would become terribly cold. The water bucket would freeze solid if not emptied before school let out.

The local school was the center of the community and many in the community fought to keep it even though it no longer best-served the children. Neighbors often stopped by to visit and sympathize with the teacher about the hard times. There was the obligatory "Hoover Bashing" though Hoover had gone out of office before I was born. Once a visitor brought word that a precinct chairperson would be calling the following week for the party donation. The teacher was visibly shaken at the suggested amount expected. She would give but at a lesser rate she said.

My parents were suspected of being Republican though I never learned if they had voted for Hoover. Most likely that had not voted at all. The required poll taxes were probably beyond their means. Grandma Miller did vote. By the 1940 election recovery from the depression still had not reached us. She said that she had helped vote Roosevelt in, but she was ready to help vote him out. Many in our area were disaffected with Roosevelt but he would remain the idol of the party faithful for generations.

Teachers seemed to think that all the poorest children came from Republican families. They were largely correct. They seemed to think also that we would have a great interest in studying about Lincoln. Actually most students shared the same "politically correct" opinions about the Civil War. We never held Lincoln responsible for it. We studied Lincoln's Gettysburg address and forgave him for being on the wrong side during the war. We regretted his assassination for in his second inaugural he had held great promise for the South. "With malice toward none; with charity for all; with firmness in the right, as God gives us to see the right, let us strive on to finish the work we are in; to bind up the nation's wounds; to care for him who has borne the battle, and for his widow and his orphan – to do all which may achieve and cherish a just, and lasting peace, among ourselves, and with all nations."

Miss Maggie Moretz taught lower grades when we were a two-teacher school. Mr. Charlie Hodges taught the older kids, up to seventh grade if I remember right. The small kids were afraid of him because of the big switches he kept at his desk. We later were to find him to be tender hearted despite his gruff ways. He was a good teacher and his students would talk to him as if he were one of their own. In the fall the boys would pester him to leave school early to go home to help cut corn or dig potatoes. I think he really knew what was going on. They had hunted squirrels on the way to school that morning. If he agreed for them to go early, as soon as they left his sight, they would retrieve all kinds of guns from under logs and in hollow trees and resume their hunt.

We were again to have a second teacher; I believe it was when Rich Mountain and Howard's Creek were combined. Her name was Bess Crawford and she was quite a case. She would come over to our classroom to talk to Miss Moretz on occasion. Mrs. Crawford knew that our moms were overworked and that the family washing could be extremely hard on them. A man might do women's work, like cooking in an emergency, but the washing was never an emergency. Unless someone could be hired, the family washing could be put off until the women either got better or died. Miss Crawford had a story on the subject that she wanted to share with us. She related that a passing neighbor once caught Abraham Lincoln doing the family wash. He was good enough to overlook what he took to be an isolated incident. Later, however, the neighbor concluded that it was a regular happening. He asked Lincoln why a man with a young and healthy wife would lower himself to do washing. Lincoln supposedly replied that he "wanted her to stay young and healthy."

After Mrs. Crawford finished the story the students were given some free time to sharpen pencils at the new crank sharpener and otherwise prepare for study. It was my job to clean the blackboard. I overheard Miss Moretz tell Mrs. Crawford that she had never read the "clothes washing" account and she would like to know where it could be found. Mrs. Crawford replied, "I've never read it either, but didn't it make a good story?"

Times were really hard in those days. For a short while there was a surplus food program in the schools. It consisted of fruit and dairy products that were eaten at the school. (Not many parents would ever admit that their children were not well fed.) The program was designed to help farmers more than to feed children. The quality was not good. The condensed milk must have been scorched in the process and the cheese could only be cut by pounding a knife through it with a stick of firewood. There was an abundance of canned grapefruit. We had never heard of grapefruit before. Most kids did not like it. Some parents even had to try it to make sure it was edible. The best of the lot was a limited supply of fresh apples from western orchards, but western raisins were full of seeds.

County support for the small schools was spotty. The new schools in the western part of the county were relatively well off. They had indoor plumbing and steam heat. Best of all there were libraries. Our school was lucky to have a functioning outdoor toilet and rarely had toilet paper. The county might have furnished it, but the people carried it off. In those days respect for public property was lacking and was paid for by everyone, and they felt it was theirs to take,

The county had promised to bring the eastern schools up to those in the west, but it was a long time coming. The war interfered and even afterwards no move was made until a state school bond passed.[1] Things took a turn for the better on July 7, 1955. The NC Board of Education came to Boone and discharged the entire Watauga County Board of Education. They then appointed a new one along with a new county school superintendent. With dedicated local support students from Green Valley and Parkway took their places among the county's best.

A one room school could be good for a basic education for the lower grades were exposed to the lessons done by the higher grades before their time. It was not well-rounded. For whatever the reason, I would always be uncomfortable before a group. My church duties often called for me to teach or lead prayer and it was difficult. I was much more at home with a pencil than behind a speaker's podium.

Practically all the Howard's Creek students came from original settler families. They were Browns, Greenes, Greers, Hodges, Millers, Norris', and Williams. Only the Christians were exceptions so far as I can now remember. (They were "old family" also but they had come, I believe, from Shady Valley, Tennessee. My mother always lamented over the disruption they caused in the tight knit little community when they came. Their large family of girls had made off with all of the most sought-after boyfriends in the community.)

We children understood that kind of thing because we experienced a similar upset in our little group at school. The Rich Mountain School was combined with our school, Howard's Creek. They came from a totally different school environment. Miss Maggie ruled her classroom with an iron fist. She tolerated no nonsense and gave frequent spankings. Though the kids of Rich Mountain were from farther up the creek, they were far more sophisticated than we were. They knew all kinds of ways to have their fun. One favorite way was to promote a fist fight between the smaller kids. When they learned that the Greer kids were quick to fight, they had a lot of fun. Once they told Elton that a much larger boy, Worth Miller, was picking on me during recess. Elton came around the corner of the building and mashed Worth's nose badly before you could blink an eye. I was nowhere around at the time. This even prompted Mrs. Clemmie Miller to pay a visit to our mother. (To her credit, she came only to arrange a truce between our families. That was the kind of lady that she was.)

Miss Maggie's strictness was also hard on the new kids who were not used to it. Her practice was to send a bigger kid to get a hickory switch for hers were frequently wearing out. (She no longer let anyone get their own hickory switch after one of the new kids ringed his with his pocketknife, so it flew apart.) Once she determined to whip one of the new boys who was as big as she was. She was whipping him for failure to complete an assignment for she whipped for poor performance as well as disobedience. She sent another new kid, Bill Ragan, to get the switch. Bill knew that the big kid was not lying when he said that he did not know how to do the work. He brought the smallest switch that he thought he could get away with. It did not work. Miss Maggie sent him to get another one that was larger. The big kid did not stay to take a whipping though. He jumped through the open window and was never heard from again.

Our school days were rough and tumble. It is amazing what good physical condition most kids were in from running, climbing trees and playing games that were not the normal school games. There were not enough of us for team sports, so we improvised. We ran in the woods and climbed trees at play. Most of us stayed in excellent physical condition playing that way. One sport involved climbing a telephone pole placed on the school grounds long before the wire was strung. You climbed up and put your hand on top of the pole. (Some of the girls could have done this but girls did not yet wear jeans.) While the playground grew weeds, the young trees near school were climbed and their tops ridden to the ground. The larger ones required a team effort or else the climber would be left hanging high above the ground and unable to get down by himself.

Not all the fun was outside. I once made a pop gun by pushing the pith out of a piece of elder to form a compression chamber. It would shoot paper wads by use of a hand carved plunger rod. It was not finished during recess and I could not resist the temptation to try it out in class. The bullet caught a fellow classmate across the room squarely in the rear. (I only got us use it that once. The teacher put it in the potbellied stove.)

Lena and I would have the same teacher the first six years. Our brothers and sisters would have three others. The last one before the school was closed was Mrs. Daisy Adams. She was much loved by both students and parents. Our early years with Miss Moretz had grounded us in the basics. She had been strict. (Grant had even been able to get a spanking while visiting before he was old enough to go to school.) In the days before school lunch programs Miss Moretz wanted her students to have a hot lunch. She would cook a rich vegetable soup on top of the potbellied stove. Once she left the lid off while she turned to do something else. A paper airplane came from somewhere, circled the hot stovepipe and made an all points landing in the soup pot. Unfortunately, the paper it was made from had brother Elton's name on it.

Miss Moretz also saw to involving us in religion by reading a Bible chapter each day before classes. Christmas programs and other special events were performed at the local Baptist church which was next door.

In all fairness to Miss Moretz, the harsh discipline she used was only a repeat of the discipline used in the homes of students of that day. She probably did not have much choice in the matter though she may have enjoyed it a little too much. After she left things were to take a drastic turn. Lena and I were already riding the bus to school in Boone, but Elton, Emma Mae, Grant, and Jack were still at Howard's Creek at the time. The new teacher was far more lenient, and the Greer children and others were quick to sense this. They began to take liberties to test the new waters. They soon lost any fear of being late for a few minutes after the bell rang for class. Elton loved to tell this story. All the boys once got too involved at play in a neighbor's field. They had found a farm wagon and were pushing it backwards as far up the hill as their combined strength could get it. They then all piled on and took a wild ride back down the hill. The teacher apparently felt it was time to make a point. She showed up demanding to know if they realized what time it was. She said she had rung the bell twice and they had paid no attention. She was expelling them all. What happened is hilarious if you know the characters involved. Calmer heads began to explain that they had no watches and had failed to hear the bell. All the while Eugene Miller was interjecting "She has expelled us boys let's go home." The teacher was losing ground fast and decided that maybe it would not be necessary to expel them after all. "Go ahead and expel us," pleaded Eugene. He had more interesting things to do. A very compromised teacher ended up almost begging them to return to class.

Compared to elementary school high school was pretty tame. It did provide much better opportunity, however, both for study and play. After playing catchup on studies I made the National Honor Society and was able to play a little football. A teacher who came from Kentucky persuaded me to apply to Berea College where I could work my way through school. I was accepted and after doing all the entrance exams was admitted with no remedial work required. That was not common for most students who came from less than ideal high schools.

High school life for me was very normal except for limited interaction with girls. We had no car nor money and there was no way I could be a decent date. It was not that the girls in the class were not great. I guess I had a crush on most of them except for sister Lena. At that time, we were being taught that early marriages led to large families that could not be properly supported. It was not only a matter of inconvenience but a moral issue as well.

There were pitfalls to be avoided. Many girls of that time lived a dreary life of drudgery at home. A misplaced sense of marital bliss would lead some to take shortcuts. A guy could find himself needing to get married and giving up all other plans. Even worse he might not be the expected child's father if the biological father ended up being a poor or unavailable prospect for marriage. The class girls usually knew all the secrets. Unless they knew the targeted male was the real father, they would tip him off, though the need did not occur often. (This only happened once, that I recall.)

I do not know just when I began to think of going to college. A Miss Alexander, high school civics teacher, was from Kentucky and knew about Berea College. They have a work program that all students participate in and she was sure I would be able to work my way through school. I was not too enthused, because it meant at least four more years of the poverty that I was growing weary of. With the encouragement of Ira Bingham, Margaret Gragg, and others I applied. They were only accepting about one in five applicants but, low and behold, I was one of them.

Leaving home was a bittersweet experience. I had never been anywhere much except for a couple of trips to the state fair at Raleigh. There was nothing at Boone except a small state teacher's college and a kraut factory that was very smelly during fall. Still it was the only home I had ever known. Arriving at Berea meant a long series of proficiency tests for the freshmen. I did quite well and was pleased that I required no remedial work.

About the fifth night there I was invited to the president's home for a reception given to small groups of freshmen by President Francis Hutchens and his family. I had already met many of the students at that time. Almost one third of Berea students were from the mountains of North Carolina. Most of them were from a place I had never heard of called Nearasheville. When I introduced myself to President Hutchins, I made the mistake of telling him I was from Boone rather than Nearasheville. "Ah", he said, "I know the place well, it stinks." Needless-to-say, this was not what a slightly homesick mountain boy wanted to hear. I managed to avoid him for the next four years.

Part of the newness that appealed to me was the opportunity to meet and talk to foreign students. Berea had several students who had lived through the war in Europe. These included a Latvian, an Estonian, a Hungarian and a former Ukrainian. These and other students met on a regular basis to discuss the world situation and foreign affairs. I was invited to attend and expected to join at the end of the program. The evening's subject was the Russian takeover of Eastern Europe and the drastic measures they used to bring those peoples into submission. That communism was totalitarian in nature was generally accepted though we had been allies with the Russians during World War II. Most, but not everyone, were ready to agree with these students who had experienced Russian communism first-hand. When the Latvian told of how the Russians broke down the will to resist in his county with the systematic rape of the women, a faculty art professor stood up and called him a liar. He said, "The Russians have a constitutional democracy superior to anything we know anything about." The foreign students began an agitated discussion, mostly in the German language, and the professor left in a huff. The point is that, regardless of what we may have been told, there was a sizeable group of people in the country coming out of the depression and World War II who greatly admired the Russian system of government. The art professor was nowhere near typical of the Berea faculty and he would go back to California at the end of the year, but he did open the eyes of a green mountain kid. I liked the group but did not join it or any other group of that type.

The McCarthy hearings were still fresh memories and it was disappointing that there were egg heads with political agendas at both ASU and Berea. I even wondered if Berea was really the place for me. I discussed the situation with John Harris, a classmate from Morganton who wanted to be a journalist. John was a character. His version of socialism was that it was only half-assed communism. Together we came to the conclusion that all college faculties probably had a few nuts, but the students were far too sensible than to be taken in.

Like many other Bereans, I would be recruited for summer employment by nationally known packing companies harvesting peas and sweet corn in Illinois and Wisconsin. The pay from Del Monte and Green Giant was not great but the hours were long. When summer's heat rolled in operations could continue around the clock. Berea was tuition free and still is but there were other expenses. Most parents could not help so we sold a bit of our youth to remain in school. I would graduate in June of 1955. By August 3rd I was in the army.

Avoiding military service was not an option in our family. Fort Jackson was hot August 3, 1955 to say the least. We arrived by bus from Charlotte, NC about 2:00 a.m. where we were issued clothing and bedding. Our first training was how to make up a bunk the army way. We were back up by 5:00 a.m. for a long day of haircuts, shots, tests, and more shots. A shot in each arm every day was the norm. In a week most of us would ship by train to Fort Knox, KY for armor training. Our arrival there was ominous. The train halted on a high trestle where we could see military police and their dogs below. They were said to be searching for someone who had gotten away.

Training at Fort Knox was on a crash basis. It was doubly hard on the reconnaissance outfit I was in. We trained hard all winter to become combat ready. Some of us got to go home at Christmas and the rest at New Years. I got five days. (It turned out to be the only leave I ever got while in the service.) I hated to go back when leave was over because of the long, cold hours in the field. We practically lived out of doors. There was never any doubt in my mind that I would go back. My family always had, and I would also.

By the time we finished our stateside training in the spring I had grown to like the army pretty well. We all felt ourselves pretty tough. Before shipping out we had marched in review at the main post at about twenty thousand strong. It was the largest formation of marching troops since World War II. Over a matter of weeks, the division was moved by train to New York City where most of us crossed on three troop ships. As we boarded, we passed under an archway with a sign. "Through these portals pass the best damn soldiers in the world." Our reaction was "So, they finally figured it out, did they?"

Germany was also continuous training with the Recon also operating on the border patrol at times. Winter training was particularly tough at Grafenwöhr. I was pulled out of my tank crew temporarily to act as a machine gunner with our infantry squads. (It seems I always drew guard posts or other assignments that required the use of live ammunition.) It was run, fall into position, set up, and shoot over and over again. If you got time to get your breath in a position you made a range card in case, you were still there at night. It was extremely cold and snowy. We counted ourselves lucky if we could find a bombed-out cellar to shelter in at night. I have since often said that you cannot get really cold in less than three days' time. Up until then you only think you are cold. After the first week or so everyone's eyes become blackened and seem to sink a little further into a person's skull. My bones began to have a continuous ache, something like having the flu and there was a ringing in my ears that would not go away.

I studied my own reactions and the reaction of others to these conditions. The loud talk and highly shined boots no longer counted for much. Some of our designated leadership sort of melted into the crowd. Others, less noticeable before, began to assume the responsibility and no one objected. I was careful to note that

271

a lot of these new leaders were quiet mountain boys and farmers. We had become "winter soldiers." I was proud to be one of them.

When training was over, we still had to convoy our vehicles back to our permanent barracks. (It would take most of two days to get the tanks back.) I was again assigned delayed party to close out our company area. We were to catch our convoy that night at Swinefurt, Germany. We were transported in an open army truck in the below zero cold. It was the most miserable night I have ever spent. It was bearable only because we had been promised that we would be allowed to pitch our sleeping bags in the heated gymnasium the army had there. But we found our outfit bivouacked in the snow outside the fence when we got there about one o'clock in the morning. The only choice was to pitch our sleeping bags in the snow also. By this time, I was long past feeling tough. My feet had been numb for hours. I normally would not let myself go to sleep until I warmed up because I always felt that I could get up and run to warm up if necessary. This time I was just too weary, and I accepted that risk that my body heat was so depleted that I might not thaw out. I went to sleep, but not before a verse came to mind.

> "I have clinched and closed with the naked north.
> I have learned to challenge and to defend.
> Shoulder to shoulder we have fought it out.
> Yet the wild must win in the end."

I had reached my limit. I always knew that everyone else had a limit, but it took a while to get used to the fact that I did also.

About three hours later someone stumbled over my sleeping bag which was covered by the wind-blown snow. The main party had had about six hours sleep, had already had breakfast, and was making one last check of the area before moving out. It was too late for breakfast, but I could rejoin my tank crew if I hurried and I knew where I had hidden a can of beans. I pulled my boots on my

272

still numb feet intending to run on the beaten down roadway until my circulation got going again. Every second or third step I would fall on my face. Very concerned at first, I found that in the dark I had put my boots on the wrong numb feet. After getting them right I was able to run until everything began to feel almost normal. The tank was much warmer than the truck and I completely thawed out while eating my beans. I had hoped no one had found them and that turned out to be the case. Most canned c-rations were full of grease except the beans. The chicken and noodles, beef patties, macaroni, and ground beef, etc. were laced with congealed grease and almost everyone found them hard to handle unless they could be heated. It seems odd now that the beans were a universal favorite.

## More Army Experience

During the early fifties, the situation grew critical in Europe. The Soviets had driven a hard bargain when American troop presence in Europe was limited for the first ten years after the end of World War II. The Russians had used the situation to overrun almost all of Eastern Europe. In the west Italy and France were getting shaky also. England had been bled dry by their war effort, so Germany became our best potential ally in Europe. Nothing was guaranteed even there. The Russians had known better than we that Berlin would always be the sentimental capital of Germany. They had tried to force us out of Berlin by blockade, but this failed due to our airlift. Had the airlift failed Germany had stood a good chance to become a Soviet republic.

The US had honored the ten-year agreement, but it became a different story as soon as it expired. I first became aware of the change that was coming when I met 101st Airborne trainees from Fort Campbell, Kentucky during Christmas of 1954. Their division was going to hold the fort in Germany until a massive build-up could take place. Little had I known at the time that in a little over six months I would be training at Fort Knox as part of the rebuilding of the famed Third Armored Division.

The task of rebuilding a heavy armored division is astronomical. Tanks and artillery pieces cost millions of dollars each and the training makes great demands upon the troops involved. A lot of things were far from being in place when I arrived for training in August of 1955. Good food was even hard for the army to come by on short notice. We ended up eating field rations most of the time. I distinctly recall one of the rare occasions when we had fresh meat. I was on KP at the time. I would have felt better if I could have identified it. The huge slices favored pork, but they were bigger than any pork I had ever seen. Others thought it might have been horse meat. I had helped butcher and cut up most classes of farm livestock except horse. The horse meat advocates could have been right. What really got my attention, however, was the letters stamped on the wooden crates. They said, "condemned as unfit for human consumption by the US Navy." Was it just part of the training? If not, I really hoped it was just good fresh horsemeat. I ate mine and I noticed that the other hungry troopers did also.

Training was on a hectic schedule. We had shots, were issued equipment, and did close order drill for two long, hard weeks. The third week found us in the field training with tanks. I had carried an M1 rifle for only eleven days before going to advanced training. We were on a wartime footing. We were given a choice of a five-day furlough either at Christmas or New Year's provided the division was manned at all times. For most of us it was the only leave we would ever get. We would likely never have accommodated such a pace except that standards were high; nineteen percent of trainees have had college experience.

Army regs will be met. We were near shipping out when someone discovered that these budding tankers had never fired the M1. Almost ten months after arriving at Fort Knox we made it to small arms ranges. Just before leaving for Germany we were given credit for basic training, something the armored infantry in our battalion had already had for months.

The Cold War was my war. I do not mean to belittle the efforts of men involved in the "hot" actions of Korea and Vietnam, but I do believe it important to see the Cold war that began with the Berlin airlift as an action that lasted until the Berlin Wall was torn down.

Budingen, Germany<br>November 11, 1956

Dear Mom and all,

I had two or three letters from home while in the field, but we were moving around too much for me to try to do any writing. I no more than get half-way caught up then we move to the field again it seems.

We got back in from the field yesterday after being out nine days. We had a lot of cold rain but outside of that it was not bad any of the time. It was more of an administrative problem than a regular field problem anyway. They had simulated dead and wounded to be recorded and taken care of just to see if the red tape was functioning right. Toward the end of the problem I was a simulated casualty. They took me over half of Germany to six or seven different field hospitals. Three days after I was supposed to have been wounded, I ended up with a replacement outfit with the 10th Inf. Div. at Weurtzburg about eight miles south of here. We were not doing anything but riding around so I did not mind.

Looks like the election went pretty well. It was two days after the election was over before I could get a paper. We were bivouacked on top of a mountain in Division Reserves and did not do much moving then. Some Germans said Eisenhower had won but I could not be sure for a while. I think most of the Germans are happier that Eisenhower won than the Americans are anyway. They really like the U. S.'s policy on the Suez Canal business. They are a little afraid of a big country that does not always live the by rules. A united Germany would be a better ally than France or England anyway.

Guess we will be in from now until the 1st of Dec. at least. We may not go out in Dec., but I believe that we will go as aggressors for the VIIth Corps when they go out next month. Will have enough to do just cleaning up all our equipment without any more field work for a while.

I know how Jack is feeling about now. If he is not going to have work this winter, it might as well count on his army time. It is a bad time to be getting into the army though. I doubt if things will improve for about two years. If the U. S. gets into a shooting war, I don't think it will be before next spring. Maybe something better will work out before then.

The ones that are in the army when a war starts always have the worst of it. But there's no way of telling when the best time to get in comes along. Jack would have been a lot better off in the National Guard where he could have done six months active duty and the rest of his reserve time. I was lucky enough to miss the Active Reserve Bill by 7 ½ days. It's for him to decide though. I don't think he will like the army, but he will probably have to put up with it sometime.

Tomorrow is a holiday for us, but I have guard as usual. Still have to give my equipment a scrubbing, before guard mount too so I had better close for now.

As ever,
Leonard

Our nation's defense was in a state of flux during the late 1950's. The Congress was now questioning universal military training as it had been begun earlier. There was a struggle between the White House and Congress and the soldier lost. All rank in the service at the time was established by Congress in the military appropriations bill, if and when one passed. New, highly technical outfits would receive no promotions for most of an enlistment period. Private E2 was automatic after basic but there was no other advancement in an outfit unless someone got busted. Privates operated tank squads in Europe with full basic load of live ammunition. It would be hard for me to visualize the situation in Viet Nam where a direct order from an officer was necessary to load a weapon. The Americans were up to it. The 3$^{rd}$ Armored Division was almost twenty percent college educated. It included several of my Berea classmates from spring graduation including a former roommate. It was a highly dedicated outfit.

## Elton Greer

Elton was the first to enter the service. He served with the Army's 1st Calvary in Japan during the Korean War era. (I do not have a picture of him in uniform.)

## Emma Mae and Elmer

Marines Emma Mae Greer and husband to be,
Elmer Kultgen, at Quantico, Virginia.

## Leonard's Service

Leonard served in the 83rd Recon, a unit of the 3rd Armored Division when it was reactivated. And he was posted to Germany in 1956. The Recon was highly mobile and performed a variety of duties, including patrolling the West German border.

## Jack in Uniform

Jack served in one of the early Nike anti-aircraft missile sites in Connecticut defending the East Coast. It must have been a small and very dedicated outfit for they kept in touch and visited each other long after their service.

## Johnny Greer

Johnny served in my old outfit, the 3<sup>rd</sup> Armored Division but with a difference. He served with the Headquarters' Brass and wore a Class A uniform, much of the time. I rarely had an opportunity to wear my Class A's.

## Joe and Clemmie Miller Sons

Shown above are their sons who were in the service:

Left to right:

First row-    Worth, Eugene, and Herbert.

Second row- Glenn, Ralph, and Baxter.

These were furnished by Baxter Miller after he entered the rest home at Blowing Rock, NC. They are the great-grandsons of Confederate veteran Jonathan Miller. A history of military service is common among Jonathan's descendants. Another set of six great-grandsons in World War II were the sons of Ed and Nellie Miller Brown.

Howard Greer
at the Old Wilkes
County Courthouse

Standing next to the
Ben Cleveland Statue

Standing next to
The "Tory Oak"

The Farm Leonard had in Virginia

Leonard Pushing Snow in Deep Gap, North Carolina

# 19

## Work Years and Beyond

There had been plenty of jobs when I went into the army in 1955. They were not plentiful when I got out in 1957. Congress had the goal of building a huge reserve of trained citizen soldiers but did not expect to pay much for it. Rank was limited and there was no more life insurance for any who might lose their lives. Discharged soldiers still had a reserve obligation, but they would get no muster out pay to replace their outgrown civilian clothing nor would they be eligible for unemployment. It was well into the sixties before a Cold War GI Bill was passed. By then it was of little or no benefit to veterans already in their thirties.

My first job after military service was teaching Shop and Agriculture in Mitchell County. I had no teaching certificate and the job was only to last until a qualified teacher became available. I liked the kids, but it was a far cry from military discipline. Mostly I missed being outside for in the service I had been in a reconnaissance unit that practically lived outside in all kinds of weather.

Returning to civilian life is hard for any veteran. It seemed harder for me than for most. I considered for a while to return to the service and about the time I decided against it I was alerted for a call-up during the Cuban Crisis. Fortunately, it was settled before any orders came down. I continued to work at any available outdoor work but mostly in timbering or construction. My spare time was mostly spent outdoors also hunting, fishing or just hiking. At one-time or another, I have stood on top of nearly every mountain in the area.

I was living with my parents when the great snows of the 1959-60 winter. In late winter, the weather fell into a pattern of two snows per week. Each new forecast was for rain, but it came to us as snow. It overwhelmed the highway department and much of the equipment failed or bogged down. There was good reason. At our house there was 44 inches of snow on the ground. There were more other places and maybe less on the south sides of mountains where the rare weak winter sun had more effect. We were concerned but not alarmed. Our biggest fears were emergencies like sickness or fire. We, like most mountain folk, had a lot of food for ourselves and feed for our animals. Miraculously, the power and telephone still worked, but there was no way repairs could be made if they went out. There was plenty of snow to shovel and we cleared our roofs in fear of moderating temperatures adding a lot of rain to our snow load.

I was still outside a lot. It was a strange, eerie time. Everything was completely quiet. Nothing made any noise because everything was shut down. Then one day I, began to notice distant sounds of heavy equipment. There was a clanking of tracks and I did not think it was army tanks. I had not thought the state would allow tracked vehicles on the roads but that must be it. Everything with a bucket or blade was moving snow. It may have started as neighbors helping neighbors, but it went on throughout the night. By about four o'clock the next afternoon a dozer driver pulled by our mailbox with a Waters Brothers' dozer. (We had not had a mail delivery in nearly a month.) He asked about houses on up the road and if the road crossed the mountain. We told him that it did, but it had not been used for years. He said he was going to cross anyway but he was only to move the snow necessary to get the dozer to the Chestnut Grove Community. He had been out two days and was starting his second night. He said he still felt pretty good though. He was expecting a truck to catch up with fuel and a relief driver the next day.

We had some helicopters flying around and we saw a lot of relief work going on television, but most mountain people expected to make it on their own. To insinuate that they could not was asking for a fight. It was told that an isolated elderly lady in Ashe County was visited by the Red Cross to offer her aid. Never guessing their intent, she apologized for not being able to give anything this year. "It has been a bad winter," she said. Watauga County had its own story. Cale Greer had moved to the grassy knob of Rich Mountain. Cale was used to bad winters because he had lived most of his life on Long Hope Creek near Bald Mountain. Cale, however, was old, a veteran of the Spanish American War. What's more, he had a cut on his head with stitches that were due to come out. R. D. Hodges and other volunteers attempted to open the Junaluska Road to bring him in. They failed the first and the second days but were sure they would get there on the third. They were too late, however. Cale had gotten over on the south side where some snow had blown off and the remainder had softened in the sun. He walked several miles into town, had his stitches removed, got a few grocery items and walked back. In his nineties he would live at the "Old Soldiers" home at Johnson City, Tennessee. He is buried at the National Cemetery there.

Politics has long been a part of my family's oral history. This was generally true for everyone else also. Irregularities were about as common as elections but were usually glossed over. Local papers were almost certain to work with the power structure and were easily intimidated. Prominent citizens and church people often saw nothing wrong with stealing an election. No one would speak to the truth of the allegations and they rarely became a matter of public record. Only oral history kept them alive.

This all began to see change when the troops returned from World War II. They were not totally responsible, but the time was right. In Boone an election night fight broke out over an extraordinary number of absentee ballots that changed the election outcome. A county in Tennessee involved firearms and homemade grenades made from dynamite. These events were quickly swept under the rug and are almost never mentioned in historical writings then or now, but they had their effect.

Democrats were ready for change also. The local Democrat primaries were now having problems getting an honest election. A hero in my mind is a local businessman who had a tremendous impact on our area, quietly and without pretention. He comes from a solidly Democrat family and was a natural to replace some of the aging party leaders. He was appointed to the local Board of Elections and there began a fight to bring modern methods and respectability to the local board. His call for scrapping the old "doctored" poll books and calling for a complete re-registration was considered heresy by many. He received a lot of flack from his own people who likely knew better than he that it would be difficult to win an honest election. His point of view would prevail at no little personal cost to him. They had even threatened to blow up his house I have heard. History does not show the fact that a momentous change had occurred. It was due in large part to his heroic stand. To my knowledge he had never had anything to do with politics since. He has been content to operate a business using local products and local labor helping to keep us from being a cash deficit area.

A majority of his party had long been taught electing Republicans was sure disaster locally. Only a Democrat Representative could deal favorably with the State Legislature. (Actually, there was little to show that a local Democrat could be effective either.) Those depending on state funding had best develop support off the mountain. It was a useful campaign tactic, however.

The worst fears of the Democrats were realized when Jimmy Holshouser became the first Republican governor of the century. He was from Boone. I was a member of a group coming from both parties who went to Raleigh for the inauguration. Surprising to many, the State survived a Republican administration. The greatest effect was probably on Republicans. They mellowed considerably just knowing that a majority of the state had been able to agree with them at least once in their lifetimes.

It was a happy, but not euphoric, group that rode the bus to the inauguration. Most Republicans expected the road ahead to be rocky and felt concern for one of their own. To the older folks Jimmy was still a boy who could have been their own son. Few expected wholesale changes immediately and the Democrats were almost certain to rebound. Those who might have expected more than this were missing the point. The significance of the event was that, with the election and the help of the courts, Jim Crow had been mortally wounded. I will never forget that among the passengers on that bus were governor elect Holshouser's real parents. They had chosen to make the trip with their friends and supporters of son Jimmy.

I truly salute these unsung heroes of my time, but the thought occurs to me that I may have drawn the lines a little too tightly concerning the divisions of my childhood. They were not altogether rooted in the Civil War as official history would have us believe. Huge segments of the Republican population did not fit the mold of being on the "other side." The large Miller, Critcher and some Moretz families were from families who fought with great dedication for the Confederacy. Actually, they seemed to have switched during the Cleveland depression of the 1890's.

By the 1960's my work was almost entirely into home construction. I worked for Uncle Roy Greer in his building business for some time but had a small building business of my own by the 1970's. In the meantime, I joined Bethelview Methodist Church. I had never been very excited about the things that seem to excite the Baptists most. When Bethelview decided to build a new sanctuary my experience in building and landscaping helped, I hope. I value highly that experience and any help I might have been to my brothers and sisters who were getting homes of their own.

By the 1980's I had another change of jobs. Inflation had become so bad during the Carter years that building material costs were often for two weeks or even less. It was so unpredictable that I took a job with Watauga County supervising a building maintenance program. I began with a large staff of mostly untrained SETA workers. It was a near impossible situation, but I felt I could do it as well as anyone else they could find. I did seem to have some talent for recognizing problem areas where something could go wrong. Some of my supervisors could not seem to understand that the success of my work was about the things that did not happen. Over the years the quality of staff improved, and I was most proud of the things they could handle within the department.

In the late 1980's I acquired an old farm north of Independence, Virginia. It had been a lifelong ambition. It gave me a reason to get out of town at least on weekends and back outdoors. I was now able to have horses, tractors, and many of the farm things that I had always wanted. My youngest sister Gail, her husband David Hayes and their two children lived on the place. We planted twenty to thirty acres of Christmas trees, but our agreement did not survive until they were marketable. My job called for long hours and was often stressful, but with help I survived the tree business.

The 1990's brought the biggest change to my life of all. As a confirmed bachelor in his sixties, I had long since given up on any thoughts of marriage. Chris Naples (later Chris Hughes) whose office was in the same building as mine, had other ideas. She had a next-door neighbor that she wanted me to meet. She arranged a dinner date for us at Shatley Springs in Ashe County. (She could not have known that my parents had dated there some seventy years before.) I found Marny to be interesting and attractive. It was not love at first sight, but we continued to date.

We also had a significant age difference. I was older by more than ten years. This would naturally be a concern for Marny. She confided to one of her friends. Her friend advised her to go ahead and marry, if she thought I would live for at least five more years. After knowing and finding our love for each other that year, we were married at a church near the farm in Virginia. We honeymooned in upstate New York and in Canada. Afterwards, we began to work-in visits to California for me to meet her people. They were farmers or had farm backgrounds, and I cherish those trips and those experiences.

Marny came with two sons by a previous marriage. John and Jamie Cole became family to me. Both were already living away from home though neither was married yet. John and wife Wendy would later provide us three wonderful grandsons. Jamie and Kim wanted children but do not have any. Marriage has now been a very rewarding experience for us for more than twenty-five years.

After a few years at Marny's Teaberry Hills home, we bought a place that we really liked on Highway 221 near Deep Gap. From here Marny continued to work at ASU, and I commuted to the farm in Virginia. In my spare time I resumed some of my building activities. I built an addition to the Deep Gap house that included a den with a rock fireplace. Next came a two-story garage apartment style building in the back. It was built with a special use in mind and was not the usual interior residential finish. The inside walls and ceilings were handmade white pine wood panels that were a full one inch thick. Brother Johnny and I had sawed them ourselves on his portable band mill at the Virginia farm. These walls had a special purpose in mind.

Marny and I had for years been adding to my collection of antique tools and household items. We frequently toured antique stores, flea markets and garage sales but were very selective in what we bought. The thick walls on the new building allowed mounting space everywhere and we needed most of it.

We had long suspected that Highway 221 would be four-laned as part of a connector to the interstate in Virginia, but we had expected it to take a cow pasture route leaving the developed area along old Highway 221 intact as a quiet country road. DOT had other plans and we lost the Deep Gap house to progress. The barn-style roof on the antique barn must have undermined its value. DOT would only give about one-third residential value even though it was nicely finished inside and passed residential codes.

We felt that there was no comparable area property available for the money we had so we began to look elsewhere. We ended up in Clayton, NC just east of

Raleigh and near the grandkids. To occupy my time, we got a fairly new place that had never been finished on the second floor. It gave us another 1,500 sq. ft. of floor space for overflow company, if we ever had any.

We had no place for the antique tools and contacted the ASU farms nearby about them. They were delighted to have them but would have to store them until a place could be made for them. (They are still in storage, I believe.) They wanted our building but could not figure a way to move it to their property. We were pleased that our house did not have to be destroyed. A neighbor was able to buy it and move it down the road to property that he owned.

These writings are not altogether about me or my life, and I hope to include tool lists and pictures of things from days past, thanks to Marny, of course.

## ICE TOOLS

1. Ice saw and handle
2. Ice spud
3. Ice axe
4. Ice tongs (old forged)

## TOBACCO TOOLS

5. Tobacco basket (small sale sample basket)
6. Tobacco cutter
7. Tobacco spear (forged)
8. Tobacco spear (pressed)
9. Tobacco sticks (hand split oak)

## TIMBER AND WOOD CUTTING TOOLS

10. One man crosscut saw – four feet
11. One man crosscut saw – five feet
12. Two man crosscut saw – five feet with handle
13. Two man crosscut saw – six feet

14. 30-inch cut-off saw

15. 22-inch cut-off saw

16. Mitre saw

17. Handsaw 10-point finish

18. Handsaw 8-point general purpose

19. Handsaw 5 ½ point rip

20. Pruning saw

21. Buck saw

22. Pulp wood saw

23. Dovetail saw

24. Meat saw

25. Large butchering saw

26. Unusual hacksaw

27. Cut off saw tooth setter

28. Small cut off saw tooth setter

29. Cross cut timber saw filer's tool

   -gauge

   -anvil

   -spider (for detecting kinks)

30. Good handsaw filer's set tool

31. Cheap handsaw filer's set tool


## OLD CUTTING-EDGE TOOLS

32. Broad axe with offset handle

33. Foot adze

34. Hand axe (polled)

35. Old Jack plane or smoothing plane

36. Coffin plane

37. Grooming plane

38. Drawknife

39. Drawknife

40. Drawknife (missing handle)

41. a) Half-hatchet

    b) Full hatchet with nail claws (not common)

42. Oversized chisel called a slick

43. Modern day froe

## FIELD CROP RELATED HAND TOOLS

44. Corn planter

45. a) Common four tine pitchfork

    b) Potato digger

46. Hoe

47. a) Small grain stacking fork (2 tines)

    b) Small grain stacking fork (2 tines)

48. Hay stacking fork (3 tines)

49. Mowing scythe

50. Five finger grain cradle

51. Four finger grain cradle

52. Hay saw

53. Hay saw

54. Corn sheller with bin

## WORKSTOCK AND LIVESTOCK RELATED

55. Oxen yoke

56. Nose tongs or "leads"

57. Cow bell

58. Roguish cow yoke

59. Horse collar

60. Horse harness hames

61. a) Horse bridle

    b) Roaching shears (for trimming horse mane)

62. Wooden stirrup

63. Small singletree

64. Metal horse harness hames

65. Logging singletree
66. Logging singletree
67. Header grabs
68. Trail grabs
69. Horseshoes (4)
70. a) Mule shoes (4)
    b) Oxen shoes (one foot)
71. Farrier's rasp
72. Breast chains (for anchoring harnessed horse to wagon tongue)

## OTHER FARM TOOLS

73. Stump puller
74. Barbed wire stretcher
75. Small bark spud
76. Large bark spud
77. 24-inch grinding wheel
78. Screw Jack (Railroad Jack)
79. Cobbler's stand with 4 lasts (a "last" is a shoe size)
80. 6-inch vise with anvil
81. Handsaw filer's vise (adjustable)
82. Fencing tool (pliers)
83. Various blacksmithing tongs (5)
84. Plow wrenches (3)
85. a) Adjustable wrenches
    b) Various steel traps (6)
86. Sears Roebuck pelt stretcher
87. Hand drill
88. Crate breaker
89. Crate breaker (iron)
90. Boring brace (antique)
91. Simple marking gauge
92. Lettered marking gauge

93. Sprit level

94. Tinner's hammer

95. Barrel tap

## PRIMITIVE AND OTHER EARLY STUFF

96. Large knot maul

97. Hand maul

98. Hand maul

99. Homemade corn knife

100. Homemade corn husker

101. Manufactured corn husker

102. Splitting wedge (3)

103. Felling wedge

104. Medium hand auger

105. Small gimlet auger with tang

106. Large gimlet auger

107. Large smoothing rasp or file

108. Small grubbing hoe

109. Large grubbing hoe

110. "Sang" digger's hoe

# 20

## Home Spun Humor

In my youth an outsider might never guess that most mountaineers had a great sense of humor. The face they were likely to see was weather worn and without much expression. Most mountain folks were slow to reveal their thoughts to strangers. In World War II state officials were said to have warned Selective Service examiners that the lack of expression exhibited by potential draftees should not be mistaken for lack of intelligence. The army found this to be true for they found that these quiet, competent men would produce a disproportionate share of the war's heroes.

Central to hill country entertainment was the art of storytelling. As children, we grew up with the traditional stories like the Jack Tales which were collected and published by Richard Chase. The art of such story telling is still being kept alive today as well it should be. Most people would find humor in everyday happenings of the day to be the best. The made-up comedy of modern days was too much like tickling your own ribs to be really funny.

As always, humor was a way of letting off steam. They would laugh at themselves but would not often tolerate being laughed at by strangers. They carried their stories to war and carried new ones back with them when they returned. Auborn Trivett, an employee in the county Maintenance Department, was one of the best storytellers I have heard. He related one story about some inductees from the western part of the county who were having their first army meal. They had been warned not to leave anything on their trays to be wasted. One branch-head boy had an extra slice of bread and he proceeded to load it from the mustard jar. The others watched while he downed it with great difficulty. Finished, he said, "Boys you don't want to eat any of the darned old army peanut butter. The stuff is soured."

Another great storyteller of my time was the widely known Willard Watson. It would not be fair to say that his stories were untrue, and one mountaineer would never accuse another of lying. It was expected, however, that the storyteller would embellish the facts enough to make a good story even better. Willard was a master at this. Willard once helped my Uncle Roy's construction crew roof some chicken houses on Wildcat Road near where he lived. I joined the crew eating lunch and listening to Mr. Watson. He had visited Idaho not too long before. He had liked Idaho and said it was foolish for a young man who like fishing and hunting not to move there. He related a story about a fishing trip to the mouth of a creek on a river. (An obviously good fishing spot.) The fish bit well late that evening and ninety-nine trout were caught that were eighteen inches long and upwards. A young crew member responded "Mr. Watson, I believe that if I were telling that story I would have made it an even one hundred fish." "What" exploded Willard, "tell a lie over one dang fish?" Willard was a favorite of my Uncle Isadore who lived in Maryland. Uncle Isadore occasionally visited him when he came down and sometimes even bought some of the "what-nots" and "whimmy-diddles" that Willard made in his shop.

Another favorite storyteller of my younger days was Jack Norris. He kept fox hounds and was full of hunting tales. Bears had been fairly common in his young days though good packs of bear dogs were no longer common in our particular area. When a bear passed through the village of Boone itself in 1890 it was hard to find dogs that would even chase it far. It had finally been trailed through Meat Camp and killed between Elk Knob and the Bald Mountain. The problem of having bear hounds was somewhat alleviated by a multiuse dog which could also be used for raccoons and even in herding the semi-wild hogs. The Plott Hound was developed especially for these uses down in the Smokies and would eventually become the state dog. Local dogs, however, were more likely to be a mix of cur and hound with maybe the predominant breed of old English black and tan thrown in. Our story is about a man who tried to develop such a pack of dogs which would be good on bear.

The dogs were just overgrown puppies but had already had some experience on the trail. Their owner's brother would lay a scent trail dragging a piece of bear skin far ahead while the owner managed his dogs. The quickest learner had been a small female that showed some of the Blue Tick breed in her background. Next was a large dark-colored brindle dog supposed to be predominantly Plott. Their owner hoped he would be the mainstay of the pack for the female was likely too fragile to mix it up much with a bear. (He called the female the "little gyp" for he respected his dogs too much to use the more common term for a female dog.) Behind the first two came two more that he called "chop" dogs because of the chop chop chop of their barking. The last dog was good sized but not yet aggressive enough. It might never be for it was a little man shy.

By pre-arrangement, the first brother began to lay a scent trail along a nearby ridge top north toward a small mountain valley. From there he was supposed to cross the mountain to the right and back into the watershed where the brothers lived. It had rained a little early that morning and the track should be easy to follow now that it was dark, and the moisture was coming back. Tired from the day's work and his earlier walk the trail layer sat on a log to rest before entering the little valley. He was dreading the steep climb out of it to another branch of the same creek now far below him.

All to soon the dogs stuck on the prepared scent trail. The little gyp was first with her excited squeal "I've found it, found it, found it." The Plott opened with "You're right, you're right, you're right." The bass of the chop dogs joined in "let's go, let's go, let's go." While the man-shy dog only managed "Don't leave me, don't

300

leave me, please." Together they told of the chase in sounds fit to warm the hearts of hound dog men everywhere. The trail-laying brother realized that he did not have enough head start for the kind of chase developing. He headed down hill in a change of plans. A devilish idea was forming in his mind by now.

Down the branch in a glade was a small church where a few of the faithful were holding mid-week prayer services. A few dog men present at the meeting had already marked with pleasure the far-off chase along the ridge while the preacher gave a rather long prayer. The preacher was more than a little disgruntled with the competition, but he had not really heard anything yet. The dogs hesitated only briefly where the trail-layer had rested. They had expected the trail to go up the branch and made a "bobble" temporarily. One of the chop dogs stuck the downhill trail first. "It's here, it's here," he yipped. The little gyp joined in, "You're right, you're right, you're right" and they were off. The leaves on the trees down the easy downhill trail fairly trembled with the sounds of their passing. In the meantime, the trail laying brother had completed his plan. The church was open under its floor and he spent some time there making sure that the scent was good and strong.

The little congregation had grown quiet as what might be the best chase anyone had ever heard approached. They still did not expect, or could have predicted, what happened next. The excited dogs arrived under their church in pure bedlam. Someone held a lantern to see if one old sister was going to faint, which she sometimes did. Not this time though. She was at what was probably going to be the best prayer meeting of her life. It was not the trail-layers intent to keep the dogs there for long though. The reception the young hounds were likely to get could ruin them for life.

A fresh scent trail had been laid at the edge of the church grounds leading a long circle to the southeast and home. Meanwhile the owner of the dogs realized that something was terribly wrong. He frantically blew and blew on his hunters' horn, but it was unheard by the excited dogs. Those church members hearing it through the open windows were undecided by what it all meant. Had not the preacher just been saying something about Gabriel's horn?

It was the man-shy pup that found the track first in the edge of the woods. "This-a-away, this-a-way," he bawled. The little gyp agreed, "You're right, you're right, you're right." The Plott and the chop dogs soon followed in full cry. The man-shy dog sounded a melodic bawl and chop and grew more confident with every jump. He would continue to lead the pack until the very end of the chase and was the first to bark "treed." The owner, on the south ridge now, swung his horn over his shoulder and headed east where he expected to find the bearskin concealed up a tree. That's where it was. He calmed the dogs and took them home, smiling to himself as he anticipated seeing his brother the next day.

The story does not quite end there, however. The preacher was very irate, and the identity of the dog owner was just too good to remain secret for long. The dog owner found himself in court for disturbing the services of a religious institution. The preacher told his story and laid it on thick. His little flock backed him for preachers were sometimes hard to find. The judge listened but wanted to hear from the dog owner before entering judgement. The dog owner was penitent saying that he was sorry and that he realized the church was not a "fitten place for his dogs to be." The judge laughed at this and the dog owner despaired. He need not have worried though. You never know where you will find a hound dog man. Some even become judges.

In recent years valiant efforts have been made to preserve the art of mountain storytelling. It seems to be having some success with several scheduled events. I believe one of the best of these is held at Jonesville, Tennessee. Jonesville is a great place for such things.

Most mountaineers were great lovers of fun-making jokes. My mother's people were no exception. Especially my mother's Uncle Noah. (It was he who made booze on the side. For medicinal purposes of course.) He was not a serious farmer and spent much of his time in the woods for he also loved to hunt and fish.

When a visitor appeared at the house Great Uncle Noah was usually in the woods somewhere. Obligingly, Aunt Jenny would yell for him. If she knew you and thought Noah would want to see you her yell would probably bring him in shortly. If she were suspicious, she could yell all day in a way that he would not come. They understood each other pretty well, but their lives were full of surprises. Aunt Jenny was once attending a daytime revival meeting at a small local church. As usual the church was overflowing, and a crowd listened at the windows. This was good for Uncle Noah if he decided to go because that was a close as he wanted to be. Inside a woman could be heard giving a testimonial and begging for prayers for an errant husband. Uncle Noah drew closer saying "There's a fine Christian woman." A little closer he was heard to say, "Why hell, that's Jenny."

One of the best practical jokes I have ever heard involved the two of them. A woman up the mountain had another child while no longer having the benefit of a husband. Aunt Jenny bribed their two young sons to make a visit to see the baby. She paid them a quarter each and must have hoped to have something to confront Uncle Noah with. He was suspicious, however. He intercepted the boys before they got there and turned them around a half dollar richer. The boys' story was that the new baby had big hands and feet and long legs like her brother, Uncle Jim, a sometimes preacher. She said, "Hush, don't say any more about it. Your Uncle Jim is a mighty fine man."

Noah had about three hundred and seventy-five acres of mostly timberland. He frequently sold small boundaries of timber, just enough to make ends meet. His real love was trading livestock, etc., but didn't bring in much money. He always began a trade by saying, "I don't reckon I would sell that at all." He also loved the excitement of making a little shine but his equipment of out of use most of the time. During the depression, his still worm got gone from where it was hidden. He said he crawled up to several operations before he found the one belonging to him and stole it back.

When Noah had timber sales going on his nephews, my uncles, and my dad, their brother-in-law, often worked the timber regardless of who bought it. Once there was a dispute with a buyer over what was considered "marketable" timber. Noah asked for a court order and took measures to slow the operation down while the matter was being resolved. He would find and hide my Uncle Jake's logging grabs after the day's work was done. Jake would call on his Indian blood and soon tracked the grabs down and returned to work without much loss of time. This went on for several days with neither ever mentioning the fact to the other.

On another occasion dad and one of my uncles were in the process of cutting a long slender tree when great Uncle Noah came up the hill all out of breath. When he got so he could talk, he said, "Where's that tree going to fall?" They pointed out a brush pile down the hill. "Hells fire," he said, "That will fall on my 'trickamado'." They obliged by working over the hill a little ways, until afternoon. With the "trickamado" removed, they then cut the tree.

In later years as other opportunities for amusement developed the occasions for practical jokes were not so plentiful. A faster pace of life meant less time for jokes and stories. The mountaineer still maintained his sense of humor, but his taste had changed. My brother Jack used to tell about a "hippie" who was chased down and dragged before a magistrate on some sort of charge. The judge seemed sympathetic as he observed the lad's disheveled appearance. "Son, I see that you have lost a shoe," he said. "No sir," the young man replied, "I found one." This joke became shorter with a sharper turn around. Jack retained a dry sort of humor throughout his life.

He was just as quick to laugh at himself. Soon after marriage he and wife Betty lived in a house on the Brown property near Boone. Wilson Brown's son Gary had a small pond nearby with maybe two dozen trout in it. Betty had bought some of the first refrigerated biscuits that came into the stores. They were not much good, and Jack decided to see if Gary's trout would eat the dough. They loved it. Unfortunately, as the dough began to rise so and did the trout. With a wry grin Jack would tell about catching those trout and squeezing the dough out of them. All survived except for one or two.

The best stories were still rooted in the day-to-day happenings of a people who continued to know each other well. One man, a good and dedicated hunter, had hiked into a remote area of Elk township to hunt squirrels. He found plenty of them and made several return trips. As was his usual practice, he cut the tails off his game and discarded them. The dogs would not eat the tails and they only added weight to his load. A few days later a man showed up at the barber shop where both were to get haircuts. He had also been squirrel hunting in the remote area. To make conversation he said, "Well I am afraid squirrels are going the same way as the chestnut." "What makes you say that?", asked the first hunter. "Squirrels don't blight." "Some varmint is killing them all," said the second hunter. "How's that?" asked the first. "I don't know what kind of varmint it is," replied the second hunter, "but it eats all the squirrel except the tail."

Early settlers appear to have been sociable and very fun loving. The predominance of fun-loving young people in a society of large families was felt. Scotch conservatism and German practicality had to be met. Dances, for example, had to follow any number of useful activities to be socially acceptable. These could range from gathering of crops, nut gatherings, log rollings and barn building. Once the countryside became more settled, community activities settled down into definable patterns. Building churches, schools and doing roadwork were necessary community activities, but many other activities had parental blessing for the gathering of young people. They included corn shuckings, bean stringings, molasses making and Christmas candy pullings. Sports also became acceptable as long as it was baseball. The community baseball teams were often surprisingly good. An occasional country boy would even make it to the majors.

One of the most popular social activities of my youth was making molasses. Molasses making operated on a fairly tight time schedule. The help of the community was often needed to strip and grind the cane and to boil the juice into molasses. Everyone wanted light, golden molasses suitable to use on pancakes. The cane was ground by passing it between two rollers rotated by a horse or mule walking in a circle while drawing a boom pole acting as a lever. The cane juice drew numerous bees and yellow jackets. I would usually still be going barefoot and would end up stepping on a bee. If the weather turned frosty the next morning, my shoes would not go on when I needed them.

The juice was boiled in a metal vat over a homemade mud and rock wood burning furnace. Two runs a day were about the limit and one of them would come off at night. These night operations were great fun for the young people. They would usually attend school during the day but would tend the last run coming off at night. Some more responsible teens would be trusted to take care of things until the run was close to ready to come off. At that time the tired adults would be called to decide if the juice was sufficiently boiled but not overdone. Taking the vat itself off the fire was an adult responsibility.

It has been often told that on one occasion when young folks were tending the batch something went slightly wrong. A young lady held the lantern lighting a skimming operation when she was unexpectedly touched in an unexpected place by an aspiring beau. She promptly dropped the oil lantern into the molasses. It was retrieved as quickly as possible and cleaned as best as cleaning could be managed. The molasses, however, had a faint kerosene taste that no one could explain.

Religion in the mountains underwent dramatic changes as I was growing up (or possibly much of the change was in me.) As very small children we remained unchurched but were still influenced by religion. Our mother's background was a curious mix from the Lutherans, Methodists, and Baptists while dad's background was predominantly Baptist if any. Early religion of the older children, however,

306

was something they developed on their own as our parents did not interfere in the process.

One of the institutions we had been exposed to was funerals. The Miller Family Cemetery was on a knoll above our house and a second funeral service usually was held there before placing a body in the ground. After our great-grandmother "Granny Marthy" died, we began to re-enact funerals. Lena elected herself to direct these services. She remembered all the details and got a pretty good service out of us except for singing. We had no radio and TV had not yet been invented. Dad occasionally sang for us and we only rarely heard the mournful singing of funerals. Elton and I did not want to sing. Hardly more than a toddler, Emma Mae was her usual enthusiastic and cooperative self. The best we could manage though, was sort of a wordless chant. Elton and I did not participate for long. There was a real danger mom would hear and think that we were mistreating our younger sister. The funerals continued, however. We developed an animal cemetery. In it we buried a pet pig that had died, a pretty fox dad had killed and numerous chipmunks and squashed toads. We drew the line on allowing a snake to be buried in our cemetery. Other animals were given an appropriate burial and the graves decorated with wildflowers in season, dogwood, azaleas, daisies, and Queen Anne's Lace.

Another religious institution observed was baptism with immersion in a pond built in the stream for that purpose. We baptized the girl's rubber dolls and all the animals we could catch. Chickens and puppies were easy, but the cats were destined to become Methodist. Somehow, we did not feel the job completed on these difficult animals. I still had some question in my mind when I became Methodist many years later. The church would have immersed me if I had wanted, but I had to find out for myself. I could not have been "more baptized. I have always been glad that I chose to be sprinkled.

Church baptismal services in Howard's Creek were always well attended. They usually took all afternoon beginning from 1:00 p.m. to 4:00 p.m. Baptized candidates would be admitted into the church at a church service about 4:00 p.m. There were large numbers of teenagers in the community then. The Baptists had borrowed a few pages from the Methodist book. Teams of counselors were sent among the teens in the audiences to bring a little pressure to bear. I always dreaded that part of the service myself. Baptists had not always been that way locally but now, with a few shouting Methodists present, they could have as good a meeting as anybody.

One baptismal service was particularly memorable. About sixteen young people were being baptized including some of my mother's brothers and sisters. Some of these branch head boys were wild and unpredictable. Few had ever been in water over their knees. One of them hung back and chanced to see a snake swimming across the upper end of the pool. He refused the preacher's invitation to come into the water. When the preacher insisted, he said "No sir, there's a blankety-blank snake in there." Needless-to-say, this did not fit the Baptist ideas on instant sainthood. A deacon's committee was convened in the shade of a nearby tree. A little later they announced that the young man had made the obligatory apology to the church and wanted to be baptized.

Not all mountain stories were intended to be taken as truth. Some were only for entertainment. The intelligent and knowledgeable would always know the difference and, in the meantime, the mountaineer would make his life and the lives of others more enjoyable. Our neighbor, Mr. Jack Norris, could make a hunting tale last for hours. You heard every yelp, bawl, and chop of the dogs as he slowly drew every morsel of the hunt into his story. After the evening chores were done, we boys would often gather at his house to hear him talk.

The ladies also had their stories to tell at quiltings, etc. These winter events were scheduled whenever possible so the young males could be out of the house. (The adult males would not be caught dead at such a function anyway.) Some ladies were invited more for their ability to tell a story than their ability to sew a fine stitch. Evidently, I reached an age of understanding before they became suspicious. Their gossip usually started out with stories of miscarriages and premature babies. Several claimed to have been born very small. One would claim to have been so small that her head would fit inside a teacup. The inevitable question would follow, "And did you live?" The answer was always, "They say I did and did right well." The meeting would get too serious if someone reported a scandalous happening such as a woman running away from her husband and family. To liven things up and change a subject someone would usually tell of fingers beginning to cramp with the sewing. This was a signal for one lady to tell about her fingers cramping on the bail of the milk bucket. To hear her tell it, it was several days before they relaxed enough to turn the bucket loose. She had slept with a milk bucket in the meantime.

There was a lot of fun and no harm in such activities. As I said before, the intelligent and knowledgeable would always know the difference between a serious tale and one that was best not taken seriously. With distant acquaintances and outsiders, one could never be sure. Looking for a news article a reporter was said to have come into the Mountain City area after Eisenhower was elected in 1952. Knowing it to be a strongly Republican area which had not elected a president for a long time, the reporter felt sure of a story. He approached an elderly man and asked what he thought when Eisenhower was elected. The man replied with a question, "was he?" "Yes, haven't you heard?" "Well I did hear something on the radio but it's just a cheap radio and I didn't know whether to believe it or not."

Even better was the story of two local boys who attended the Saturday afternoon westerns when they came to Boone. In one scene a sheriff's posse chased an outlaw who rode under a tree and was swept off his saddle. As the outlaw approached the tree one boy bet the other a quarter that the outlaw would be knocked from his horse. The loser offered to pay but his money was refused. The winner admitted that he had seen the movie before. The loser said, "I have too but I thought the dang fool would know better this time."

Mountain folk had a healthy suspicion of new things that they did not at first understand. When hand-held calculators came out young people adapted to them and trusted them. Older people would use them but would check the calculation long-hand to make sure the contraption was working right.

In the days before commercial entertainment many stories survived generation after generation. Jack Tales and other folklore was often repeated before bedtime. The stories and their language were said to be Elizabethan of centuries before. It may have been so but with a Scottish twist. The Lowland Scots spoke English but never would be content to be second-class Englishmen. It showed in some surprising places. A popular flower grown then was called "Sweet William." The Scots oftentimes called it "Stinking Billy."

# 21

## Religion-Race-Politics

There can be little doubt that a predominance of Colonial settlers had religious freedom high on their lists of things to be desired. Separation of church and state was their idea of how to achieve this as many had suffered under a state church. The Scots were the most vocal. They had a burning hatred of anything Episcopalian. As British subjects they were forced to pay taxes to the official Anglican church even in America. Scottish religion was much more than loyalty to the Presbyterian Church. In America it became a common culture that influenced most Protestant denominations. (Except maybe for the Lutherans and Episcopalians.) It set a style of emotional worship that really transcended denomination in the south and has been called "Southern Church." Robert Burns wrote of the dramatic flair of the Scottish evangelical preachers in:

"The Holy Fair"[1]

"Hear how he clears the points o' faith
Wi' rattin' an' thumping'
Now meekly calm now wild in wrath
His stampin an he's jumping."

Scots Presbyterians would often fail to keep pace with frontier worship with an organized church. Not surprisingly the Baptists would often adapt their preaching style within widely varying degrees. Will Rogers once said, "I am not of an organized religion, I am a Baptist." Author and Appalachian State University professor, Howard Dorgan, sorts them out best in his book, *The Old Regular Baptists of Central Appalachia*.

Both my paternal and maternal ancestors were among the first members of Three Forks Baptist Church. It was the first and only church on the upper New River for many years. Both ancestors were eventually removed from the church roll. Benjamin Greer for attending the horse races at Sycamore Shoals and "drinking to excess" without making satisfaction. (Apologizing to the church. Drinking must have been tolerated except when done to excess.) William Miller was more likely removed for lack of attendance. He found his property below the mountain on Lewis Fork Creek more hospitable, especially in winter. Three Forks Church became the mother church of many area Baptist churches. It drew worshipers form miles around inspite of primitive conditions. The log church was not heated and in winter breaks were called so worshipers could warm at outside bonfires.

Religion in the mountains underwent dramatic changes as I was growing up (or possibly much of the change was in me.) As very small children we remained unchurched but were still influenced by religion. Our mother's background was a curious mix from the Lutherans, Methodists, and Baptists while dad's background was predominantly Baptist. Early religion of the older children, however, was something they were allowed to develop on their own. Early exposure was mostly Baptist.

"Once in grace, always in grace" was not always a solid principle of the Baptist Church in our area until the 1930's. An area preacher named Dan Graham is credited with promoting the idea. It was well taken, for large successful revival meetings were held in the area. They ran for as long as they had any success, sometimes for two weeks. Some small churches baptized twenty to forty people at a time.

Graham was ahead of his time in one thing. He was much against the use of tobacco. He said it would kill you. Dad's friend pointed to him and said, "It killed this man's grandpa." Graham said, "See there, tobacco killed this man's grandpa." Dad said, "Yes, but it took 102 years to do it."

Prior to this era mom's Aunt Matt Hodges would attend the local revival much to everyone's delight. Mom said that when Aunt Matt shoved over her old black pocketbook, she was getting ready to shout. Aunt Matt had the practice of spending at least one night with every young family in the community. When she came to our house the lamp had to be cleaned and placed on the Bible table for Aunt Matt must read from the Bible before going to bed. She did not come empty handed. She brought her own brand of coffee and a jar of strawberry preserves.

My first Sunday School teacher was also Methodist until someone decided it was not proper. I thought they should have given the news to her privately, and not as she walked in with her class materials. They met her before the whole congregation to tell her that her services would no longer be needed.

Aunt Frances, a sister to Aunt Matt, probably had the most to do with my attraction to the Methodist Church. She remained Methodist though the family had moved some six or seven miles away from her beloved Hopewell Church. She would walk those miles to church if the weather was promising. She sometimes stopped at our house to invite the children to go along. There would have been nothing wrong with us going except that we did not think we could keep up. She wore long skirts all her life but had a long stride. It seemed that she could hardly wait to get there. She had a great outlook on life and was optimistic through depression, war, or any other difficult time. Her favorite quotation was "All things worketh to the good for them who love the Lord."

Aunt Frances' religious principles were never compromised. They governed everything for her. Her brother Coy once came to give her a ride to vote. She said, "I have to walk to church and I'll not ride to vote." She was seen later in the day walking to the polls.

The Baptist Church sometimes acted unchristian it seemed to me. I suppose other churches do too. In fairness, however, I must say that no other church has made as much progress in the last 50 years. It, I, or both of us have changed a lot during that time.

My family inherited great religious diversity. "Granny Marthy" was born Lutheran and no amount of persuasion ever changed her. Her children were both Methodist and Baptist. Aunt Frances, a devout Methodist, put it this way. "Brother so and so was immersed, sister so and so was sprinkled, the thief on the cross had no water of any kind that we know anything about, but" she said, "I have confidence in all of them." She was a great old lady and I found myself more and more drawn to her beloved Methodist Church. Some of the things which excited the Baptists so much I just could not find to be important. Years later when asked to explain I would say "I was born Baptist, but it did not take."

Methodists were said to be more tolerant and less set in their ways. Part Indian, the bear hunter Wilburn Waters, was a well-accepted Methodist lay preacher. This was less likely to have been accepted in most Baptist churches. But the message was the same. I offer one of his widely quoted sermons for example. The word seems always to come through regardless of denomination or version of the Bible.

I would like to give you an account of Wilburn Waters' experience at a camp meeting which took place in Ashe County, North Carolina. In 1858 or '59 the Holston Conference held its annual session in Abington, Virginia. The friends of Wilburn Waters, knowing that he had never been in such a gathering as this, influenced him to go along with them to the meeting. He came and attended the sessions regularly and punctually. He was at the preaching every day and night. Bishop Early, who presided over the deliberation of the body, became acquainted with him, and was also very much interested in him. One evening the Bishop asked Wilburn what he thought of the ministrations and other exercises of the services of the sessions.

"Well Bishop", he said, "I will answer your question by giving you a bit of history of my own religious experience. About three years ago I heard of a camp meeting in Ashe County, North Carolina, some twenty-five miles from my cabin, and on Friday night, I made up my mind to go. I fixed up my plunder, greased my boots, and started in that direction very early one Saturday morning. On the way I passed a store and as the hat I had on was rather shabby, I concluded to stop in and buy a new one, as much to honor the Lord as to look more respectable myself. I bought one that suited me, paid pretty high for it, and put it on, and left the old one and my gun at the store till I returned.

I arrived at the campground early in the afternoon. When I arrived, a preacher was in the stand preaching a cold and spiritless sermon and I quietly took a seat as near the altar as I could get, putting my new hat under my seat for safety. Just as I was about to raise my heart in prayer, I heard someone's feet shuffle under my seat and I moved my hat and laid it on the ground beside my seat for I knew that my new hat was in danger.

This cut my prayer short, and I moved my hat and sat it on the ground beside me and went to praying again, but just then a man behind me spurted amber all around it, and I began to think that it would be ruined if I did not put it on my head, which I could not well do in a congregation. The preacher preached on, but that hat was on my mind and in my way. When I would try to be

315

devotional something would whisper, 'You had better take care of that hat!' The meeting was over, and sunset came, someone suggested that since the Lord had not blessed the meeting that they should go out into the grove to pray. We went – I with my new hat in my hand fearful all the time that I would get my hat mashed in the crowd or injured in some way. We prayed, sang and prayed, but our prayers did not seem to rise higher than our heads and our songs higher than the treetops.

At last a good old father of Israel said, 'There must be an Arian in the camps, the Lord refused to bless us, and we might as well return to our tents.'

I stood musing a few minutes, not knowing what to do, with my hat still in my hand, when I heard a man utter a deep and bitter groan. Looking around, I saw that all had left except that man and myself, and he seemed to be in great agony. I asked him what was the matter? When he replied, he said that he was a great sinner, and he did not believe that the Lord would pardon him.

'Yes, he will', said I! 'If you will call upon him as you should with your whole heart and soul.' He said he had prayed, but it did not seem to do any good, and asked me if I would pray for him. I told him, 'Yes, bless God, I would.' I laid my hat carefully away in a clump of bushes where I thought nothing would get to it, and I went to prayer, and with my might, soul and spirit. How long I prayed I don't know, but when I came to myself the stars were all out, the whole congregation had returned, and the despairing man was shouting and praising the Lord. All the believers were happy and clapping their hands with joy, and for the first time after the man asked me to pray for him, I thought of my new hat. Looking for the clump of bushes, the people had trodden down and a black spot in the dust was my new hat.

And now Bishop, there is more to this story. There are too many new hats in this conference."

Wilburn Waters was a Methodist in his religious faith and was a devout Christian gentleman. He was born in 1812 and died in 1879. He was also an uncle to my Great Grandmother Lula Waters Greer, and I will give that more space later.

Extremes in churches are to be found in churches most anywhere you look. I recall the death of the only Catholic I ever heard of in our early community. Our church would agree to have the funeral if the body were left outside the church. (Someone said this was the way Catholics did Protestant funerals.) My favorite though concerned an event at an Obid's church in Ashe county. A man of good standing had built a nice brick home after long years of hard work and saving. He was "turned out" of the church because the Bible said, "A rich man cannot enter heaven", or so they believed.

To me the organized churches all had their extremes. In my younger years I attended several on different occasions and was not impressed with any. In my forties I began to feel drawn to the faith of my Methodist elders. I joined Bethelview United Church determined not to be discouraged by human failures, even my own. I was never disappointed. There could have been extremes there, but they were never made part of any worship. Neither was there any pressure to be a judge of anyone or any group. This church family is a rewarding aspect of my life.

Church activities became an important part of my life. Not because I was the best available but because I often seemed to be the only one available. My years of teaching Sunday School were hard for me for I always remained somewhat backward and never really enjoyed being before a group. My greater pleasure was when the church added a new sanctuary. That was more my kind of work. I was pleased that when we had to move away, qualified people took over the work.

When I met Marny, my wife-to-be, we were fortunate to agree on churches. She had been brought up Episcopal but had become Methodist in her teens. I was much pleased when she became active in our Bethelview Church. She remains active in our Christ Community Church today.

I have always felt that any valid religion had to affect a person's values and actions. It is soon apparent that this is not universally believed or practiced. I accept that, for the Lord did not see fit to put me in charge of those things.

# Race

My association with black people was rather limited during my childhood. Nevertheless, that limited contact was traumatic and would influence the way I thought about issues of race for all my life. I cannot honestly say that I was a crusader for equal rights, but I do say that my experience was unique and some different from my peers.

During the 1930-40's era there was a prison camp near Boone that housed convicts. It was for blacks only for the prison system in the state was segregated, as was everything else at the time. These convicts were doing "hard time" and were worked on the county's dirt roads. They were hauled out to work in the back of a covered truck that towed the guard trailer with its armed guards behind. One of the two guards went to the local church so the community would know when to expect the work gang in the area.

The work gang used an area near my grandmother's mailbox to assemble. A mule drawn grader would make a few trips over the immediate road ahead until the desired results were achieved. It was up to the road gang to do the finish work. They trimmed the right-of-way, opened drainage ditches, and beat up the rock jerked loose by the grader. Jobs were assigned according to how well the individual prisoner was felt to be trusted. Right-of-way trimmers worked to the sides of the road and were given axes and other sharp tools. The rest worked in the roadway itself and used shovels and rock hammers. Of this group maybe two or three would be chained to heavy iron balls. When one of these completed his area, he would ask permission to move up. The boss guard would instruct him to pick up his ball and chain and move up the middle to the road until told to drop it. It was awkward to have more than a couple in chains. Any others considered to be dangerous would wear targets on their backs. Reputations would be established by experience and not by sentence for some relatively good people could end up on the chain gang. A few were so trusted that they were called "trustees." They were allowed to visit neighboring farmhouses to fill the water bucket and maybe to buy eggs, milk and the like to supplement their meals. I do now know what the prison sent out for midday dinner, but I guessed it would rely heavily on cornbread and beans. (If a prisoner was confined to solitary, he would get only cornbread and water.)

My uncle would take me with him to visit the worksite. He was friends with the chief guard. The trusted prisoners were allowed to sell a few items to the locals to raise money to buy food or for some other need. They had handmade belts, wallets, cheap rings, and a tobacco allotment. My uncle preferred the chewing tobacco that they sold.

The locals loved to hear the work gangs sing as they worked. The gangs could not be ordered to sing and would not if they found it demeaning. They were more likely to sing on some lonely stretch of road away from any houses or maybe if a storm were brewing.

> Steal a-way, steal a-way home
> I ain't got long to stay here.
> My Lord calls me.

He calls me by the thunder.
The trumpet sounds within my soul.
Ain't got long to stay here.

Needless-to-say, as a child I found these things hard to understand. Later in life, I would find that it was only a part of a larger something that felt altogether wrong. In *Appalachia – A History*, John Alexander Williams describes in detail the use of convict labor to build railroad tunnels and various other hazardous jobs. Convicts were part of contracts in numbers hard to deliver. Persons with only minor offenses or even innocent persons, were frequently sentenced. Living conditions provided by the contractors usually were poor and the work too dangerous for local hire.

The churches of my youth were segregated also, only rarely were any church functions combined. One exception, at our local church, was a songfest by black singers from their church in town. It was new for them also, and they had no means of travel. Arrangements were made to bring them out on a couple of farm trucks. The music was memorable, but so were the preparations. Most people favored the visit, but the opposition was loud, as you might expect. The congregation voted in favor with conditions. The visiting choir was all the program, but some of the choir ladies were opposed to having the visitors sit in the choir section. This was solved by using a similar seating area across the room known as the "amen corner." ("Proper" procedures had to be followed.)

The visiting choir drew a good crowd that wanted to hear, "Go Down Moses," but the visitors were reluctant.

They did a universal favorite first instead.

Swing low sweet chariot
Coming for to carry me home.
I looked over Jordan and what did I see

A band of angels coming after me.
Coming for to carry me home.

Another one that they liked was:

O Mary don't you weep don't you mourn.
O Mary don't you weep don't you mourn.
Pharaoh's army got drowned.
O Mary don't you weep.

And finally, after some others:

Go down Moses
Way down in Egypt's land.
Tell Old Pharaoh
Let my people go.

## Politics

These few contacts had a lasting impression on my life. I don't claim to have been an ardent desegregationist, and I was nearing middle-age before I could feel good about any church. Things changed and so had I. Toward the end of World War II, I mentioned to a neighbor lady that it hurt to see black soldiers in their country's uniform being forced to go to the back of a bus. She said that, "They are no better to fight than my boys." I did not pursue the subject further, but the war had a lot to do with change. Returning veterans no longer felt the same about fraudulent elections and the power structure that had written so much of North Carolina's history. It was now losing favor. Sometimes it took violence, but elections finally were largely cleaned up. It even involved the use of dynamite at Athens, Tennessee. Glenn Beck's *Miracles and Massacres*, "Actions by Veterans Brought Change."[2] The "Great Generation" kept on being great.

Race had finally become a religious issue. Actually, color had become a religious issue for Ashe and other counties had also discriminated against Indians. So were poor whites, though they did not always recognize it.

The 1950's saw the country struggling with integration laws. (President Eisenhower probably never received full credit for his actions to enforce law and order.)

Berea College resumed integrated studies peacefully at the time after repeal of the Day Law. It happened during my first year at Berea. It was never a problem to me or anyone else that I knew of. (The Day Law had stopped Berea's mixed-race classes for decades.)

To me there has never been any way to separate race and religion. I was well-aware that many of my neighbors saw it differently. How I never quite understood, but then I have never felt appointed to be their judge. They were still good people and kind neighbors for the most part.

I do not know if race was a factor when the state discharged the entire Watauga Board of Education, July 7, 1955. Hardy indicates that it was for poorly qualified teachers, crumbling buildings and deteriorating conditions that were not being dealt with. My own experience confirmed this.

Things were changing statewide also. Luther Hodges became governor. State money would no longer be kept free of interest in big banks that were political friends. Neither would the party "shake down" of state employees for campaign funds, at least not openly. Locally the one lane farm-to-market roads built during Kerr Scott would be widened for two-way traffic. Democrats were not universally happy with their governor. Some referred to him as a "Republican in Democrat clothing." I believe he was one of the best governors of the century, but his legacy was not outstanding. It was still hard to go against the traditional power structure and receive public acclaim. The media in those days did little to oppose the power structure. Newspaper early files often do not reveal an accurate picture of things as they really were. (Hodges deserves much credit for the beginning of the Research Triangle.)

In my opinion, there is no way to separate race, religion, and politics, but many seem to find it easy. As of yet, there seems no end in sight. In this day candidates seem to select a party affiliation that offers the best chance of election. Practices and principals often remain very much "old school" in some quarters regardless of political affiliation. Unfortunately, the real hard core still think fraudulent voting practices are a God-given right.

It would be fair to say that my early views of race, religion and politics were distorted to say the least. The traditional views on race have seen wholesale changes for most people in my time. This has been good but can be overdone. A fair and balanced democracy would not provide advantages for anyone. Religion has also undergone more change than most church people would admit. The church structures of my youth were very limited in scope and not much different in beliefs from one denomination to the next. Many prominent denominations of today were unknown not too many years ago. One of my dad's favorite stories was about a traveling preacher who found himself in a rural area of Watauga County. He inquired of a woman he saw if there were any Episcopalians in the area. She replied that she did not rightly know but her husband and the dogs had caught something while hunting a few nights before. "It's hide is tacked on the barn wall if you want to take a look at it." I cannot help but think that today's diversity has been good for it is a great thing when a person finds a church where he can really fit and serve.

Politics during my early years were definitely one-sided, due to the Depression. The political "spin" promoted misconceptions that went all the way back to the Civil War. One was that Republicans were a poor and lower class of people. This had never been quite true. The other was that Republicans were disloyal to the state and the country. Actually, many local families had made great sacrifices for the South. By the 1890's the Millers, the Critchers, the Blairs, some of the Moretz's and many others were dependent upon the economy for they were that day's middle class. Their status and well-being were severely tested during President Cleveland's Depression of the 1890's and they desperately wanted change, even if it meant becoming Republican. A story Grandma Greer told reveals the depth of that feeling. Her grandfather, Andrew Yonce, was seen going at a fast walk on election morning. When asked why he hurried, he replied, "I'm off to the polls to show my true colors. No more Cleveland soup kitchens for me." And he smacked his right fist into his left palm for emphasis. Such events never became a part of our history. By the time I was in high school it would still have been sacrilege to admit that the South had ever done anything wrong. Republicans were not true and loyal Southerners and must have "Yankee" backgrounds. It is still popular today to associate counties such as Wilkes, Avery and even Mitchell with the North. I am sure that they did have Union sympathies, but I would not bet that history is that accurate. Our elders did not always think so.

It would be hard to give any of the churches of my childhood a good grade on race relations. Mostly they all sprang from a Scottish religious culture that grew up wild on the frontier. Religion in the area was best described as "Southern Church" regardless of denomination. Some denominations, the Methodist and Baptist in particular, split into Northern and Southern factions during the Civil War but the split was about which government was to be preferred rather than on race. The Methodist Church that I joined was made up of the two divisions that came together in the 1950's. The church that they became, I thought, had a good attitude on racial issues. I cannot say that there was no prejudice, but I can say it was never a part of any church service of my time. Progress has often come in unexpected ways during my early years it was not uncommon to hear Republicans referred to as "Black Republicans", though the party had officially become a "White Man's Party" some years earlier. This had been a necessity more than choice. Democrat election laws and coercion at the polls had all but eliminated a Black electorate. The only chance for Republican growth was to attract disgruntled Democrats. This eventually worked well for the Republicans but was not without problems. It has been hard at times to make Lincoln Republicans out of former Democrats. Perhaps the biggest effect was on the remaining Democrats. It soon became apparent that they could no longer win elections, except by attracting a large Black vote. This they did inspite of the fact that earlier they gave us slavery, rebellion, and Jim Crow.

# 22

---

# Lost Institutions

## The County Post Office

Every community once had its own post office. The volume of mail did not require a lot of them, but the methods of delivery did. Mail was delivered either by foot or on horseback. By my time the local mail was delivered by car but there was still evidence of delivery by mule. Some mailboxes were still high enough to be reached from the saddle and some of these bore battle scars. The postman, a man by the name of Houck, delivered the mail astride a mule. To signal the mule that it was time to move on Mr. Houck wore one spur on his right boot. The mule associated being spurred with the mailbox and would sometimes try to kick it off its post. Over the years the mailboxes would be gradually lowered as the mail carriers' cars would be lower, but a few mailboxes still bore signs of an earlier time.

Stories were told for years of Mr. Houck and other mail carriers who had to be helped to break the ice off their clothes before they could get out of the saddle. Carriers who later used cars would also build huge reputations for themselves. One of the most notable would become a legend in our area. Her name was Miss Addie (Clawson). She was as dependable as any male.

It was often hard to name a new post office. The "Maggie" (Maggie Valley, NC) post office was said to have been the third choice, name of a store owner who wanted a post office. His daughter was surprised to have a post office named for her. Locally, a committee labored unsuccessfully into the night to name their new post office. They finally agreed to use the next word spoken for the name. Everyone sat quietly until late into the night. Finally, a sleepy committee member yawned loudly saying "Aho." Aho became the name of a little post office on the Blue Ridge.

The postal system soon tired of so many small post offices. They began a long struggle to eliminate them wherever politics would permit. People were proud of and defensive of their post offices. It is said that the postmaster of the Triplett post office in Watauga County became incapacitated or died. When the postal inspector learned of this, maybe weeks later, he came to check on things. He flew into a tizzy when he found postal fees, stamps, etc. on a table in the back of the store. There people had bought stamps and made change. He laboriously counted stamps, money, etc. and reconstructed a record. All the time he was rubbing the storekeeper the wrong way with his constant complaints about the situation and the neighborhood in general. Finally, he expressed amazement that everything balanced with a penny or two. The disgruntled storekeeper replied, "People around here may not know much but, by God, they're honest."

## Watauga County Community Post Offices in 1896

| | | |
|---|---|---|
| Yuma (Deep Gap) | Valle Crucis | Silverstone |
| Stoney fork | St. Jude | Sugar Grove |
| Triplett | Harmon | Vilas |
| Penley | Beech Creek | Deck Hill |
| Aho | Leander | Boone |
| Deerfield | Hattie | Rutherwood |
| Blowing Rock | Sweetwater | Sands |

| | | |
|---|---|---|
| Green Park | Reese | Yerger |
| Kelsey | Zionville | Norris |
| Grandfather | Mabel | Moretz |
| Foscoe | Greer | Soda Hill |
| Banner Elk | Tracy | Meat Camp |
| Dark Ridge | Mast | Todd |
| Watauga Falls | Amantha | Breakside |
| Bamboo | Matney | |

## Ashe County Community Post Offices in 1896

| | | |
|---|---|---|
| Gap Creek | Wagoner | Ash |
| Idlewild | Transou | Garnet |
| Obids | Laurel Springs | Clifton |
| Nettle Knob | Creston | Grimsley |
| Riverside | Fig | Idol |
| Baldwin | Graybeal | Algier |
| Beavercreek | Grigsby | Blevins |
| Southerland | Grayson | Southside |
| Trout | Thaxton | Nathan |
| Todd | Pinkston | Crumpler |
| Scottsville | Jefferson | New River |
| Wheeler | Linney | Silas Creek |
| Lansing | Apple Grove | Bud Eye |
| Stergills | Helton | |
| Hermitage | Robert | |

## The Country Store

The church was a social institution that was rivaled only by the country store. There the various denominations, and even the few unchurched, came together as a community. There you would learn the news both foreign and domestic. Local gossip was always a hot item as customers took time to sit around the potbelly stove or to whittle while they kept an eye on their teams out front. These country stores were not only a source of staples not produced on the farm, they were a stopping place on the way to the mill, to work or even fishing.

They offered many goodies also. A father would often buy ten cents worth of candy from one of the candy barrels, especially if the children had been sick. Here you could get a Nehi Orange or a Moon Pie. (The first soda I ever had was a Royal Crown, "RC" Cola at the school picnic. I had been advised that it was larger, and it was. Unfortunately for today's kids neither RC nor Moon Pies are available today.) Not everything was as it seemed, however. Andy Griffith would later write that he was almost old enough to vote before he knew that you could drink a Seven-Up without slipping around to the back to do it.

Most country stores would deal in furs, roots and herbs, eggs, and butter at least, since most of their patrons were cash poor. The furs, roots and herbs were usually sold to buyers who traveled from store to store while butter and eggs were traded locally. Every county seat would have one or more small hotels and some with permanent residents. Most had an overflow crowd on court week. Stores that prospered would add a line of dry goods. It was here that the locals would first learn of manufactured clothing.

## Water Powered Mills

The grist mill was once at the very heart of the early community. Old land entries often mentioned the presence of a mill seat on a property. This would have been a place on a stream where a dam might be built that would provide water to turn a water wheel. The state had long recognized the need for a grist mill convenient to every community. By 1715 the provincial government had offered a fifty-acre grant free of taxes to anyone who would file on a mill seat and build there. A mill keeper would also be exempt from militia service.

A mill had to be custom designed to fit the locale and meet the needs of the community. No two were ever alike. Like old barns, old mills have a lot of character. In their day they likely influenced other developments, the first of which would be roads. Chances are that a blacksmith shop and country store would be somewhere nearby. (In extreme cases these things would go if the mill closed. The mill on lower Howard's Creek closed, for example. Even road maintenance was discontinued.) If business warranted it the water wheel or turbine might also mill lumber and card wool. Wool cleaning was a messy chore that the early families were glad to get out of the home.

The mill was normally the men's domain. They chewed, whittled, and talked politics and horse trades while waiting on their corn meal or feed to be ground. This probably went back to an even earlier day when distilleries were common and legal. What better place to run a still than from a place where a toll of grain was realized? Few ever complained even if they had to wait awhile. Each expected to wait his turn. In fact, a bag of corn to make the family meal became known as a "turn."

Most mills have now fallen into ruin or washed away by floods. Oddly, more seem to have survived off the mountain. It could be that more of those in the mountains washed away. There is now a Society for the Preservation of Old Mills. It would be a shame to lose any more of them. Meadows Mill in Wilkesboro made, and still may make, the mill stones used to grind corn. At least in 1990 they were said to be the only manufacturer of mill stones on the North American continent.

My folks were likely to patronize the Crit Norris mill about two miles down the creek. It had roller mills for flour as well as stones for grinding corn meal. They even milled their own brand of buckwheat flour. It was available in their own brand name bags. Horses and wagons often had to wait hours for their turn at grinding. Sometimes they would be there much of the night and would be fed the evening meal by the Norris'. It was a great spot for visiting and learning the news. The first time I was there I went with my Uncle Jake Miller. It was early spring and we were very interested in the suckers trying to run upstream to spawn. Earl Norris, who was later to become my brother Elton's father-in-law, was later to tell about growing up there. He said he became a good judge of human character. It was as simple as observing the condition of the horses and mules driven to mill. If a man's horses were poorly fed or mistreated, the man himself could not be trusted.

This mill figured big in the life of the community. Children too young to work or who were not well were often sent to mill. The large volumes of bread people consumed required frequent trips. Once after my mother moved in with the Hardins as a young girl, she was asked to ride a farm horse to mill. She did not mind because she had long been used to horses and mules and it was only about a mile. The line was long, and the horse grew impatient for its feed long before her meal was ready. Someone tied her bag of meal and the horse was off in a run. He had a hard mouth and there was little she could do but hold on for dear life. The horse got even faster as it neared the barn, but she held on until it stopped at its stall and snorted for its grain to be put into its feed trough.

The most distressed I ever saw mom was when dad went to the mill some years later. He too had a long waiting line and his wagonload of grain was still not ready at dark and a tremendous thunderstorm was in progress. Mom paced the floor without ceasing because no one could tell how a young team of horses would react to a storm. Dad too was getting uneasy for the creek was beginning to rise. He finally figured a way to keep some, much needed corn meal dry and started home. He never told what that ride was like in front of the kids, but we knew our parents were very glad to see each other.

The Winebarger Mill is one of the few mills still existing from the scores which once straddled the headwaters of the New River. These mills were an essential part of every community, but few now have survived mountain floods or have been replaced by store bought meals, flours, and breads.

## Tanneries

In the days before rubber and plastic, leather was one of the most useful products known to man. It enabled him to have shoes, harness for his horses and belts for his machinery. It was especially vital during wartime. The country was still very dependent upon hides in World War I. Green hides brought the unheard-of price of fifty cents per pound. They brought good money also in World War II and even after.

Many small tanning operations existed in the early settlements. There was said to be one at Boone for years. As a youngster I sometime fished the tan-trough hole at the Tom Watson place on New River. The tan-trough name had come from the wooden troughs used to process hides long before anyone still living could remember. Early on, the troughs were logs that had been chopped out with an axe or a foot adze. Lime or wood ashes were used to take off the hair. After that, the hide was scraped free of flesh and placed in a trough of water laced with crushed bark of chestnut or oak to tan.

Eighteen ninety-five saw the beginnings of a huge corporate tannery at North Wilkesboro. After much research in the area, C. C. Smoots and Sons of Maryland began a tannery operation on the Reddies River in North Wilkesboro. By 1904 it was credited with being the largest in the south. It worked as many as two hundred hands. It consumed a lot of chestnut, oak, and hemlock bark in the process. Farmers peeled the logs to be used for fencing, firewood, and a multitude of other uses in the spring while the sap was up. (Among my antique tools is an old bark spud used for this purpose.) At the tannery farmers would be paid in a rare commodity, cash. From one hundred to three hundred wagons a day loaded with bark would deliver their loads in the "bark season."

Smoots and Sons was sold out in 1925 to International Shoe Company. Business continued as usual for about five years. The great chestnut blight wiped out the source of chestnut bark. Fortunately, they were able to convert to grinding chestnut wood from the millions of now dead chestnut trees. Millions of cords of dead chestnut wood went into "extract" wood in my younger years. The International Shoe Company did a great business until the 1940 flood. Then their private power source on the Reddies was washed out. They did resume processing the extract wood for another five years but did no tanning. After the wartime demand was over, they closed in 1945. I believe a plant in Galax, Virginia still bought the chestnut wood for a few years longer, but an era of our history drew to a close.

## The Railroads

The era from 1910 to 1920 was one of the most promising in history for the nation's farmers. The year 1914 would be used as "parity" to base farm price supports on for decades. This prosperity was slow in reaching the mountains, however. Tennessee had authorized a railroad from Johnson City to Cranberry, NC. I suppose the iron works there were still operating. This road opened in 1881. Its narrow-gauge tracks would eventually reach Boone about 1918. Even then the big interest was area timber. Boone was only a spur. The real action was in the removal of timber by a line back of Howard's Knob reaching all the way to Rich Mountain. The railroad hauled logs to a big band mill on the upper Watauga River. The village of Boone was envious. Someday Boone might be as big as Shull's Mills. (The Watauga Democrat carefully avoided giving Shull's Mills any publicity.)

The railroad had reached Shull's Mills about 1916. Difficulties with rights-of-way kept it out of Boone for two more years. Shull's Mills had boomed in the meantime. By August of 1917 it had a depot, mercantile, feed and grain store, a hospital, doctors office, two large boarding houses and a hotel. Over one thousand people worked and serviced the mill operation. But the good times would last just shy of ten years. I have found no estimate of the lumber produced but it had to have been many millions of board feet. The Whiting Lumber Company began moving its operations to Tennessee in 1925. From there it eventually went to Kentucky where the logging train was again used to extract timber

After the timber was gone the railroad struggled to stay in business. There was not much going on in the area yet. But the area was very dependent on the railroad. Ashe and Watauga had long been called the "lost provinces." (Enough volunteers went to Johnson City in the Spanish American War and World War I to help Tennessee become the Volunteer State.) But now they had grown even closer to East Tennessee. Johnson City was a source of goods and had doctors for serious ailments which could not be treated locally. But too much track was lost in the 1940 flood to ever repair it fit to resume service. The locals had many fond memories of outings to Johnson City. They would sorely miss the sound of the engine's whistles until the Robbins brothers returned Tweetsie to Blowing Rock. Stories about Tweetsie once abounded. One involved my Grandfather Miller. It reveals his sentimentality. The Bryant family across the mountain was noted for pretty girls who tended to marry young. One of them, with her beau, came by grandpa's one day on their way to Boone. They were eloping. Shortly after, a distraught father came by looking for them. Grandpa talked him into taking a rest and delayed him in every way he could devise. By the time the father got to Boone, the couple was aboard Tweetsie well on their way to Johnson City, Tennessee to be married.

Ashe County was blessed with a standard gauge railroad. Its first leg was built to the Damascus, Virginia area in hopes at the iron ore there would turn into a big business. (Damascus was named because of the name association with Damascus steel.) The tracks were extended from Abingdon to Damascus in 1900. It had followed the same trail that Daniel Boone had used on his first trips to Kentucky. It began to extend along the same trail toward White Top, Virginia in 1906. Construction in stages would follow timber operations for it too was largely a lumber train in the beginning. No other enterprise would have been profitable enough in itself to pay for track laying in the mountainous area. Terrain was so difficult and trains so slow that the Virginia Carolina letters on the rolling stock were becoming known as the "Virginia Creeper" railroad. Lumbering operations at White Top, Virginia in the 1920's caused a boom there as they had at Shull's Mills. White Top once had a population of about 500 with a police force, a mayor, and a justice of the peace.

The railroad reached the present site of West Jefferson in 1914. It had missed the county seat by two miles. Real estate interests were already in place and a new town began to take shape. Hard feelings between the towns existed in some quarters for years to come. From West Jefferson the tracks were pushed on to Fleetwood and to Elkland by May of 1915. (It created a lot of excitement in Watauga County for many fully expected it to come on to Boone and put the narrow gauge out of business. They might have saved their breath. Only a spur was built up Gap Creek to take out lumber and that was the closest it ever got to Boone.)

For eighteen years the Virginia Creeper made its way to Elkland (now Todd, NC) to take out timber and to supply what had become a center of commerce. (Todd grew fast and rivaled Boone, but it was not resented quite as badly as the upstart, Shull's Mills.) The Creeper was a friendly train. It could be stopped anywhere along its tracks. Some children even used it as a school bus. It also increased ties to Virginia and Tennessee only this time the source of wholesale goods was Bristol, Virginia rather than Johnson City, Tennessee. Ailments that were untreatable before could now often receive attention. (Irene Morphew related that Cecil Miller rode the Creeper from Riverside on the South Fork to Baltimore, Maryland to have an appendix removed.) But boom times were not to last. The tracks from West Jefferson to Todd were dropped in 1933. Much maneuvering was required to keep the train coming to West Jefferson until 1977. The railroad then ended in the high country.

Just recently there was a move to convert the old tracks to the Virginia line into hiking trails. Virginia had already successfully done this with many of its old railway lines. The arguments were long and bitter and the measure in Ashe County finally failed. It was sad that it did. I would have enjoyed walking the White Top along the railroad grade that my grandfather had helped to maintain in his youth. Boone has its Greenway. Wilkesboro is developing some flood plain areas into parks and walking tails. They are such a blessing. Somehow, they make an area seem far more civilized.

There is little left of either railroad but memories. One would think that every man who grew up in Ashe county had at some time helped grease the tracks to stall the Creeper. (The engineers had soon learned where they had to speed up to coast over the greased tracks. Boyhood was all too short, and these boys would soon move on to bigger things.) Today thousands of children and a few oldsters know what it is like to ride Tweetsie once more. Today West Jefferson and Ashe County have a thriving artist colony. Their favorite subjects seem to be the Creeper, the old depot, and the New River.

## Mail Order Catalogs

The advent of convenient local post offices ushered the country into a new era of merchandising. Mail order houses like Sears, Spiegel's and Montgomery Ward became some of the biggest businesses in the country. The coming of a new catalog created more excitement than the arrival of a super Wal-Mart does today. The mail order houses introduced many new products and made them available on a huge scale. The women's clothing and household linen section would be in front. The men's clothing section would follow because the women were also charged with clothing the men and boys. The farm section in back was simply amazing. You could order honeybees or day-old chicks, fence wire or horse harness, pocketknives or guns, kerosene lanterns or Delco plants, all kinds of tools or farm wagons. You could even order a car from Sears.

The mail order houses would not only change our economy, they would change our whole society by introducing new products and even new ways of seeing things. Early on young boys were instructed not to be looking at the front part of the catalog where scantily clad models displayed woman's under-garments. They had better stick to pocketknives, pocket watches and steel traps. In time all would become less modest. A new catalog would come every year if you were a customer and the old one would be used in the outhouse. The story was often told of a lady who attempted to order a new product called toilet paper without a catalog. She received a letter concerning her order. She was instructed that a catalog number was needed to assure that she would get the product that she wanted. It was said that she wrote them back that if she had a catalog, she would not need the toilet paper. In my family not all the catalog went to the outhouse. My old maid aunts would carefully divide the mysterious front section with women's clothes and put it on a high shelf at the back door where the ladies would carry it with them out back. We boys carefully never let on that we might have been short changed.

## The Family Lamp

In the days before electricity every family had to have at least one kerosene lamp. Its normal location was in the living room, but it could be moved to the kitchen for cooking and the dining area for eating. If the family prospered a second lamp or a lantern would stay in the kitchen. A lamp could cause a serious fire if dropped and broken. The head of household would move it to the dining room table when the meal was ready. Meals were usually eaten in silence, but talk was in order when they were over. The lamp would have to remain in the kitchen until the table was cleared and the dishes washed for next day.

We got electric service a little before Christmas in 1940. The house had been wired for months and the lines strung but the actual hook-up was done on a cold December night. Every room had a single twenty-five-watt light bulb. We could not believe so much light for it took five lamps to equal one bulb. The electrician said you will probably want bigger bulbs later. Mom said, "No, we will never need more light than this."

## Dinner for the Preacher

Most established families expected to have the preacher for dinner (lunch) at least once a year. It was an extended family effort that began taking shape days before the actual event. Smaller boys would begin special efforts to swat all the flies. Flies were a huge, huge problem then and if they could be killed on the outside porches so much the better. Some were sure to get inside though and had to be minded away from the food. Newspapers were attached to a rod and the pages cut into a fringe to frighten the flies away from the food. Sometimes tree branches with leaves on them were used. Usually the girls drew the chore of minding the flies.

Not everyone would get to eat at the preacher's table. Children would eat at a second setting hoping (usually in vain) that the preacher would not be long winded. By the time the limited supply of dishes and silverware were washed and reset, any surviving food was apt to be cold. Children did not look forward to preacher's dinner.

## Pocketknives

A pocketknife was once considered essential to a boy's normal development. If delayed too long, he was sure to be labeled a sissy. It was also a necessity to trim a pencil at school. The county did not see fit to provide us with a pencil sharpener until about fourth grade. A wall mounted crank sharpener greatly improved the process. It was such a novelty that pencils did not last near so long. For a while it became necessary to show the teacher a dull pencil before you got to use the trimmer.

Having a pocketknife was a symbol of responsibility. That responsibility had limitations. School property belonged to no one individual and therefore it belonged to nobody. Every desk seemed to need someone's name carved on it. This was also true of the trees around the building. Every tree was carved. Some of them with a boy's name and that of his favorite girl.

Early on a boy with a pocketknife could arm himself with a homemade sling shot or a bow. As an adult the experience of using his hands would be beneficial. When hiring carpenters Uncle Roy Greer would often say that a man who knew how to use a pocketknife was worth more than a man with a lot of tools that he did not know how to use.

## The Slingshot

One of the best incentives to having a good pocketknife was the slingshot. Boys usually made their own and a new and improved version was usually under way. Time spent in the woods oftentimes involved keeping an eye out for the perfect slingshot fork. The homemade product was not expected to be extremely accurate but was a lot of fun to shoot.

Target selection was a part of growing up and being responsible. Sisters were not to be targets even with soft ammunition. Neither were family chickens, dogs, or cats. Snakes and ground squirrels were considered pests and called for a round and accurate pebble. It was hard to get the water snakes any other way. Brother Elton and I had great fun with another target. Hornets, black jackets, and yellow jackets liked to build under an overhanging bank of the nearby roadway. We hid in the bushes on the opposite bank and shot at their nests. The bees would swarm into the roadway but seemed to never figure out where we were. It did not enter our minds that this might be a problem for we never walked that section of the road. Our neighbor did. He would have to get out at night to burn the damaged nests so he could use the road the next day.

# The Hound Dog

The hound dog as an institution may be fully understood only by hound dog men; but this dog was once firmly entrenched in the family lifestyle. He was part of nearly every household and let everyone know if company had arrived. One could track the progress of the mailman or every peddler by the different barking of the dogs at every farmstead. He might be a mountain cur, a Black and Tan, a Walker, a Redbone, a Bluetick, a Plott or a mix of any of the above but hound was the common denominator. For untold generations, the hound had been bred for the chase. At the signs of an impending hunt he was beside himself with joy. He might have laid around almost half asleep for days but now he could almost turn cartwheels. It was more than a master gathering hunting gear for he and master seemed to share an unspoken excitement for the hunt.

By the 1900's the hunt meant fox hunting for the deer were long gone and the bear was almost extinct in the area. Raccoon hunting awaited the introduction of a prolific Florida stock. Hunting of the fox was not riding to the hounds. The mountains did not permit that kind of hunt. Neither did it call for the catching of the fox. The hunters could often identify a particular fox by its territory on the game trails that it ran. To take one of their favorites could be a fighting offense and was at least once in my memory.

The hunting party would meet at a prearranged spot on top of a ridge that afforded good hearing in all directions. There they gathered firewood and built a fire while waiting for the dogs to strike a warm trail. When the fox was jumped the trail became "hot" or was sometimes said to be "sweet." Dogs and men alike became excited. Every man's dog bark was recognized by its owner and probably by the others also. A running account of what was happening dominated the conversation. If the chase led to the far side of a mountain it might not be audible for a while, but the fox would usually return to its home territory if the trail was not lost. Sometimes individual dogs did become lost or were too footsore to return that night, but lost dogs would almost always find their way back to the campsite. There he would find that his owner would have left some recognizable article such as a hunting coat. He would curl up on it and wait however long it took for his owner to return.

By my time, the old hunters and their hounds were fading into the past. The hound of choice had now become a beagle and the hunt was for rabbits. The beagle was a happy little hound with a great personality, and he had just as good a voice on the trail as his larger cousins. Unfortunately, his time was also limited as the countryside developed. The smaller the property the bigger the house dog and the little hounds did not have much chance.

The racoon population exploded after Florida coons were released. Just down the road from the Virginia farmhouse was a favorite spot for coon hunters to release their dogs. Usually the dogs were retrieved at the end of the hunt but not always. Once a young dog with no collar identification stayed there faithfully for over a week waiting for someone to pick him up. Occasionally he would give a long "lost dog" bark. (Almost all dogs had a "lost dog" bark to aid in their recovery.) This dog would not respond to strangers. I hope the rightful owner got him. His dog still had a lot to teach him.

## The Bookmobile

Our little mountain community with its one teacher school was almost lost in the wilderness of isolation and the Depression. The new WPA schools in the western parts of the county were relatively well off for they had steam heat and indoor plumbing. We were lucky to have a functioning outdoor toilet and it never was furnished with toilet paper. More importantly the new schools also had libraries. Someone at the county level came up with a partial solution. Surprisingly, the idea was funded, and the county bookmobile was born. The bookmobile was a van-type vehicle with double doors in the back that opened to expose revolving shelves. It was much like the modern-day peddler's car except that the shelves were loaded with books from the county library. The driver was a local lady named Mary Cook Brown. She came to the school maybe twice a month so the students could check out books. In the summer she was not limited to the school. She would show up anywhere it was convenient for a few children to gather. She knew her patrons. To most she would say, "I have a book I know you will want to read."

## Hitching Rails and Upping Blocks

The most common mode of travel in the mountain community was by foot. Trails and footpaths were often quicker and avoided the mixture of mud and horse manure of the public roads. In those days crossing over neighboring lands was accepted and expected. The public roads were also used for walking and were necessary for horses and oxen. Travel by surrey, buggy or covered wagon kept passengers out of the mud and provided some shelter for sun and rain.

The farm work horses would find off-farm use to go to the store, the mill or to church. Much of the first two was done by children who were too young for the heavier farm work. Most children could ride before they were big enough to mount a horse by themselves. Mounting for girls and women would be a problem at any age because they did not wear slacks and rode sidesaddle. Most public facilities, including churches, made accommodations for the horses and riders. A hitching rail was often provided but was not universally used. Some horses were anti-social and some wee too sociable. Many owners preferred to find a place in

342

the shade that afforded their horses some privacy. Surprisingly, the hitch rail still survives at a few churches that provide for Sunday horseback riders. The one that I know of is the United Methodist Church at Grassy Creek in Ashe County, NC. The "upping block" seems to have gone out with the sidesaddle. It was a large block of wood that children, ladies and the infirm mounted so they could get into the saddle.

## Home Weaving

The better-established settlers would usually provide for weaving flax and wool into cloth to clothe the family. This was nothing new to many emigrants for they had been weavers in the old countries. It was different in that the weavers were now women of the household rather than the men. These women not only provided for their own, but often produced cloth for a local market.

My Miller ancestors provided weaving facilities elaborate for their time. The loom room was in an adjoining building with lots of windows, and its own heating stove. Great-aunt Frances once said that she wove 105 yards of cloth there one winter. Such work brought in good money or goods from many of the larger country stores, but the market only lasted a few decades.

Weavers often sang as they worked. For most it was probably hymns. But those in a hurry, a faster tune probably came over from the old countries. Its' music perfectly fitted the rhythm of the loom.

> Half a pound of tuppenny rice.
> Half a pound of teacle.
> That's the way the money goes.
> Pop goes the weasel.

Every night when I go out
The weasel's on the table.
Take a stick and knock it off.
Pop goes the weasel.

These were only two of perhaps dozens of such verses. We still sang Pop Goes the Weasel in elementary school. We neither read nor understood the lyrics we sang. In our version a real monkey chased a real weasel.

# 23

---

# Mountain Ways and Speech

One of the most significant changes that I have noted in my lifetime is in the way people talk. Talking and the telling of a good story is almost a lost art. Even a good story now has lost much of its character. Once there was much more variety and character to the highly individualistic ways of talking. When I was a young boy many area people brought saws and other tools to my dad to be sharpened. They came from diverse and somewhat isolated homes and had their own ways of talking. A few even used a lot of hand motions but not often. They were more reserved than today. They loved fun and jokes but did not show it much. Loud or raucous behavior was considered disrespectful and somewhat stupid. Today's comedy would likely seem too foolish to them to be funny. At best it would be like tickling your own ribs.

Traditional mountain speech had many words and expressions that might not be understood today. Some individuals I remember used such different speech that it was notable even then. One character named Richard used "whar", "thar", etc. so much that he was known as "Thot ar Dick." Many others had individualistic expressions that made their speech unique. One was Great-Uncle Cornelius Woodring. He began most sentences with a long, drawn-out "By the Gracious." My Uncle Calvin Miller had come back from the west and bought Grandma Miller one of the first TV sets in the community. Local preachers were preaching that the things were evil and had no place in the home. A curious neighbor asked

Uncle Calvin if this were not true. True to his devilish nature, Uncle Calvin had replied "Yes, it's true. Mine has naked women on it." A few days later we passed by where Uncle Cornelius was sitting on the front porch of his daughter's home. He said, "They say that Calvin Miller has one of them new television sets and that it has naked women on it." The only answer was "Yes, I've heard that too." At this, Uncle Cornelius gave out a long drawn out "Well, by the Gracious." We were true to our upbringing. We did not laugh until we got out of sight.

Everything now seems to be molded by TV and other institutions into a very common mold. In my childhood days individuals were so different as to be very interesting. Aunt Frances Miller was a good example. Her limited travel and the span of her years made her different, but she also had a lot of interesting local history. She used words and expressions that seemed odd even then. She would say "hayo" instead of hello. "How you come on?" came next. (It was obligatory to say, "How are you?" in some form or fashion.) The usual reply was expected to be "common" or "just common." If a person felt well this covered the subject without boasting about good health which could often be temporary. People who understood the old ways of talking were getting scarce, even back then. Once a classmate, Bill Ragan, and some of his friends rode bicycles some distance from home only to stop and rest at Aunt Frances' gate. "Hayo" she said, and "How you come on?" Bill, being consumed with the excitement of a new bike, replied "On a bicycle."

We were fortunate to be exposed to Aunt Frances in our formative years. In her peculiar way she taught us much about our heritage and about religion. Her speech was slow as was nearly everyone's then. Speech patterns today are more standard. Old ears now often have problems understanding young people and the TV that taught them for they are now so fast.

A little Scots blood goes a long way I have always said. Ten generations after the first settlement we still have a lot of Scots-Irish in the way we talk. At least those of my generation do. Those who grew up in front of television sets may not talk the same way. Some would say that these children were educated by TV. Some would, but I would not. In my day if you did not know the difference between a gill, a pinch, or a smidgen you could not speak the language. People who remember the old ways of saying things are becoming rare, but dictionaries for mountain speech are now common though not always accurate.

A few words commonly used and universally understood in our area were:

abide – meaning to put up with or endure
afeared – scared or apprehensive
ailing – sick
aim to – intend
airish – windy
ary – to have one or any
ballhoot – to free slide down a bank or mountainside
biggety – conceited
blackberry winter – unseasonable cool spell in spring
blow-down – trees uprooted by the wind
boundary – track of land or timber
branch – small stream
brickley – brittle
burying – funeral
chuffy – short and stout
contrary – opposed to
coon – to climb
cow brute – a large cow or bull
dotey – senile
eats good – tastes good
falling weather – rain or snow
favor – resembles, looks like
fetch – bring
feisty – impudent

fitten – suitable

fleshy – overweight

follow – practice a trade or profession

frail – to beat or flog

fur piece – long distance

guam – smear or mess

get shet of – dispose of

gip – female dog

give out – tire beyond continuing

granny woman – midwife

gum – beehive or container

hear-tell – to hear of

hick – an ignorant person often overly impressed with other cultures

hickory – a switch used for discipline

hippins – diapers

hog wild – riotous

holp – to help

jag – small amount

juberous – dubious

jumper jacket – a denim jacket

lamp oil – kerosene

lap of a tree – the top or branches

leather britches – dried snap beans

let on – pretend

light out – leave in a hurry

make out like – pretend

mast – tree nuts, acorns, etc.

mess – a lot of

nary – none or not any

nigh – near

outlandish – overstated

pay no mind – ignore

peart – well and lively

point blank – direct and to the point

play pretty – a toy used for child's play

plumb – very or completely

plunder – goods or household effects

poke – a paper bag

pone – a cake of bread

poorly – not well

prong – a branch or fork

puny – indisposed or not well

right smart amount – a goodly number

ruction – a fight or riot

sallet – cooked greens

scandalous – extreme or exceedingly

scooch – to slide nearer to a companion

scouting – hiding in the woods to avoid the law

shucky beans – beans dried in the hull for winter

sich – such

smidgen – small amount – at our house less than a pinch

sorry – poor or worthless

spell – a period of time

still – a device for making spirits

stockbrute – a bull kept for breeding purposes

stout – strong or well

swag – low spot in the ground or saddle in a ridge

tacky – shabby or out of style

tetched – feeble minded or mentally impaired

tetchous – irritable

time about – alternating

tote – carry

tree – cause to take refuge in a tree

up and done – acted immediately

way off – far or remote from here

wear out – to flog or whip

wider woman – a widow

woods colt – illegitimate child

work brittle – industrious

worn out – tired or exhausted

yourn – yours

Placed back in my Grandmother Miller's living room the average child of today probably would have problems understanding the conversation. It was not because people talked fast like they do today, however. Unbelievably slow drawls were common in those days.

Mountain folks were generally very modest and mannerly. Few of them were heard to curse and at most would use a mild expletive such as "dadgum it" or "dadblamed." Even polite words were sometimes believed to be too rough for mixed company. A man would not use the word "bull" in front of a lady. This could be a problem when the family milk cow needed to visit a neighbor's bull and the owner was away from home. The phrase "gentleman cow" was used instead. It could also present a problem if your favorite chew was Bull of the Woods chewing tobacco. The Burkett brothers of the Big Hill area once came to the general store at Sands to replenish their supply. There was a problem. The owner had gone fishing for the day and his wife was keeping the store. Learning that the owner would likely come home late, they solved the problem by asking for "Cow in the Bresh" chewing tobacco. There were many other brands such as Red Juice, Red Coon, Days o Work, Black Mariah, Beech Nut, and many others, but only Bull of the Woods would do.

In the days of my youth people were much more modest. The mail order catalogs were far too explicit for mixed company. They were generally kept from the boys and men except for the back pages where the watches, pocketknives, guns and farm items were to be found. When the catalog became outdated and was ready to go to the outhouse the women's wear portion was torn off and kept in the house so only the women folk would have access to it.

One of the most used phrases in my youth described a very frequent and normal occurrence. Expectant mothers were not said to be pregnant, at least not in mixed company. She was said to be "in a family way."

A lot of men came to our house in winter with saws for dad to sharpen. Winter wood cutting chores needed sharp tools. These people were invited to warm at the fire. Winters were also a time for colds and sickness and the visitor was always asked if he and the family had been well. The answer was almost always "common" or "just common." Men in those days seemed reluctant to give out information on the family health. Later in the conversation he might volunteer that the kids had whooping cough earlier but asking for information not freely given was prying.

Much of the way of thinking and talking was preserved from harder times. My Grandmother Miller, for example, still made her own soap. She even had an ash hopper to leach out the lye rather than buying it. It was not so much about money as it was about being self-sufficient and capable of dealing with any and every need.

The ingrained mountain ways of doing things were hard to break. Most of those I recall would have to concern my Grandmother Miller. Grandma Miller's place was just a short way down the path, and we saw her almost daily. But it was more than just the contact. She was a strong traditionalist. Her ways of coping with the hard facts of life went back to settlement days and further. The Indian blood she likely carried in her veins showed in her actions as well as in her appearance. There were ways things were to be done and that was that. Her pride and joy were her smokehouse and the cellar. Though she had her own large family, the destitute knew she would always have good, albeit, pretty plain fare.

One day in late spring about 1940 I remember being at grandma's place when two young cousins came by. Grandma asked them if the corn had come up good. The teenage boys were clearly embarrassed and finally admitted that they had not planted any. Grandma was astounded and the boys felt they just had to explain that they had all been sick with measles and had missed doing the plowing early when the sod turned good. In fact, they said, their father was still sick, and they had decided not to plant any corn this year. To my grandmother, this was unbelievable heresy. "You boys go home," she said, "you are big enough to do that plowing and planting yourselves. You may not make a big crop unless fall frosts are late, but at least you will have enough to make bread. I tell you people starves that don't plant corn." On another occasion one of her sons had returned home from working in the lumber camps of Idaho. He was relating how lumberjacks ate a hearty breakfast that included huge helpings of hash brown potatoes. He was of the opinion, that hash browns would be a good addition to the family breakfast. Grandma did not see it quite that way. She said "It seems a shame to me to have the same thing for breakfast that you have to depend on so much for dinner and supper. Where would a body be if he ever got tired of 'taters'".

In the mountain south dinner had always been the noon meal. Supper was the evening meal. This was understood by everyone and there was no good reason to change it. To change it would have been stupid by mountain standards. As late as 1994 when my wife-to-be and I were dating this was still my understanding. She invited me to dinner, and I promised her that I would come as soon as I could after church was over. (The relationship was not yet serious enough to take her to church with me.) I arrived about 12:45 p.m. I did not see any preparations for dinner but was not concerned. A lot of people ate late dinners on Sunday. She, being originally from California, might be later than most. We spent the afternoon visiting until I noticed I was close to 4:00 p.m. It was then that I decided to leave. Any women who would delay dinner so late probably did not eat three full meals a day and was an unlikely prospect for anything serious.

Needless-to-say, mountain beliefs and practices have changed tremendously during my eighty-odd years of life. Television has speeded things up and also standardized everything to a large extent. Not so in my early childhood. The slow-spoken men who brought their tools to dad to be sharpened in winter would not fit well into today's society. They were friendly but not overly so. The man of that day did not reveal his emotions to people he did not know well if at all. For example, few men of that day could say "thank you" though a woman might. A man would say "obliged" or "much obliged." A man could, however, express great surprise or emotion by word. The most common was "Great Scots." Where this came from, I do not know, but perhaps it had something to do with family origins.

A list of sayings and beliefs of my day follow below

## Truths, Half-Truths and Lies

---It will always stop raining in time to do the milking. Not so. This was said to be a saying of my Grandfather Miller, but he could be careless about his milking times.

---If the owls hooted before good dark, it would snow before daylight. We lived in owl country and this was a good indicator.

---If the chickens stayed on the roost on a rainy morning the rain would end soon. This was true. If it was going to rain long, they would get out and get wet early.

---If the rooster crowed long before daylight you would hear of a death soon. Not true. It only meant he was having a restless night. If he had many of them, he would end up in a pot of dumplings.

---If your nose itched before breakfast, you could expect company that day. Not true. It merely meant that you needed to rub your nose.

---If the groundhog saw his shadow on February 2$^{nd}$ look for six more weeks of winter. Not true. If man made in God's image could not predict the winter, what could you expect of a groundhog? Winter lasted at least six more weeks anyway.

---If a stolen dirty dishrag was rubbed on warts and then buried in the woods the warts would come off. Not true. Just wishful thinking. My father had one he like better. Find a hollow stump holding rainwater. Hold your warty hands in the water and say:

> Barley Corn, Barley Corn
> Indian Meal Shorts
> Stumpwater, Stumpwater
> Swallow these warts.

---Handling frogs caused warts. Not so. Warts seemed to be mildly contagious in the days before good hand hygiene. Boys did have them more often than the girls but not because they handled frogs.

---If a lizard or turtle bit you it wouldn't turn loose until it thundered. I was careful not to try this, but I doubted if thunder meant anything to a turtle.

---Someone heard a panther scream in a particular locality. Not true. Panthers were believed extinct. In those days people felt free to travel other people's lands. A panther's scream meant the area had a clandestine use.

---If the hornets nested high off the ground it would be a hard winter. More likely it was a good year for polecats and nests were not safe near the ground.

---You could predict the coming winter by black bands on the wooly worms. There seems to be a lot of truth to this, but it is not infallible.

---Lightening never strikes in the same place twice. Partly true. Lightening may strike trees, etc. more but for people and livestock once is usually enough.

---Crops should be planted by the signs of the moon. I never seemed to have time to keep to a moon schedule but there is likely something to this. I noted that weeds sprayed with weed killer sometimes wilted down in two or three hours. A day or two later using the same mix at the same time and the same weather it might take days. Something had to make the difference.

---Animals stir more before bad weather. Yes, and people too. A long line of farmers at the mill grinding cattle feed was a sure sign.

---Hurts and wounds during mid-March were slow to heal during the Ides of March. I am sure this came from Aunt Frances Miller for she was the only one in the family with a knowledge of Shakespeare.

---Count the foggy mornings in August and you would know how many snows to expect that winter. Not so. If you lived at Deep Gap the snows would not have melted all summer.

---A halo around the moon meant falling weather soon. This was usually reliable.

---If the fire in the fireplace crackled falling weather was on its way. True, but not always reliable. If you burned chestnut firewood it popped and crackled all the time anyway.

---All weather signs fail during a drought. This was very true.

---If the children were too rowdy a rising cake baking in the oven would fall. This sometimes happened at our house, but we enjoyed the cake anyway.

## The Hillbilly Mountaineer

Unfortunately, much of what has been written about the Appalachian South does not come first-hand. A notable exception is *At Home in the Heart of Appalachia* by Franklin, West Virginian John O'Brien. His work fills a void that many native mountaineers have long felt and is very readable. Among many other things mountaineer O'Brien finds fault in is the popular Hillbilly Mountaineer image. He says it does not exist and probably never did. He credits the once numerous charity schools, orphanages, and hospitals with cultivating the image to draw funds from their congregations and businesses mostly in the north. He notes William G. Frost of Berea College in Kentucky as being one of the most successful. It would be hard to say that these institutions were not of great benefit but the picture they portrayed was searched out and promoted to the embarrassment of the natives.[1]

At long last the portrait of the Hillbilly Mountaineer seems to be fading, but such practices are more common than ever, especially in politics. The portrait of a poor downtrodden black sharecropper or mountaineer is very much alive. Anyone expecting to be elected must promise something for those who hold these images. Promise but not always to deliver. When delivered they eventually come with an unseen cost in respect and more years of the same.

# 24

## Other Family and Friends

### Edmund Miller

No account of local Miller family origins would be complete without mention of Uncle Edmund. He was a brother to my Great-Grandfather Henry Miller and was a legend in his own time. My mother could remember him. Great Aunt Frances had many stories about him. Aunt Frances either did not believe, or chose not to tell, some of the more outlandish ones. I will not either, though an entire book could be written. That should be the prerogative of one of his direct descendants I believe.

Uncle Edmund was born October 8, 1850. He grew into an unusually tall man, at least for his times. He was said to be near seven feet tall. In his day many would feel called to challenge him to a fight. They wanted to be known for having fought the biggest man in the territory. It was said that Uncle Edmund was accommodating. Aunt Frances once told that a noted fighter came from Wilkes County to challenge him. At the time Uncle Edmund was clearing trees from property he owned in the high gap leading to the Longhope Creek area. (Some called the location Miller's Gap, but it was called the Fire Scald Gap in my youth.) Uncle Edmund agreed to see which was the better man but only if the challenger rested first from his climb up the mountain. Edmund kept chopping at a warm-up pace until the challenger got cold then he gave him a good thrashing. Afterwards they shook hands and the stranger went on his way.

Edmund and Great-Grandpa Henry were said to have been two of Watauga County's largest landholders. (Mom used to say that the reason Uncle Edmund's family was small was that he was away trading on land so much of the time.) Aunt Frances told that he once went so far as Kentucky looking to buy land. Two suspicious characters took him back into the hills to a cabin where they were to spend the night before looking over the property the next day. Edmund managed to overhear their plan to take his money after he went to sleep. They were afraid to try when he was awake. Edmund pretended to be getting ready for bed until they got their shoes off. He then beat them over the head with a riding boot and escaped. One of them shot him in the hip as he was mounting his horse. He later picked the bullet out with a horseshoe nail and returned home to North Carolina.

Everyone seems to have had an "Ed Miller" story. Luther Moretz, my brother Jack's father-in-law, had a favorite. A local family had cattle dying one winter. They believed in witches and thought that to be the cause. Uncle Edmund knew better than to dispute this belief in witches. Instead, he offered to shoot the witch if they had some silver coins to make bullets. When the day came, he went alone to the barn. There he fired into the air and then swatted the wall with a stalk of pokeberries. Calling the family, he showed them where he had shot the witch. Edmund then asked what they were feeding the cattle. They replied that their cows had all the rye straw that they could eat. Uncle Edmund said "Law! Law! (his by-word) Nothing is worse to cause witches to take up at a place. Some good hay and a little grain would most likely solve the problem."

During Edmund's time the Millers were active supporters of Teddy Roosevelt. According to a local news article, Edmund toyed with the idea of forming his own company of soldiers to help Teddy in Cuba. (Edmund's son "Bob" was already in the army.) When Roosevelt ran for president Big Ed campaigned actively. Mom said he rode his stud horse, Old Frank, throughout the countryside singing a campaign song that he wrote. He had a strong voice and sang from hilltops so people on both sides could hear him. Mom did not remember the words except for the last line, "Vote Republican and save the country." I do not know the family's attraction to Roosevelt, but he was a great conservationist and supporter of anti-trust laws.

In Roosevelt's day the big timber interests and miners exploited public lands almost at will. Senators and congressmen openly worked in their interests. Roosevelt opposed them so they passed a bill overriding his stop sales order. But Roosevelt had not been idle. He had secretly had surveys made of all remaining government lands. It was said that he stayed up all night prior to the deadline signing orders to create the nation's great system of national forests. Big timber would no longer get to log public lands at ten cents per tree.

Roosevelt's ideas on conservation of natural resources were revolutionary for his times and drew powerful opposition. (Mark Twain called him "that damned cowboy.") This did not deter Roosevelt. I cannot say if Miller support was due to Roosevelts personality or his policies or a combination. Aunt Frances was well into those events but did not offer much detail. (Perhaps she did not expect her audience to understand.) She would give every nephew or niece a buffalo nickel. She always called it a "Bull Moose" nickel. She made some connection to Roosevelt that I never understood.

Uncle Edmund was unusual to say the least. He once spent time in federal prison for being part of a counterfeiting scheme. (Some say he took the blame for others.) Legend has it that he created an unhealing sore on his leg by rubbing it with a copper penny. He was released from federal prison in Georgia because they thought he had cancer.

Edmund died December 4, 1916. He was buried on his home farm beginning what is now the Bethelview Methodist Church Cemetery. (We have made arrangements to be buried there also.) One account related that he owned about

7,300 acres. His great grandson once told me that the family did not claim it all. They were land poor and did not contest another claim unless the property was local.

My father never knew mom's great-uncle Edmund, but he had heard of him before he ever met mom. Dad said that Edmund regretted any involvement in a counterfeiting scheme, and he took the printing plates to a site on Elk Knob. There he undermined a boulder and buried the plates. Then he used levers to pry loose the boulder which filled the site and could not again be moved by any ordinary means. He did not want anyone to ever be tempted to use them again.

Joseph J. Miller, the son of Edmund Miller, had a huge family near us on Howard's Creek. They were kin, friends, and neighbors, and we spent many Sunday afternoons playing with them in the field in front of their house. The best description we have of this family is in Volume 2 of the *Watauga Heritage* book entered by Jane E. Penley.[1] (Ms. Penley did a lot of the research that went into this book.) In part she says Joe was born January 27, 1891. He married Clemmie Gentry in 1911. They moved from the Bethelview area about 1916 to the old Jonathan Miller homeplace. They had seven sons and three daughters. Six of their seven sons and three grandsons served in the Army or Marines during World War II or the Korean Conflict. Mr. Miller was highly respected and was elected the county surveyor several times. Mr. Miller died June 11, 1970 and his wife died February 8, 1976.

## Parlier Family Including Greer Descendants

### First Generation

Jean (1) Parlier was born about 1640 in LaTremblade, Saintonge County, Maritime Providence, France. There he married Marie Arnaud, November 27, 1667. His occupation was that of a ship's pilot. During this time there was a great turmoil in France as Louis XIII came to power and ordered the Huguenots (French Protestants) to cease and desist. Children were taken from their parents and put into Catholic homes, parents were persecuted, and all too frequently put to death. The Perliers were Huguenots, and in order to keep their freedom of worship, planned to flee to the New World as many Huguenots were doing. It appears that Jean met an untimely death as only Marie and her sons sailed for American in 1686. It has been told that they hid in hogsheads which had holes bored in them and were stored with the freight in the bottom of the ship until they were out of reach of the inspectors. On the ship Marie met Pierre Traverrier and they were married in the church, January 4, 1688 at Frenchtown, Narragansett, Rhode Island.

## Second Generation

Jean (2), son of Jean and Marie Perlier was born October 16, 1669 in LaTremblade, Saintonge County, Maritime Province, France. Jean and his brother Andre accompanied their mother to the New World, arriving in America in the year 1686. Jean was declared a freeman of New York in 1695. He married in the French (*Huguenot) Church, New York City on December 25, 1696. He married Anne Rezeau, the daughter of Renier Rezeau and Anne Coursier of Staten Island, New York. She was born (date unknown) in Isle de Re, Maritime Province, France. Two daughters and a son, Jean, were baptized in the Huguenot Church. Jean's occupation was that of a carpenter. It has been told that he once owned the land that the Woolworth building now stands on in New York City. Jean served in the French and Indian War in 1711 and in the South Company of the local militia in 1715. Jean died in Fresh Kill, Staten Island, New York, September 14, 1723. His will was probated October 28, 1723. "In the name of God, Amen. I Jean Perlier, of Staten Island, being very sick. I leave to my wife all my estate, real and personal, during her widowhood. I leave to my son John all my carpenter tools. If it is necessary to pay debts, my wife shall sell the salt meadow that I bought of Jerome Deslin. I leave to my sons, John, Peter, and Abraham, all my lands and Plantation. I leave all my movable estate to my six daughters, Ann, Elizabeth,

Mary, Sarah, Esther, and Martha. My sons shall pay to their sisters 100 pounds sterling. I make my wife and my beloved friend, John LeCounte executors."

### Third Generation

Jean, son of Jean and Anne Parlier, was born September 5, 1703 in Staten Island, New York. He was baptized in the French (Huguenot) Church in New York City on September 29, 1703. He married about 1733 Abigail Jones, baptized April 22, 1722, daughter of Edward Jones and Catherine Decker of Staten Island. They were residents of Staten Island, New York where sons Edward and Peter were baptized in St. Andrews Church. It is believed that they moved to New Jersey after his father died and had other children possibly while in New Jersey.

Jean and Abigail went with a group of residents of Hunterdon County, New Jersey to the Abbots Creek area of Rowan County, NC (Davie County). The settlement was called the Jersey Settlement. The move probably took place between 1750 and 1760. We find the Vannoy and Green families in this group that came from Hunterdon County, New Jersey. Later they are in Wilkes County, NC along with Isaac Parlier, the son of a John Parlier (Rowan County).

"The Vannoys in France were Huguenots and to escape persecution for their religious beliefs, fled to Holland. From Holland they went to England and then to the New World. A John and Rachel Vannoy left from Scotland September 5, 1685 on the ship Henry and Francis. They settled on Staten Island New York. John died May 13, 1699. A land grant of 18 acres on the "south side of Fish Kill" was made on March 17, 1700 to the widow Rachel Vannoy. Their son Francis Vannoy was born 1688 on Staten Island and died August 15, 1774 in Hunterdon County New Jersey. His son John Vannoy left Hunterdon New Jersey sometime after his marriage in 1740 to Susanna Baker Anderson. They came to the Jersey Settlement in Rowan County NC where others from the Hunterdon County New Jersey area had come. The Jersey Settlement Church, a colony of Baptist, moved from Hunterdon County New Jersey between 1747-1755."

The history of the Green family of Wilkes County is as follows:

"The Green family is reported to have come to the New World from England in the late 1600's. The progenitor of the Green family of Wilkes County NC was William Green born circa 1660 in England, who came to Staten Island New York. He married Joanna Reeder of Staten Island about 1692. They moved to Hunterdon County New Jersey shortly afterward where he died June 16, 1722. Their son Jeremiah Green was born circa 1715 in Hunterdon County New Jersey and married a Hannah Hunt circa 1740 in Hunterdon County. By 1756 they were in the Jersey Settlement of Rowan County NC, joining others from Hunterdon County new Jersey area."

I believe this John Parlier is the same as the Jean Perlier of Staten Island and Hunterdon County New Jersey. The age is the same and the number of families that surrounded him in the Jersey Settlement were from Hunterdon County New Jersey. Also note the family names such as Isaac that appear in both families. However, there has not been found today any proof that this John Parlier is indeed the same as the one from Hunterdon County. If this is the same John, then it appears that Abigail may have died, and John has married a woman by the name of Ann?

John Parlier children of local interest are:

4. Isaac (4) Parlier b. about 1745, Davidson County, NC/Abbotts Creek; d. about 1835, Wilkes County, NC.
6. Jacob Parlier b. about 1751, Davidson County/Abbotts Creek; d. about 1791, Iredell County.

Note: Isaac Parlier lived on the Lewis Fork road crossing the Blue Ridge. The Wilkes County court appointed him overseer for a portion of this road.

Note: Jacob Parlier lived in the Brushy Mountain area of what became Alexander County. Some of his descendants would later move to Watauga County.

## Fourth Generation

Jacob (4) Parlier was born about 1751 in Davidson County/Abbotts Creek, and died about 1791 in Iredell County. He married Rachel.

4.  Jonathan Parlier, b. about 1785, Wilkes County; d. July 21, 1845, Wilkes County, Parlier Family Cemetery, Pores Knob.

## Fifth Generation

Jonathan (5) Parlier was born about 1785 in Wilkes County, and died July 21, 1845 in Wilkes County/Parlier Family Cemetery, Pores Knob. He married Rebecca Shinn February 12, 1811 in Wilkes County, daughter of Levi Shinn and Hannah Deboard.

7.  James Wesley Parlier, born about 1830, Wilkes County, died January 23, 1869 Wilkes County, NC/Parlier Family Cemetery.

## Sixth Generation

James Wesley (6) Parlier was born about 1830 in Wilkes County, and died January 23, 1869 in Wilkes County, NC/Parlier Family Cemetery. He married Phoebe Cook about 1849 in Wilkes County, daughter of Ephraim Cook and Levina Marlow.

Children of James Parlier and Phoebe Cook are:

6.  John Noah Parlier, born December 12, 1860, Wilkes County, died February 13, 1936, Watauga County/Moretz Cemetery.

## Seventh Generation

John <u>Noah</u> (7) Parlier was born December 12, 1860 in Wilkes County, and died February 13, 1936 in Watauga County. He married (1) Elizabeth Nancy Younce about 1880 in Watauga County, daughter of Andrew Younce and Emily Greer. He married (2) Mary Carlton about 1926 in Watauga County.

Children of John Parlier and Elizabeth Younce are:

(My grandmother Emeline)

1. Mary <u>Emeline</u> (8) Parlier, born June 18, 1881, Watauga County; died August 11, 1954, Watauga County/Laurel Springs Cemetery.
2. Lula Belle Parlier, born May 21, 1884, Watauga County; died May 7, 1951, Watauga County/Laurel Springs Cemetery.
3. James Jackson Parlier, born February 16, 1886, Watauga County; Died June 21, 1955, Watauga County/Laurel Springs Cemetery.
4. Etta Lillian Parlier, born October 15, 1902, Watauga County; died February 1980, Akron, Ohio.

## Eighth Generation

Mary <u>Emeline</u> (8) Parlier was born June 18, 1881 in Watauga County, and died August 11, 1954 in Watauga County/Laurel Springs Cemetery. She married Ivory Ward Greer June 23, 1908 in Watauga County, son of Elijah Greer and Lula Waters.

Children of Mary Emeline Parlier and Ivory Greer are:

1. Jacob <u>Roscoe</u> (9) Greer, born May 27, 1909, Watauga County; died Watauga County. Mt. Lawn Cemetery. (My father.)

2. William <u>Roy</u> Greer, born September 15, 1910, Watauga County; died Watauga County, Rutherwood Cemetery.

3. Thomas <u>Isadore</u> Greer, born December 13, 1912, Watauga County; died January 23, 1979, Bel-Air Cemetery/Bel-Air, Maryland.

4. <u>Ina</u> Louise Greer, born July 21, 1915, Watauga County; lives in Baltimore, Maryland, buried at Laurel Springs, Watauga County.

5. <u>Docia</u> Lina Greer, born July 15, 1918, Watauga County; died November 29, 1979, Watauga County/Mt. Lawn Cemetery; married Ronald Ragan.

6. Ora <u>Dare</u> Greer, born February 22, 1921, Watauga County; died December 15, 1954, Watauga County/Laurel Springs Cemetery.

7. Nellie <u>Frances</u> Greer, born January 10, 1924, Watauga County, lived in Boone, NC; married Emmette Harrison Dollar. Both are deceased and are buried at Laurel Springs.

## The Philyaws

Grandma Miller's father was John Philyaw, a son of Gideon Philyaw. Her mother was Fannie Lane Philyaw. Fannie had a brother, named Govan Lane, who lived on present day Rainbow Trail Road near Boone, NC. Grandma Hattie was said to be one-fourth Indian and her appearance verified it. I suspect the Indian blood came from the Philyaws rather than the Lanes because of the Philyaw appearance. Hattie's mother died of a malady called "milk-sick" when Hattie was about four. She had numerous relatives most of whom lived in West Virginia and mined coal. They came visiting about as often as the miners went out on strike.

Grandma Miller was not brought up by her blood kin who had mostly moved to the coal fields to find work. She was adopted by John and Bessie Barnes who had no children of their own. They reared at least two other adopted children, Joe Church and Mary Greene. Grandma Miller looked upon these two and their adoptive parents as her real family and she kept in touch with them throughout her life. Her birth father, John Philyaw, remarried Elizabeth "Liz" Doneho and they had the following children:

Bessie who married a Coffey

Roy

Stella who married a Greer

Cecil

Cuba

Felix

Lonnie

Oma who married an Archer

# I. G. Greer

Another mountain man who gained much respect from me was a distant kinsman, Dr. I. G. Greer. Dr. Greer began his career as a teacher at a small school in western Watauga County in 1900 at nineteen years of age. He followed a course of self-improvement until he received a degree from Appalachian Training School in 1906. He would later join the staff of that school after receiving a degree from the University of North Carolina in 1910. He had an outstanding career there until he left in 1932. While at Appalachian Dr. Greer pursued an interest in Southern Appalachian studies on ballad collecting. He was widely sought after as a speaker and a singer. It was upon this foundation that Cratis Williams would continue to build.

Dr. Greer did not leave Appalachian to retire. He left to pursue a lifelong interest in the welfare of children. He became superintendent of the North Carolina Baptist Orphanage at Thomasville, NC. Children were plentiful and many became orphans in those days. Also, a Baptist preacher, Dr. I. G. was chosen president of the North Carolina Baptist Convention in 1942. Wake Forest bestowed an honorary degree upon him in 1944 for his humanitarian work. His success in fund raising was noticed by the University of North Carolina and they persuaded him to become vice president of their business foundation in 1948. He retired for good in 1954.

Dr. Greer had a large following across the state. Locally ASU named a building for him. He was once an alderman of Boone and a representative to the state legislature. Many thought him so able and so respected as to be electable as a candidate for governor. This speaks volumes for the respect that they held for him.

I had many other local heroes or persons I greatly respected. Among them would be teacher Margaret Gragg and Ira Bingham, but I must move on.

## Howard Greer

Howard Greer and I have several things in common though we are only distant cousins. We are both descendants of Benjamin Greer; he from Benjamin's son James and I from son Samuel. Howard grew up on West Mill Creek of Ashe County and I on Howard's Creek of Watauga. We both graduated from Berea College with degrees in Agriculture; I in 1955 and he in 1959. Howard pursued his professionally with advanced degrees. He has long been retired now and lives in Stillwater, OK.

Howard usually visited family in Ashe County each summer and we occasionally did family research together in the area during those visits. My line of Greers, Benjamin's Samuel, is fairly-well documented in the area. Howard's line, Benjamin's James, moves in and out of NC, TN and VA and is more difficult. Howard has done a lot of research and provided me with good evidence of the James Greer line.

---James Greer married Mary Sallie Hampton and moved to Carter County, TN. (Where they lived later became Johnson County.)
--- Son Alexander Greer married a Lydia Curd. They had ten children. Five of their sons were confederate veterans which was somewhat unusual for the area.
---Son Benjamin married a Lydia Calhoon November 4, 1866. They moved back to Ashe County, NC and reared nine children.
---Son William A. Greer married Samantha Jane Shepherd August 21, 1895.

---Son Avery Lester Greer married Ethel Ina Elliot October 21, 1931.

---Howard A. L. Greer married Ava Joan Adams June 1, 1958.

## The Jacksons

The Jacksons were long-time friends and Bethelview Methodist Church family when we lived at Boone. They were not of the original James Jackson "Meeting House" Jacksons, but they have a long and interesting area history themselves. Retired teacher, John Jackson still lives on the Jackson ancestral farm not far from the church. John and Glenda reared four beautiful children in that church. They have now married and gone their separate ways, but I am sure this will always be home.

This Jackson family arrived in the area during the Civil War era. Theirs is a very interesting story. The one I have most heard tells of confederate soldier Jesse William Jackson who came home with fellow 58th NC Infantry soldier, J. B. Miller, where he met his wife-to-be, Sara Melinda "Sally" Miller, a sister of J. B. This account may not be completely accurate. Most units of that day were raised locally, and Jackson was from Randolph County. This would not, however, rule out the possibility that they had met and arrived together as J. B. could have been on leave.

John seems to have collected the most reliable records of his ancestor's service. His unit was the 22nd NC Regiment C.S.A. He was detached with Longstreet's Corps to East Tennessee during the South's unsuccessful attempt to drive Burnside out of Knoxville. While on foraging duty in the East TN/West NC area, he was captured by Unionists. He was able to escape and was making his way to more friendly surroundings when he ended up at John Miller's home at Meat Camp in Watauga County. Jackson was able to rejoin his unit and fought at Gettysburg. He was still in service at Appomattox.

John has furnished a copy of his father's family tree. I will include it if space allows. He has also provided a copy of his mother's line. Miss Marie was a gracious and inspiring retired school librarian. (I believe John once told me that she too descended from a confederate soldier of Ashe County.) Marie was a dedicated member of our church after her retirement.

# Dad's Genealogy

William Jackson – Clarissa Wall

Jesse William Jackson (Confederate Veteran) – Sarah Melinda Miller

    John W.

    James C.

    Edward L.

        Nancy

        Thomas Jefferson

        Charlie Ross

        "Mary C." (real name was Margaret E.)

        George R.

        Robert B.

    Jesse Frank – Minnie Lillian Johnson

        Lizzie D.

        Hazel F.

        Thomas R.

        Dora L.

        Robert Orville – Nola Marie Francis

            John R. – Glenda C. Gentry

                Jessica L. Jackson (m. Wyatt)

                Justyn M. Jackson (m. Carlton)

                Johnna R. Jackson (m. Church)

                Jordan R. Jackson (m. Lindsay Kaudelka)

                Grandchildren of John and Glenda:

                Nathan and Ethan Carlton;

                    Brently, Bowen, and Barrett Church;

                    Morgan and Caleb Wyatt; Griff Jackson.

# Mother's Genealogy

<u>Henry Francis – Melinda Koontz</u>
Martha Francis
Coy R. Francis – Zelpha Malana Wiles
<u>Nola Marie Francis – R. O. Jackson</u>
    Colonel E. Francis
    William E. Francis
    Herbert B. Francis
    Vergie Francis (Cox)
    <u>John R. – Glenda C. Gentry</u>
        Jessica L. Jackson (m. Wyatt)
        Justyn M. Jackson (m. Carlton)
        Johnna R. Jackson (m. Church)
        Jordan R. Jackson (m. Lindsay Kaudelka)
Grandchildren of John and Glenda: Nathan and Ethan Carlton; Brently, Bowen, and Barrett Church; Morgan and Caleb Wyatt; Griff Jackson.

John Jackson clings to an earlier age in some respects. He has long been a hound dog man. He keeps Plott hounds. They are a bear hunting breed developed in the North Carolina mountains. They are also the state dog. If you have ever seen the Daniel Boone sculpture on the ASU campus in Boone, you have seen Daniel's dogs as modeled by John Jackson's Plotts. Sherry Edwards was a personal friend of wife Marny and mine. We went with her to take measurements of the dogs.

If time and space permitted, I would dearly love to include many others, but both my time and resources are limited. Among those I must leave out are:

---The Clint Miller Family
---The Glenda Stephans Duncan Family
---The Norris Family
---The Winklers and many, many others

## Daniel Boone Sculpture

Photos of the Daniel Boone sculpture on the Appalachian State University campus. It was created by Sherry Edwards, the head of the Art Department.

It was our privilege to be of some help to her during the planning stages. We arranged for her to see John Jackson's Plott hounds, where she carefully measured tails and ears. We also arranged for her to see and measure Walter Lewis' collection of muzzle loaders.

Sherry was well known for the many sculptures she had on the campus and on display at various locations off campus, including Washington, D.C.

Sherry was a great friend. She lived to complete the work but die of cancer before the statute could be cast and dedicated.

## Daniel Boone Statue Site

A wonderful tribute to Daniel Boone and Sherry Edwards, and a great addition to Appalachian State University and to the Boone area.

The statue is located on the Appalachian State University campus just beyond the large statue of Yosef and facing River Street.

## The Calloway Cemetery

This is in the Calloway Cemetery near the crossing of Hwy 163 and the south fork of the New River in Ashe County near West Jefferson, NC. The tall rock seen over my left shoulder is called, "The Daniel Boone Camp Rock". Legend has it that Daniel Boone often used this route through the mountains. He is said to like this spot so will that he wanted to be buried here. The cemetery is said to have already been an Indian cemetery. Thomas Calloway was Boone's close friend and was trusted to keep the camp rock until Boone returned. This did not happen, and Calloway used the stone to mark his own grave.

## The Squire Boone Grave

This is the Squire Boone gravesite at the Old Joppa Cemetery at Mocksville, NC. The Greers in this are not direct descendants of Daniel Boone, but his father, Squire, is a distant Grandfather, if you go back far enough. Howard Greer, a distant cousin, took this photo as we toured the area together.

SQUIRE AND SARAH MORGAN BOONE
PARENTS OF DANIEL BOONE
SQUIRE BOONE DEPARTED THIS LIFE THEY
SIXTY-NINTH YEAR OF HIS AGE IN THAY
YEAR OF OUR LORD 1765 GENEIARY THA 2
SAH + BOONE DEPARTED THIS LIFE 1777 AGED 77 YEARS

## John Jackson's Antique Bear Trap

This bear trap is said to have been owned by Wilburn Waters, "The Bear Hunter". It is now owned by John Jackson of Boone, who furnished pictures of the trap and his Plott dogs. John, himself, is a modern-day bear hunter who owns pedigree Plott hounds.

The Plott was developed in the North Carolina mountains for bears, hogs, raccoons, and anything else that requires a lot of grit. It is now the State Dog.

Photo courtesy of John Jackson

John Jackson After "The Hunt"
with One of His Plott Hounds

Two of John's Other Plott Hounds

Photo courtesy of John Jackson

Home Sweet Home

Leonard and Grandsons

    Harley
       Tanner
         Braden

Putting up the flag in front
of our house in
Archer Lodge, North Carolina

2012

## Old Bethelview United Methodist Church

This is the old Bethelview United Methodist Church before it was enlarged. The Jackson's were much in evidence here. Marie Jackson, John Jackson's mother, was a retired school librarian and created the church library, which was named for her.

Other names frequently found in this church were: Brown, Carroll, Hollers, Miller, Norris, Ragan, Stanbery, Vaughn, Walls, and Winkler.

## Today's Bethelview United Methodist Church

# 25

---

# Postscripts

## The Naming of Boone

Why the name "Boone?" It might just as well have been "Council" for early settlers of that name; or "Burrell" for Howard's black herder who was Boone's first resident. (Summer resident of course.) It was Burrell who showed Boone the way across the Blue Ridge and around the area. Boone did not really discover the place any more than he discovered most of the places where he plied his trade. Men like Reubin Stringer, Benjamin Cutbirth, Benjamin Cleveland, Benjamin Greer, and others fairly wore the mountain trails out during and prior to Boone's time. Like Boone, most would follow the frontier west. Only a few like Lewis, Ward and Greer would remain in the area from hunting and trapping days on.

Boone could just as easily have been named Cutbirth. "Cutbirth's Smoke Hole" was the name of the steep hollow on eastern Howard's Knob even until my grandparent's day. Cutbirth was at least the equal of Daniel Boone but never received the publicity. Yet Boone was a great choice for a name, and I have no problem with it, though we are probably less than accurate when we place it on his most traveled routes. Boone likely would have had no more reason to remember it than the thousands of other spectacular scenes he had witnessed. The area would

380

likely have been special only if he made short hunting trips across the Blue Ridge with his sons or the nephews he was rearing. Some believe that he did.

Bryan did show a stroke of genius in choosing the name. No doubt it added name recognition to the area. Bryan was Boone's first Chamber of Commerce and Director of Tourism. His hotel business benefited, no doubt. He set the tone for area promotion both then and now. Most needed today is to tie the area to the broader national history, the formation of a national character and the settling of the west. No one better portrays this than Daniel Boone himself. But so do the ten or so generations of local people who stayed behind. They can claim kin to a huge portion of the nation's population.

That huge portion of our population is also Scottish though we are more likely to call ourselves English these days. The term Scots-Irish does not quite describe us. Its original intent appears to have been to distinguish the early Scots from the "Shanty-Irish" or "Bog-Irish" who came largely after the potato famines. Neither are we Highland Scots for they came later, settled in the lowlands, and remained loyal to the crown. Yet all true Scots are a peculiar people. Unlike England and Ireland, Scotland was never overrun by the Roman empire. The Romans chose instead to build a wall across the island to protect themselves. Often persecuted and largely forgotten when history books are written, their ability to endure and willingness to fight for their principles has marked their presence wherever they go.

## Early Inspirations

Locally one of the most important people in my estimation to come into my life was Cratis D. Williams. Williams had been a mountain boy himself near Blaine in Lawrence County Kentucky. He had overcome the usual hardships of a mountain boy to go to attend Cumberland College at Williamsburg, Kentucky.

From there he went to Caines Creek, also of Lawrence County, to become teacher of a one-room school. He would soon become an English teacher and principal at the Louisa High School, again Lawrence County. He introduced an innovative program but seems to have lost some favor locally. I am not sure of the reasons, but they could have been, at least in part, political. He arrived in Boone, NC in 1942 where he taught English and dramatics. To his boss Dr. Wey's credit, little of Williams' background followed him to Boone. He left a tubercular wife in a Huntington, WV sanatorium and had an arrested case of the disease himself. (She would later be moved to Beckley, West Virginia.) With Wey's encouragement Cratis Williams became known as America's foremost scholar on the Appalachian experience. Wey, in return, received his help and advice in setting up a most innovative program at Appalachian High School, the college demonstration school.

My appreciation for the man has nothing to do with credentials. I had no classes under him. But Dr. Wey saw to it that Williams often entertained us in assembly. He sang ballads (which he collected extensively) and told stories in mountain dialect. (He only discovered when he needed a birth certificate that the "D" for his middle name had stood for, "Darrel." He went through life using "Derl" because of mountain pronunciation.) Cratis gave many a mountain boy and girl an appreciation for his or her heritage. He was one of us.

The Cratis Williams collection of ballads and other cultural works may have been the best in the land. Unfortunately, it was destroyed when the old campus administration building burned.

## To Oral History

Probably the most outstanding social institution of mountain folks was the art of storytelling. Most family history passed from generation to generation this way. A goodly portion of the population was actively involved in the events of their times and were knowledgeable of local, state, national and even international events. Mountain folk were never as ignorant as many portrayed them to be. However, they did have a healthy distrust for the printed media and even the state selected textbooks. Grandpa's version often varied from the official version and grandpa was not known to lie. The official version, on the other hand, sometimes favored the politicians in power at the time and could be slanted, and sometimes was.

The local paper usually had its own axe to grind but had a hard time leading the skeptical mountaineers too far from the truth. The papers were usually laced with snake oil or patent medicine advertisements and stories about two-headed calves, Siamese twins, and the like anyway. The average mountaineer kept his own close observations of the courts and county officials. News needed to be verified by family or friends to be believed. I am often surprised at how often the version related by my family has proven true one hundred or more years after the fact. As a county employee I was still amazed at how different some of the written versions of reporters could be from what I had heard said. I sometimes wondered if the reporters had attended the same meeting that I went to.

Oral history has long been a great part of mountain life and usually related a correct account. However, in recent years, I have observed a tendency to lend a lot of credence to history related stories by locally prominent persons, many of whom have never verified anything they have to say in local records. I am sure mountaineer skepticism is handling their stories as well as ever but there is a danger that the university people and other newcomers will be misled. Fortunately, many publications seem now to make great efforts to dig deeper for more accurate facts.

## Afterwards

This work was begun as a simple history of my Greer ancestors. I soon found that no family history can be very simple. This first became apparent when I first looked at my mother's side of the family, the Meat Camp Millers of Ashe and Watauga Counties, North Carolina. Somehow, I expected the Greers to be different. My father had always said that "A Miller can set out across country and, wherever nighttime catches him, he can find someone to claim kin with to spend the night." On the other hand, "Greers rarely claim kin even among themselves." There is some truth to this, but both families share a common problem in tracing kin. There is simply no stopping place. Every question answered raises two more and nothing is ever quite complete.

In this effort I have felt it very necessary to find a stopping point. Other interests also make demands upon my time and, even though I am now retired, I cannot find the time to spend on research and writing that I would like. I am diabetic and need the physical exercise, in order, to stay healthy. I also enjoy working on the family shrubs, flowers, and lawn.

My original work has expanded tremendously. I have found that we have many misconceptions about our early history, and I feel obligated to point these out wherever I can. How can you find a stopping point with a story that seems to expand every day? How can I keep my efforts from becoming a pile of notes, etc., which no one will ever be able to make sense of? I believe I have devised a strategy to avoid a complete loss if I do not survive until the finish of the work. I will attempt to write up people, places, and events in chapter form. These chapters will be completed as I believe the subject matter is well covered and not necessarily in chronological order. Chronological order seems to be the best order for the final completed product, but this will give me the option of leaving chapters open until they can be developed properly. They can always be inserted later in the appropriate order.

Early on I realized that my family's history was also, in large part, the local history and the history of our nation. I hope to provide family and historical data that will encourage others to do their own research. The record sources and authors I am using will be plugged into my finished copy as my work becomes complete. I hope others will find my efforts to be a good resource. But there is also the family's oral history, especially that of my great aunt on my mother's side. She did not expect history, as she had experienced it, to agree with the accepted versions of her day. Neither do I expect what I have learned in my day to always agree with other versions available. Too often those writers have listened to only those who talked. In mountain society this is often a very limited resource. To my knowledge not much has been done by one who has actually "lived the life." I hope I have something worthwhile to contribute.

In this final analysis, if only my family and friends find these efforts informative and helpful, I will feel my efforts vindicated. My greatest obligation is again neighbors in Ashe and Watauga Counties, North Carolina. It is they who would truly understand what I have to say about our heritage.

## My Appalachia

My roots are in old Appalachia.
It's a fact for which I'm proud.
It's not always popular to say it,
But I will say it long and loud.

The people here are old-time.
They came from foreign lands.
The mountains were still wilderness,
Awaiting strong and determined man.

They helped to create a new nation,
Of people longing to be free.
Always steadfast in principle,
As noble as free men can be.

Not all of them would stay here.
Many would move on to the west.
But they were to be a changed people,
They were some of America's best.

People like Lincoln and Jackson,
Had roots that once grew here.
But there were many other others,
Who moved on to far and near.

They would build a national character.
Patriotic, where-ever they went.
These mountains somehow changed them.
They were leavening heaven sent.

Those who chose to stay here,
Remained steadfast in their thoughts.
A bastion of strength for the country,
In every war it has fought.

During times of National peril,
Mountain men were in much demand.
They would make buddies over the country,
As they fought to defend their Land.

They took their music with them.
The sounds they loved the most.
It would now be called "country",
And it's heard from coast to coast.

Life could be very hard here.
Generations would move away.
Others would seek work in far places,
As they searched for better pay.

The country rarely noticed them,
But they left changes in their wake.
These were not always visible,
But they helped make the country great.

They seem to alter the country,
Others they have begun to win.
No part of the country is excepted.
The country is now a healthy blend.

Some still may not always own it,
But others believe it to be so.
For they now find biscuit and gravy
Near every place they go.

----J. Leonard Greer

# END NOTES

Chapter 1 - <u>A New Land</u>

[1]  Ted Franklin Belue, *The Long Hunt – Death of the Buffalo East of the Mississippi*, p 12

[2]  John Lawson, *A New Voyage to Carolinas*, pp 51-52

[3]  Ballard and Weinstein, *Neighbor to Neighbor*, p 108

[4]  Ted Franklin Belue, *The Long Hunt – Death of the Buffalo East of the Mississippi*, *p* 163

Chapter 2 - <u>Our Ancestors</u>

[1]  James Webb, *Born Fighting*, p 10

Chapter 3 - <u>Patterns of Settlement</u>

[1]  Marjoleine Kars, *Breaking Loose Together*, p 73

Chapter 4 - <u>Independence</u>

[1]  Arthur Herman, *How the Scots Invented the Modern World*, p 229

[2]  Rufus Myers, *North Carolinas Northwest Frontier*, p 96

[3]  Pat Alderman, *The Overmountain Men*, p 115

[4]  Max Dixon, *The Wataugans*, p 59

Chapter 5 - <u>Crossing the Blue Ridge</u>

[1]  Stansberry, *Old Wilkes County Land Records*

Chapter 6 - <u>Frontier Life</u>

   [1]   Ted Franklin Belue, *The Long Hunt – Death of the Buffalo East of the Mississippi*, p 71

   [2]   John Lawson, *A Voyage to Carolina*, p 50

   [3]   John Preston Arthur, Western North Carolina, A History, p 9


Chapter 7 - <u>The Homestead</u>

   [1]   Ballard and Weinstein, *Neighbor to Neighbor*, p 108


Chapter 8 - <u>Always Cash Poor</u>

   [1]   Inscoe and McKinney, *The Heart of the Confederate Appalachia*, p 91


Chapter 9 - <u>Homegrown Medicine</u>

   [1]   David M. Oshinsky, *Polio: An American Story*


Chapter 12 - <u>Miller Ancesters</u>

   [1]   Curtis Smalling, *The Heritage of Watauga County North Carolina: Vol II*, pp 149-150

   [2]   Marjoleine Kars, *Breaking Loose Together*, p 73


Chapter 13 - <u>The Civil War</u>

   [1]   Martin Crawford, *Ashe County's Civil War*, P 72

   [2]   Martin Crawford, *Ashe County's Civil War*, P 102

   [3]   John Preston Arthur, *Watauga County NC- A History*, P 171

   [4]   Ballard and Weinstein, *Neighbor to Neighbor*, P 24


Chapter 14 - <u>The World Wars</u>

   [1]   Pat Beaver and Sandra Ballard, *Voices From the Headwaters*, p 52


Chapter 15 - <u>My Grandparents' Day</u>

   [1]   Leland and Mary Cooper, *The People of the New River*, p 97

   [2]   "Find a Grave" Website

Chapter 18 - <u>Days of My Youth</u>

[1]  Michael C. Hardy, *A Brief History of Watauga County*, p 189


Chapter 19 - <u>Work Years and Beyond</u>

More recollections


Chapter 20 - <u>Homespun Humor</u>

More memories


Chapter 21 - <u>Religion-Race-Politics</u>

[1]  Glenn Beck, *Miracles and Massacres, p 200*


Chapter 23 - <u>Mountain Way and Speech</u>

[1]  John O'Brian, *At Home in the Heart of Appalachia*, p 249


Chapter 24 - <u>Other Family and Friends</u>

[1]  Curtis Smalling, *The Heritage of Watauga County North Carolina: Vol. II*, P 147

# BIBLIOGRAPHY

The views and opinions expressed in this work are primarily those of the author only. Tradition and the oral history of the author's family play a large part in what is recorded here. Otherwise, he would only be parroting the view of others. However, those personal opinions have in many instances been reinforced by public records and the heritage books of Wilkes, Ashe, and Watauga Counties. The public libraries of these counties have been invaluable resources.

It would also not be fair to neglect the mention of numerous authors who may or may not have influenced the personal view expressed by this author. For those wishing to do a documented account of our local history, the following books are recommended:

Alderman, Pat. *THE OVERMOUNTAIN MEN Battle of King's Mountain-Cumberland Decade-State of Franklin-Southern Territory.* Johnston City: The Overmountain Press, 1986.

Arthur, John P. *A History of Watauga County North Carolina with sketches of prominent families.* Johnston City: The Overmountain Press

Arthur, John P. *Western North Carolina: A History FROM 1730 to 1913.* Johnston City: The Overmountain Press, *1996.*

Ballard, Sandra L. and Leila E. Weinstein. *Neighbor to Neighbor: A Memoir of Family, Community, and Civil War in Appalachian North Carolina.* Boone: Center for Appalachian Studies, 2007.

Beaver, Patricia D. and Sandra L Ballard. *VOICES FROM THE HEADWATERS STORIES FROM MEAT CAMP, TAMARACK (POTTERTOWN) & SUTHERLAND, NORTH CAROLINA.* Boone: Center for Appalachian Studies, 2013.

Beck, Glenn. *MIRACLES AND MASSACRES TRUE AND UNTOLD STORIES OF THE MAKING OF AMERICA. New York:* Threshold Editions, 2013.

Belue, Ted Franklin. *The Long Hunt.* Mechanicsburg: STACKPOLE BOOKS, 1996.

Cooper, Leland and Mary Cooper. *The People of the New River.* Jefferson: McFarland & Company, Inc, 2001.

Crawford, Martin. *Ashe County's Civil War.* Charlottesville: University Press of Virginia, 2001.

Dixon, Max. *The Wataugans.* Johnston City: The Overmountain Press, 1989. Reprint.

Dorgan, Howard. *The Old Regular Baptists of Central Appalachia: Brothers and sisters in Hope.* Knoxville: University of Tennessee Press, 2001

Draper, Lyman C. *Kings Mountain and Its Heroes: History of the Battle of King's Mountain, October 7, 1780, and the Events Led to It.* Johnston City: The Overmountain Press, 1996. Second Edition.

Dunaway, Wilma A. T*he First American Frontier: transition to capitalism in southern Appalachia, 1700-1860.* Chapel Hill: The University of North Carolina, 1996.

Durkerly, Robert M. *The Battle of Kings Mountain: Eyewitness Accounts.* Charleston: The History Press, 2013. Fifth Printing.

Faragher, John Mack. *Daniel Boone: The Life and Legend of an American Pioneer.* New York: Henry Holt and Company, 1992.

Fink, Paul M. *Bits of Mountain Speech.* Chapel Hill: The University of North Carolina Press, 2017. Print.

Fletcher, Arthur Lloyd. *Ashe County: A History (Contributions to Southern Appalachian Studies).* Jefferson: McFarland & Company, 2006.

Gaffney, Sanna Ross.[1] *The Heritage of Watauga County, North Carolina: Vol. I.* Winston-Salem: Hunter Publishing Company, 1984.

Gregory, Peggy H. *Judd: A Compilation of Judd Families, Primarily Descendants of Rowland Judd, Esquire, of Wilkes County, North Carolina. Madison: University of Wisconsin, 1984.*

Hardy, Michael C. *A Short History of Watauga County.* Blowing Rock: Parkway Publishers, Inc. 2005.

Hayes, Johnson J. *Land of Wilkes.* Jefferson: Wilkes County Historical Society, 1962.

Herman, Arthur. *How the Scots Invented the Modern World.* New York: MJF Books, 2001.

Johnson, Patricia Givens. *The New River Early Settlement.* Blacksburg: Walpa Publishing, 2003. 2nd Printing.

Kars, Marjoleine. *Breaking Loose Together: The Regulator Rebellion in Pre-Revolutionary North Carolina.* Chapel Hill: The University of North Carolina Press, 2002.

Lawson, John. *A New Voyage to Carolina.* Chapel Hill: The University of North Carolina Press, 1967.

Miller, Danny. *The Miller Families of Ashe County.* (Unknown): D. L. Miller, 1988.

Morgan, Robert. *Boone: A Biography.* Chapel Hill: Algonquin Books, 2008.

Moss, Bobby Gilmer. *The Patriots at Kings Mountain.* Blacksburg: Scotia-Hibernia, 1900.

Myers, Rufus. *1799: North Carolina's Northwest Frontier.* Kearney: Morris Publishing, 2005. Second Printing.

O'Brien, John. *At Home in the Heart of Appalachia.* New York: Anchor Books, 2001.

Oshinsky, David M. *Polio: An American Story.* New York: Oxford University Press, 2005.

Rouse, Parke Jr. *The Great Wagon Road from Philadelphia To the South.* Richmond: The Dietz Press, 1995.

Smalling, Curtis, Editor.[2] *The Heritage of Watauga County North Carolina Volume II.* Winston-Salem: Hunter Publishing Company, 1987.

Stansberry. *Old Wilkes Land Records.* (Wilke County Library)

Webb, James. *Born Fighting: How the Scots-Irish Shaped America.* New York: Broadway Books, 2005.

Williams, John Alexander. *Appalachia A HISTORY.* Chapel Hill: The University of North Carolina Press, 2002. The June, 2019 issue of <u>Scotland Magazine</u>

CPSIA information can be obtained
at www.ICGtesting.com
Printed in the USA
LVHW061219130323
741490LV00002B/19